DRIVING

AUSTRALIA

Macmillan • USA

CONTENTS

Written by Anne Matthews

Edited, designed and produced by AA Publishing.

Published in the United States by Macmillan Travel A Prentice Hall Macmillan Company 15 Columbus Circle New York, NY 10023

Macmillan is a registered trademark of Macmillan, Inc.

ISBN 0-02-860073-8

Color separation: Daylight Colour Art Pte, Singapore

Printed and bound in Italy by Printers SRL, Trento

Title page: *Aerial view of Surfers Paradise*

Above: *Bondi Beach lifeguard*

Opposite: *Preparing for a ceremony*

INTRODUCTION

This book is not only a practical touring guide for the independent traveller, but is also invaluable for those who would like to know more about Australia. It is divided into four regions, each with its own city tours and motoring tours. Some of these itineraries are circular, but the large distances to be covered, as well as the variability of what is appealing to visitors, mean that many of the tours are linear – from A to B.

The eight major city tours are designed to show you the best of Sydney, Brisbane, Cairns, Canberra, Melbourne, Hobart, Adelaide and Perth, and there are special features on the Gold Coast and the Great Barrier Reef, the unique flora and fauna, Aboriginal history and culture and Kakadu National Park, Ayers Rock and The Olgas.

Each motor tour has details of the most interesting places to visit en route – again, due to Australia's vast area we have not attempted to cover the entire country: merely the most historic and scenic destinations. Side panels cater for special interests and requirements and cover a range of categories – for those whose interest is in history, natural attractions or walking, and for people who have children. Other panels highlight scenic stretches of road along the way, or give details of special events, crafts, customs and foods. Where applicable, these are cross-referred to the main text.

The easy-to-follow directions are accompanied by a simple map of the tour, and addresses of local tourist information centres in some of the towns en route. Simple charts show the approximate distances from one town to the next in kilometres and miles – these can help you decide where to take a break and stop overnight.

Before setting off it is advisable to check with the information centre or bureau at the start of the tour for recommendations on accommodation and where to break your journey, additional information on what to see and do, the best time to visit, and details of road conditions for outback areas.

EMBASSIES AND CONSULATES

All of the major high commissions and embassies are located in Canberra, while some countries are also represented in Sydney, Melbourne, Brisbane and other cities. The following embassies can be contacted in Canberra:

Canada	(06) 273 3844
Ireland	(06) 273 3022
New Zealand	(06) 270 4211
UK	(06) 270 6666
USA	(06) 270 5000

ENTRY REGULATIONS

All visitors to Australia require a valid visa, with the exception of New Zealand passport holders. Normal visitor visas are valid for either three or six months, while young people aged 18 to 25 years from the UK and some other countries can stay for up to 12 months on a working holiday visa. Visa regulations vary from time to time, so check with your nearest Australian consulate or embassy for full details.

Note that a departure tax (currently A$25 per person) is payable on leaving Australia.

CUSTOMS AND QUARANTINE REGULATIONS

Visitors over the age of 18 may bring in 250 cigarettes or 250 grams of tobacco or cigars; one litre of wine, spirits, beer or other alcoholic beverages; plus other dutiable goods to the value of A$400 per person. There is no limit on the amount of funds for personal use.

Australia's island nature means that the country is free of many plant and animal diseases, such as rabies, and quarantine regulations are very strict. Animals are placed in quarantine for at least six months, and all foodstuffs or goods of plant or animal origin must be declared on the form provided – anything suspect is likely to be confiscated. Drug smuggling is treated extremely harshly.

ACCOMMODATION

Australia offers every type and price category of accommodation – from backpackers' hostels (from around A$15 per person per night) to international standard five-star hotels (A$250 plus per night for a twin/double room). In large cities and major holiday centres such as the Gold Coast you also have the choice of self-catering serviced apartments. For those on a budget, bed and breakfast guesthouses, hostels and caravan parks are very reasonable.

Country towns generally offer three-star motels, the usually cheaper local hotel (pub), and caravan parks. The island resorts, particularly in Queensland, are generally excellent and there are many wilderness-style lodges in the more scenic regions. Tasmania offers a special style of accommodation – historic and colonial houses and a great many country-style self-contained cottages.

For more details of rates and what types of accommodation are available, contact the State Tourist Offices listed on page 6.

BANKS

Banks are generally open from 9.30am–4pm Monday to Friday, with a one-hour extension to 5pm on Fridays in major cities. Travellers' cheques and banknotes in major currencies can be cashed at hotels and many other outlets, such as American Express and Thomas Cook, outside these hours and on weekends.

CLIMATE AND WHEN TO GO

Australia's vast size means that the climate varies considerably from north to south, and across the continent. The seasons are also the reverse of those in the northern hemisphere – summer is from December to February, autumn from March to May, winter from June to August, and spring from September to November.

For all areas other than the tropical far north (which experiences hot, wet summers) and the heart of the continent, the best months to visit are generally from October to March. It can be very hot from December to February in Queensland, New South Wales, South Australia and Western Australia, but this is the ideal time for touring the cooler states of

Victoria and Tasmania. The best time to visit Central Australia and the far north is from April to October, when temperatures are much lower and there is less rain in the tropical regions.

CREDIT CARDS

All credit cards are widely accepted in the major cities and towns, but you might experience difficulty in some country and outback areas if your card is not of the MasterCard, American Express, Visa or Bankcard.

CURRENCY

Australia's currency system is based on dollars, comprising 100 cents. Banknotes come in $100, $50, $20, $10 and $5 denominations (the latter two are plastic), while there are coins for 5, 10, 20 and 50 cents (all silver coloured), and $1 and $2 (gold coloured).

EMERGENCY TELEPHONE NUMBERS

Calling the police, ambulance service or fire brigade from anywhere in Australia is very simple – just dial 000. Emergency telephone calls are free of charge.

HEALTH

Australian health care standards are excellent and you will be well looked after in the event of sickness, dental problems or an accident. However, medical, dental and ambulance costs are quite high, and most overseas visitors are not covered under the government-operated Medicare scheme, so it is strongly recommended that you take out a personal sickness insurance policy before leaving home. British and New Zealand visitors are, however, entitled to 'immediate necessary treatment' under a reciprocal arrangement.

Tap water is safe to drink everywhere, and the only medical problems you are likely to experience are sunburn and mosquito bites (make sure you have good supplies of 15+ blockout and insect repellent and wear a hat), while marine stingers in the water can cause problems – particularly in Queensland and along the northern coast during the summer.

MOTORING

Hiring a vehicle is very easy in Australia and you will find outlets in all cities and most major towns. Petrol, both leaded and unleaded, is inexpensive compared to most countries and is sold by the litre. Distances on maps and road signs are in kilometres.

Striated mounds of eroded sandstone: the Bungle Bungles

PUBLIC HOLIDAYS

Some public holidays, such as Labour Day and Bank Holidays, vary from state to state, but the major national holidays are as follows:
1 January – New Year's Day
4th Monday in January –
   Australia Day
March/April – Good Friday and
   Easter Monday
25 April – Anzac Day
2nd Monday in June –
   Queen's Birthday Holiday
25 December – Christmas
   Day
26 December – Boxing Day

School holidays in most states occur in April, June/July, September/October, and mid-December to late January – the latter period is peak summer holiday time in most areas, when all transport, accommodation and tourist facilities are heavily booked.

TOURIST OFFICES

Each Australian state operates its own tourist bureau – the following are the head offices which can be contacted for information, maps and details of accommodation, and also to make advance hotel reservations:
Australian Capital Territory Tourism Commission 330 Northbourne Avenue, Dickson, ACT 2602. Tel: (008) 026 166 (freecall outside the ACT), or (06) 205 0044/205 0666.
New South Wales Travel Centre 19 Castlereagh Street, Sydney, NSW 2000. Tel: (008) 817 987 (Freecall outside Sydney), or (02) 231 4444.
Northern Territory Government Tourist Bureau 33 Smith Street Mall, Darwin, NT 0801. Tel: (089) 81 4300 or **Northern Territory Tourist Centre** GPO Box, Darwin, NT 0801. Tel: (089) 84 4493.
Queensland Government Travel Centre Corner of Adelaide and Edward Streets, Brisbane, QLD 4000. Tel: (07) 221 6111.
Tourism South Australia 18 King William Street, Adelaide, SA 5000. Tel: (08) 212 1505.
Tasmanian Travel Centre 80 Elizabeth Street, Hobart, TAS 7000. Tel: (002) 30 8233/30 8250.
Victoria Royal Automobile Club of Victoria, 230 Collins Street, Melbourne, VIC 3000. Tel: (03) 790 3333/650 1522.
Western Australian Tourist Centre Corner of Forrest Place and Wellington Street, Perth, WA 6000. Tel: (09) 483 1111.

Documents

Overseas driving licenses are valid throughout Australia, but an international permit can make life easier.

Vehicle hire

Major car, 4WD, campervan and motorhome outlets such as Hertz, Avis, Budget and Thrifty are widespread throughout the country. You must be over 21 to hire a vehicle and compulsory third party insurance is included in rental prices, which are generally quite reasonable and often competitive.

As distances are so vast in Australia, some of the tours described are of the fly/drive variety – an example is to fly to Alice Springs, hire a car and then undertake Tour 20 around the southern part of the Northern Territory. It is recommended, particularly in peak holiday periods, that you pre-book a vehicle before arriving at your destination. Note that sections of some tours in this book require a 4WD vehicle and this is indicated where applicable.

Road rules

The general idea is to drive on the left and overtake on the right, but Australian drivers can be somewhat reckless and do not always stick to the latter, especially on multi-lane freeways. Speed limits vary from 60kph in built-up areas to 100kph or 110kph on freeways. Wearing seatbelts in front and back seats is compulsory and drink-driving laws are strict – random breath testing is very common. The general legal permitted limit for alcohol is 0.05 per cent (0.08 in the Northern Territory).

Full details of road rules can be obtained from the National Roads and Motorists Association (NRMA) at 151 Clarence Street, Sydney (tel: 260 9222).

Driving conditions and tips

Although Australia's major highways are generally of a good standard, driving in the outback is another matter. Many roads are unsealed and some areas require a 4WD vehicle. Driving at night on these roads can be particularly difficult for the uninitiated, with wildlife presenting frequent hazards. Road trains of up to 50m long create another difficulty on many northern and outback roads. If you intend to drive on isolated roads make sure you have plenty of water (at least 20 litres) and fuel, carry spare parts and check the repair kit before setting out. Breaking down in very remote regions in summer can be fatal, so stay near the vehicle and wait for help to come.

Breakdowns

The NRMA and various state organisations such as the Royal Automobile Club of Victoria (RACV) offer a 24-hour breakdown service, and members of most international motoring associations are entitled to receive certain service arrangements – check with your organisation at home.

Accidents

If you are involved in an accident the incident must be reported to the local police, and you should exchange contact and insurance details with the other driver.

POST OFFICES

Post offices are generally open from 9am to 5pm from Monday to Friday. Stamps can be purchased from hotels and some newsagents and souvenir shops.

TELEPHONES

The minimum local call charge from public telephones is 30 cents (some are 40 cents) for unlimited time and 20 and 10 cent coins can be used. STD, or long-distance calls in Australia vary considerably in price, but you should have a good supply of 50 cent and $1

coins. Phonecards are a much better idea and these come in values of $5 and upwards. Codes for the capital cities are as follows:

Adelaide	08
Brisbane	07
Canberra	06
Darwin	089
Hobart	002
Melbourne	03
Perth	09
Sydney	02

International calls can be made from many public telephones by dialling 0011, followed by the country code:

Canada	1
Ireland	353
New Zealand	64
UK	44
USA	1

TIME

Australia has three time zones – Eastern Standard Time (EST), which is 10 hours ahead of GMT (Greenwich Mean Time) and applies to Queensland, New South Wales, the Australian Capital Territory (ACT), Tasmania and Victoria; Central Standard Time (CST) for the Northern Territory and South Australia (half an hour behind EST); and Western Standard Time (WST) for Perth and Western Australia (two hours behind EST). Things become even more complicated between the months of October and March when most (but not all) states go on to Daylight Saving Time for differing periods. Essentially, this means advancing the time by one hour in the eastern states – with the exception of Queensland.

ELECTRICITY

The standard electricity supply in Australia is 240–250 volts AC and a flat three-pin adaptor will be required for most non-Australian appliances. Hotels provide 110-volt shaver sockets.

THE EAST COAST

Australia's east coast could well be described as the 'Holiday Coastline' – from southern New South Wales to the deserted beaches north of Cairns there are hundreds of coves, capes and headlands; abundant surf and sand; dozens of resort towns and fishing villages; and a glorious sunny climate. The coastline includes the major holiday centres of the glossy Gold Coast, the more restrained Sunshine Coast and lovely Fraser Island – a World Heritage site that provides a complete contrast to the high-rise and fun parks further south. The gem of this wonderful region, however, is the Great Barrier Reef, stretching for over 2,000km off the coast and providing island resorts, scuba diving, game fishing and reef experiences without comparison.

Behind the coast lies a narrow plain, backed by the Great Dividing Range, which lends a great diversity to this region. The contrast between golden beaches and surf, and the green, eucalypt and rainforest-clad hills and slopes of the range is remarkable. In these upland areas there are many opportunities for bush-walking, bird and wildlife spotting, and simply enjoying the cooler climate of picturesque hill towns and villages. Temperatures vary considerably from the north of Queensland to southern New South Wales – as a general rule, the area south of Fraser Island can be visited from September to May, while northern Queensland is best avoided in the very hot and humid months of December to February.

Australia's eastern coastline was first explored and charted by Captain James Cook in 1770. Cook's explorations eventually led to the establishment of a convict settlement at Sydney Cove under Governor Arthur Phillip in 1788 and, despite the hardships and difficulties of those early years, Australia has never looked back. By the early 1800s pastoralists were heading west to farm beyond the Blue Mountains and small villages, and whaling or sealing stations were dotted along the New South Wales coast.

Brisbane was founded as another penal settlement in 1824, but the development of the remainder of what is now Queensland came much later. A few towns such as Maryborough existed as pastoral centres in the 1840s, but it was not until the 1860s and 1870s that the discovery of gold and fertile farming lands opened up north Queensland.

City Tour 1

Sydney – Australia's first and premier metropolis – has transformed itself in 200 years from the forgotten city at the end of the earth to a vibrant and exciting place to live and visit. Explore the inner city, the historic Rocks area, Sydney Harbour, the unmistakable Opera House – and much more!

Tour 1

One of Sydney's major attractions is its proximity to the harbour and wonderful sandy beaches that stretch for 60km along the city's eastern fringe. This tour includes parts of the harbour foreshore and famous Bondi Beach, and then takes you to the city's northern beaches and the yachting paradise of Pittwater.

Tour 2

West of Sydney, the heavily forested Blue Mountains formed an impenetrable barrier that was not crossed until 1813 – today the area is one of the city's favourite weekend destinations. *En route* are the historic settlements of Parramatta, Richmond and Windsor, and to the west, farming plains and the wine-growing area of Mudgee.

Tour 3

To the south of Sydney you will visit historic Botany Bay, named by Captain Cook, and the delightful Royal National Park – the world's second oldest such reserve. Beyond here is Wollongong, the state's third largest city, and a long stretch of mostly unspoiled and uncommer-

cialised coastline, all the way to Batemans Bay.

Enthusiastic snorkellers discover the Great Barrier Reef

Tour 4

This long tour north to Brisbane includes some of the eastern seaboard's best beaches and coastal resorts, but also takes in the city of Newcastle, the hilly wonderland of Dorrigo National Park, and NSW's premier wine region – the Hunter Valley. Once you cross into Queensland the scene changes with the glossy and ever-popular Gold Coast, and the temperatures start to soar.

City Tour 2

Laid-back, sub-tropical Brisbane has made great strides to change its image from a sleepy riverside settlement to a modern, vibrant city. The warm climate means lots of outdoor living and there are new developments, such as the exciting South Bank complex, to enjoy as well as some more historic landmarks.

Tour 5

In complete contrast to Brisbane and the coast, the upland farming and grape growing region of the Darling Downs and Granite Belt is charmingly rural. Toowoomba, the 'Garden City of Australia', dates back to the 1860s and is full of history, while the area contains some rugged uplands, preserved as national parks.

Tour 6

North of Brisbane there are more wonderful beaches and holiday resorts, but these are far more low key than the Gold Coast. The high-light here is World Heritage listed Fraser Island – the world's largest sand island. Inland, the Blackall Range is full of picturesque villages and lovely scenic drives.

City Tour 3

Cairns, Australia's tropical northern tourist mecca, offers every imaginable form of water and beach activity and provides the best access to that wonder of the world, the Great Barrier Reef. Diving, snorkelling, coral viewing, cruises, rafting, and even bungee jumping are all available here.

Tour 7

Beyond the charming resort town of Port Douglas, far north Queensland is totally unspoilt, with a perfect coastline, the World Heritage-listed Daintree rainforest and the small settlements of Cooktown and Laura. There is a wealth of ancient Aboriginal rock art here, and you can also tour the uplands of the Atherton Tableland and the hill town of Kuranda.

Tour 8

Filling in the gap between Tour 6 and Cairns, this sugar cane growing coast offers many wonders – lovely Hinchinbrook Island, the watery playground of the Whitsunday Islands, delightful island resorts and more of the Great Barrier Reef. Historic towns and cities include Townsville, Mackay and Rockhampton, on the Tropic of Capricorn.

SYDNEY

Circular Quay • The Rocks and Observatory Hill Sydney Opera House and Sydney Harbour Bridge • Royal Botanic Gardens • Art Gallery of New South Wales • Macquarie Street • College Street and Hyde Park • Darling Harbour George Street and Pitt Street • Circular Quay

Australia's oldest city is just over 200 years old, but a remark-able transformation has occurred in this relatively short time. The convict tents at The Rocks have given way to high-rise hotels; the colony at the end of the world has become an important, go-ahead city; and the reluctant first convict and soldier 'tourists' have been replaced by enthusiastic visitors. Despite the rapid modernisation in the last two decades, Sydney has retained many old buildings and historic districts, as well as a great deal of parkland surrounding the harbour. There is so much to see and do in the city centre that this walk is best split into two sections, and perhaps undertaken on two different days. A suggestion is to conclude the first part at the Art Gallery of NSW, starting with Macquarie Street on the following day.

RECOMMENDED WALK

2 For a wonderful view of the city and harbour, take a walk along the Sydney Harbour Bridge to the south-east **Pylon Lookout**. The bridge walkway is accessed via Argyle and Cumberland streets in The Rocks and you can climb the pylon's 200 steps for a bird's-eye view of the city's superb location. There is also an interesting exhibition on the bridge's construction.

ⓘ NSW Travel Centre, 19 Castlereagh Street, or the information booth at Circular Key

Start the tour at Circular Quay.

Circular Quay

1 The hub for buses, trains and fer-ries, Circular Quay is one of the city's busiest areas and a great place to sit and watch the world go by. From here you can take a ferry to **Darling Harbour**, **Manly**, the zoo and many other points on the north side of the harbour. The area behind the quay is where the First Fleet landed in January 1788 – in front of Alfred Street's grand 1885 **Customs House**.

There are several harbourside cafés and plenty of busker entertain-ment here and you can walk around Circular Quay West to visit the **Museum of Contemporary Art**. Housed in the 1930s art-deco style

The billowing-sail contours of the Opera House mark a venue that hosts many free performances

Maritime Services Board building, this relatively new museum contains over 4,500 paintings, sculptures and other pieces of modern art. Further along the walkway, the **Overseas Passenger Terminal** is the mooring place for the huge liners that fre-quently visit Sydney.

From Circular Quay West, cross the street to Cadman's Cottage.

The Rocks and Observatory Hill

2 You are now in the historic Rocks area, so named originally because of the rocky shoreline. This was Australia's first 'village' – First Fleet convict tents were pitched here in 1788 and the area developed into an important site, with the nation's first fort, windmill, hospital and wharves. The Rocks later became a slum, and the domain of thieves, drunks and prostitutes. It was almost demol-ished after an outbreak of bubonic plague in 1900, and again during the development-crazy 1960s and 1970s, but thankfully much of this historic and picturesque area has been pre-served and restored.

Simple, whitewashed **Cadman's Cottage**, the city's oldest surviving building, was built in 1816 as a bar-racks for the governor's boat crew and now houses a National Parks and Wildlife information office. Walk up the steps beside the cottage to enter **George Street** – the main thoroughfare of The Rocks. There are many 19th-century buildings here, but head straight for the old **Sydney Sailors' Home** (1864) at 106 George Street. This is The **Rocks Heritage and Information Centre**,

which contains a shop, information desk and an excellent display on the history of The Rocks. Further along George Street you will find the 1848 **Merchants' House** (no 43), a museum for children, while the fascinating **Earth Exchange** – a geological and mining museum – is around the corner on Hickson Road.

Continuing along George Street, you reach **Dawes Point Park**, beneath the Harbour Bridge and, to the left, historic **Lower Fort Street**, with its 19th-century houses and the the oddly shaped 1844 **Hero of Waterloo** hotel. At the end of Lower Fort Street lies **Argyle Place** and its village green – from here you can walk up **Observatory Hill** (the city's highest point at 44m) to see the 1858 **Sydney Observatory** and take in the view of the harbour. The **S H Ervin Gallery**, with an excellent café and National Trust shop, lies just behind Observatory Hill and is housed in the 1815 Military Hospital.

Return to George Street by walking down Argyle Street – with its historic warehouses, the Argyle Centre shopping precinct and the charming old houses of **Playfair Street** and **The Rocks Square**.

Walk down George Street and turn left into the Circular Quay area, continuing around the waterfront of Circular Quay East.

Sydney Opera House and Sydney Harbour Bridge

3 Sydney's world-famous landmark, the Opera House, stands with its glittering, sail-like roofs at the end of

Right: Cadman's Cottage is the oldest house in the city
Below: Circular Quay, revamped for the 1988 Bicentennial

Bennelong Point. Prior to its construction between 1959 and 1973, there was an unattractive tram depot here but the foresight of the New South Wales government has created a wonderful addition to the already glorious harbour. The project was fraught with technical and political problems, however, with the Danish architect Joern Utzon resigning from the scheme in 1966. The spectacular exterior contains the Opera Theatre, Concert Hall and three other performance halls, as well as restaurants, bars and an exhibition hall. The Opera House is the home of the national opera and ballet companies and presents an excellent range of attractions throughout the year. The best way to view the interior is to take one of the daily guided tours.

From the plaza beside the Opera House there is a wonderful view of the water and the Sydney Harbour Bridge. Completed in March 1932 and replacing the ferries which plied their way across the harbour, the bridge has become far more than a mere access route to the northern

FOR HISTORY BUFFS

2 There is so much to see in the history-packed Rocks that it's easy to miss some of the less well-known gems. If you are interested in the area's history, a short Rocks Walking Tour is highly recommended. Details are available from The Rocks Heritage and Information Centre on George Street.

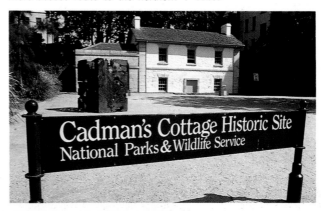

BACK TO NATURE

4 There is no better spot to rest and appreciate Sydney's natural beauty than the harbourside **Royal Botanic Gardens**. In addition to tree-fringed pathways, lovely vegetation, ponds and floral displays, the gardens contain the Sydney Tropical Centre, a fernery and the National Herbarium.

side of the city. This unmistakable Sydney icon is the world's widest long-span bridge – 502.9m long and 48.8m wide – with eight traffic lanes, two railway tracks, a footpath and a cycleway.

Continue walking around the waterfront from the Sydney Opera House.

Royal Botanic Gardens

4 Founded in 1816, the lovely Royal Botanic Gardens provide a tranquil haven with a marvellous variety of plants and trees from Australia and around the world. There are statues, ponds and an excellent restaurant here, and the **Sydney Tropical Centre** – housed in the Arc and the Pyramid Glasshouse. The gardens are fronted by Farm Cove, so-named by Governor Phillip who established a Government Farm here in 1788. Prior to this time, the area was a site sacred to the local Aboriginal people. At the far side of the gardens Mrs Macquarie's Point, named after Governor Macquarie's wife, provides excellent views of the water and Sydney Harbour Bridge.

From the Point, follow the road back towards the city, skirting the Botanic Gardens.

Art Gallery of New South Wales

5 Beyond the Botanic Gardens lies the 1885 Art Gallery of New South Wales. The gallery contains a wonderful permanent collection of European, Australian and Aboriginal

art – the latter is particularly recommended, as is the excellent Australian painting collection featuring works by artists such as Tom Roberts and Arthur Streeton. High quality travelling exhibitions are shown regularly and the bookshop is also worth a visit.

In front of the gallery lies **The Domain** – a large green area, surrounded by enormous Moreton Bay fig trees, which was originally laid out as the 'domain' of the governor in 1810. Today, the area is used mainly by lunchtime joggers, as the venue for summer open-air concerts, and, on Sunday mornings, as Sydney's 'Speakers' Corner'.

Cross the Domain, walking towards the State Library.

Macquarie Street

6 Sydney's most elegant thoroughfare dates back to 1810, when Governor Macquarie began to lay plans for the city. Most of the early 19th-century buildings are, unfortunately, long gone, but the eastern side of Macquarie Street still contains some wonderful examples of colonial architecture. The old section of the **State Library of New South Wales** dates back to 1910, while next door the **State Parliament House** (1810–16) is one of Sydney's oldest structures – it was originally a wing of the 'Rum Hospital', completed in 1816 and built with the profits of the lucrative rum importation trade.

Sydney Hospital replaced the old

FOR CHILDREN

8 The vast **Powerhouse Museum**, within walking distance from Darling Harbour (or accessed via the Haymarket Monorail Station), contains everything from decorative arts and old photographs to aeroplanes and motor cars. There are many educational and technological hands-on displays here that children in particular will enjoy.

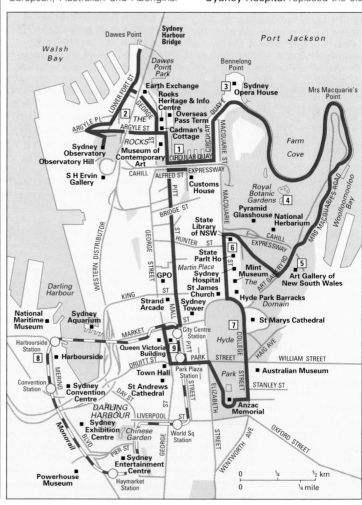

Rum Hospital, while the next-door colonial Georgian-style **Mint** building was another wing of the original hospital and dates from 1816. This simple but elegant structure now contains a museum of decorative arts, stamps and coins.

The gem of Macquarie Street, however, is elegant **Hyde Park Barracks** – built as convict accommodation in 1819 and designed by the brilliant ex-convict architect, Francis Greenway. The Barracks is a fascinating museum of the colony's early history. Across the street, **St James Church** is another Greenway design, dating from 1822 and the city's oldest church. It is hard to imagine now, but the spire was once a major landmark for ships entering the harbour.

Walk around the eastern side of Hyde Park and into College Street.

College Street and Hyde Park

7 The first building in College Street is the Roman Catholic **St Marys Cathedral**. Dating from 1868–82, this Gothic revival church features lovely stained-glass windows. Across William Street, the **Australian Museum** is a must. The original 1849 building, and more recent additions, contain Australia's best collection of natural history and ethnographic material and has a particularly good Aboriginal display. The Australian mammals section is also of interest and the museum has an excellent gift shop.

On the other side of College Street, Hyde Park is one of the city's oldest reserves, dating back to 1792 when Governor Phillips declared it public land. The formal gardens include fountains and tree-lined walkways and provide a great spot for a sightseeing break. From the Australian Museum, cross College Street and head for the distinctive art-deco style Anzac Memorial, built in 1934 to commemorate those killed in World War I.

Cross Hyde Park diagonally, walk down Park Street and turn right into Pitt Street to the monorail station. The monorail will take you to Darling Harbour.

Darling Harbour

8 The lively Darling Harbour complex has transformed the neglected dockyard area that long existed here. Darling Harbour has many attractions, including park areas, the shopping and eating extravaganza of the **Harbourside complex**, and the tranquil **Chinese Garden**. The **Sydney Aquarium** contains over 5,000 fish in 50 specialised tanks and two vast floating oceanariums, where visitors actually walk beneath the ocean. There are sharks, turtles and crocodiles here, and a special display on the Great Barrier Reef. Across the bay, the **National Maritime Museum** is an excellent tribute to Australia's maritime past and present and includes interesting displays and photographs, as well as several vessels moored outside the museum: these include the destroyer *Vampire*, which can be boarded.

Above: space-age Sydney Tower takes a back seat to the elegant 1892 Strand Arcade
Right: in the midst of a modern metropolis, the Chinese Garden invites meditation on the timeless beauty of nature

Rejoin the monorail at any Darling Harbour station and return to the Park Plaza station. Walk down Park Street to the Town Hall.

George Street and Pitt Street

9 These major city thoroughfares are lined with many important buildings and innumerable shops. On George Street, the **Town Hall** dates from 1868. Next door, **St Andrews Cathedral** was begun in 1837 and designed by Edmund Blacket, the colony's most important church architect. It's impossible to miss the **Queen Victoria Building**, which takes up an entire city block. Built in the 1890s, the complex has been meticulously restored and is now a delightful shopping mecca. The restoration prompted designer Pierre Cardin to declare this 'the most beautiful shopping centre in the world'.

From the QVB, cross George Street and walk along Market Street to the **Pitt Street Mall**. This shopping precinct is dominated by 305m-high **Sydney Tower**, completed in 1981 and the city's most distinctive landmark. Taking the lift to the observation level is a must – the view over Sydney and the surrounding countryside is nothing less than astounding! Back at ground level on the mall, have a look at the 1891 **Strand Arcade** before continuing along Pitt Street. On the way to Circular Quay you will pass **Martin Place**, the city's largest pedestrian plaza, with the grand 1874 **General Post Office**, and many high-rise modern buildings.

Continue walking along Pitt Street to return to Circular Quay.

132km (81 miles)

SYDNEY'S COASTLINE

Sydney Harbour • Watsons Bay • Bondi Beach
Centennial Park • Manly • Northern Beaches
Whale Beach and Palm Beach
Church Point and Pittwater • City Centre

While central Sydney offers many attractions, no visit to this maritime city is complete without a tour of the harbour foreshores and the surrounding coastline and beaches. The Sydney metropolitan area coastline stretches north to south for 60km, but this drive (which can take up half or an entire day) takes in a section of the Sydney Harbour foreshore and world-famous Bondi Beach, before crossing the Harbour Bridge to reach Manly and travel north beside the beautiful northern beaches. As a guideline, the drive from the city centre to Bondi Beach takes approximately 15 minutes, while Palm Beach is around 40km from the city

SPECIAL TO ...

Sydney's beach suburbs know how to put on a good show and there are many festivals on offer. Two of the most popular are the spectacular September kite-flying **Festival of the Winds** at Bondi and the **Manly Jazz Carnival**, held in October.

RECOMMENDED WALK

2 From Camp Cove at Watsons Bay a 15-minute walk takes you to South Head, the southerly guardian of Port Jackson, the official name for Sydney Harbour. The headland, part of the Sydney Harbour National Park, is capped by the **Hornby Lighthouse** – there are wonderful views across to Manly and dramatic North Head, and out over the Pacific Ocean.

ℹ NSW Travel Centre,
19 Castlereagh Street

Start at the Town Hall on George Street, turn into William Street, passing under the Kings Cross tunnel and continue via New South Head Road to Rose Bay.

Sydney Harbour

1 At Rose Bay the road closely follows the harbour foreshore. This attractive residential suburb is also home to the Royal Sydney Golf Course, while protected **Shark Island** can be seen offshore. On the hill just beyond Rose Bay, leave your car to enjoy the view to the Bridge and Opera House.

Continue along New South Head Road to Watsons Bay.

Watsons Bay

2 This charming harbourside suburb was founded as a fishing village and military base in Sydney's earliest years. The road from Sydney Cove was constructed in 1811 and some cottages date from the 1840s. Today, the suburb offers quiet harbour beaches, a waterfront café and pub, and waterside and cliff walks.

Return up the hill, turning left into Old South Head Road. Follow this road until you reach Curlewis Street, then turn left towards Bondi Beach.

The wealth of the sea awaits you at Doyles restaurant, Watsons Bay

Bondi Beach

3 The most famous of Australia's beaches is a fascinating mixture of sand, surf, sun, cafés and outdoor living. Even in winter Bondi is a popular surfing, jogging and walking spot. The cafés are excellent and the **Bondi Pavilion** regularly hosts art exhibitions and festivals.

Follow Campbell Parade south around the beach, then continue on Bondi Road and the Bondi Junction By-Pass to Oxford Street and Centennial Park.

Centennial Park

4 Centennial Park is one of the city's largest expanses of parkland. It was created in 1888 to commemorate Australia's centenary, while the 1901 Federation ceremony, which established the Australian Commonwealth, was held here. A drive around this tranquil 220-hectare park reveals lakes, birdlife, horseriders, joggers, roller-bladers and cyclists, and an excellent café.

Rejoin Oxford Street and follow this road through Paddington and Darlinghurst. Just before Hyde Park, turn right into College Street and Macquarie Street and take the Harbour Bridge exit. Once across the bridge follow the Freeway and take the Manly exit. Drive to the Spit Bridge, then follow the signs to Manly.

Manly

5 Named by Governor Phillip in 1788 (due to the particularly masculine appearance of the local Aborigines), Manly was established as a fishing settlement in the 1820s. By the 1850s the suburb had become a seaside resort, attracting large numbers of city folk. This is still the case today and Manly offers harbour and ocean beaches and a lively seaside holiday town atmosphere. The short walk from Manly's main beach to lovely Shelly Beach and its café is recommended.

Take Belgrave Street opposite the Manly Wharf (this becomes Pittwater Road) and drive through the suburbs of North Manly and Brookvale to reach Collaroy.

Northern Beaches

6 Sydney's northern beaches form an almost continuous chain from Manly to Palm Beach and provide a magnificent aquatic playground. Collaroy and Narrabeen join to create a long peninsular finger of surf beach, and are backed by the **Narrabeen Lagoon**, rich in birdlife. Further north the road travels inland through **Mona Vale** – turn right here into Barrenjoey Road. **Newport** and **Avalon** are two more beach suburbs with good surfing, interesting cafés and craft shops.

North of Avalon, turn right into Whale Beach Road and follow the scenic clifftop drive.

Whale Beach and Palm Beach

7 These two fine surfing and bathing beaches are surrounded by some of Sydney's most desirable residences – this is millionaire film star and artist country! Palm Beach has an ocean beach, while to the west lies Pittwater and, across the waterway, unspoilt **Ku-ring-gai Chase National Park, which remains in its wild state** – boat trips are on offer from the jetty. Other Palm Beach attractions include a vigorous walk up **Barrenjoey Head**, trendy shops and cafés and famous fish and chips!

Leave Palm Beach by Barrenjoey Road and return to Mona Vale. Turn right here on to Pittwater Road and follow this waterside drive to Church Point.

Church Point and Pittwater

8 The small village of Church Point is located on Pittwater's southern shore and is the starting point for ferry trips to scenic waterside settlements. Opposite Church Point lies the unusual residential 'suburb' of Scotland Island.

Return to Narrabeen North via Pittwater Road, then turn right on to the Wakehurst Parkway, eventually rejoining the main route back to the city at Seaforth.

Sydney Town Hall – Rose Bay 7 (4)
Rose Bay – Watsons Bay 5 (3)
Watsons Bay – Bondi Beach 7 (4)
Bondi Beach – Centennial Park 5 (3)
Centennial Park – Manly 20 (12)
Manly – Collaroy 10 (6)
Collaroy – Whale Beach 18 (11)
Whale Beach – Church Point 22 (14)
Church Point – Sydney Town Hall 38 (24)

Surf lifesaving boat

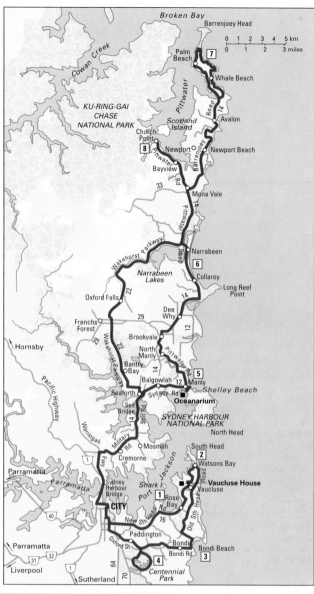

FOR CHILDREN

5 Children will enjoy the many delights that Manly has to offer. There is a safe harbourside beach; an ocean pool at Shelly Beach; the Manly Oceanarium, with its large collection of marine life; and a motley selection of buskers and street entertainers in The Corso.

FOR HISTORY BUFFS

Vaucluse House, one of Sydney's most historic residences, is a short detour from the main route to Watsons Bay. (From the hill above Rose Bay, turn left into Vaucluse Road instead of following New South Head Road.) Set in 11 hectares (27 acres) of delightful gardens, this gothic-style mansion dates from the 1830s and was the home of the 'Father of the Australian Constitution', William Charles Wentworth. The house contains 15 lavishly furnished rooms and there is an excellent tea-room in the gardens.

3/4 days – 684km (391 miles)

THE BLUE MOUNTAINS & BEYOND

Sydney • Parramatta • Lower Blue Mountains
Leura and Katoomba • Upper Blue Mountains
Jenolan Caves • Mudgee • Bells Line of Road
Richmond and Windsor • Sydney

This tour from Sydney includes the famous Blue Mountains and Jenolan Caves – one of Sydney's favourite holiday playgrounds, and a lovely region of sandstone plateaux, deep gorges, rivers and eucalypt forests. The wine-growing region of Mudgee lies further northwest; while in the Sydney metropolitan area, Parramatta (Australia's second oldest settlement), Richmond and Windsor (both dating back to 1810) are some of the nation's most historic towns.

Jenolan Caves: guided tours, graded for strenuousness, take in nine of the caves

Start at the Town Hall on George Street and follow the signs to the Great Western Highway (Route 32) and Parramatta.

Parramatta

1 Parramatta was founded in November 1788, 10 months after the First Fleet's arrival. Located 22km from Sydney, the site was chosen for the good farming land that was so sadly lacking at Sydney Cove. Parramatta is now a city in its own right, but has retained many of its historic buildings. Don't miss the 1793 **Elizabeth Farm**; **Old Government House**, dating from 1799; and **Experiment Farm Cottage** (1835). There are many other old buildings and churches to explore on the Parramatta walking tour – details from the information centre.

i   Prince Alfred Park, Market Street

From Parramatta, take the Western Motorway (F4) towards Penrith and follow the Katoomba signs.

Lower Blue Mountains

2 Explorers Blaxland, Wentworth and Lawson, who crossed the mountains in 1813, are all remembered by the names of small settlements in this lower mountains region. The main attractions are at **Faulconbridge** (the Norman Lindsay Gallery and Museum), and **Wentworth Falls** – which, in addition to the falls themselves, is home

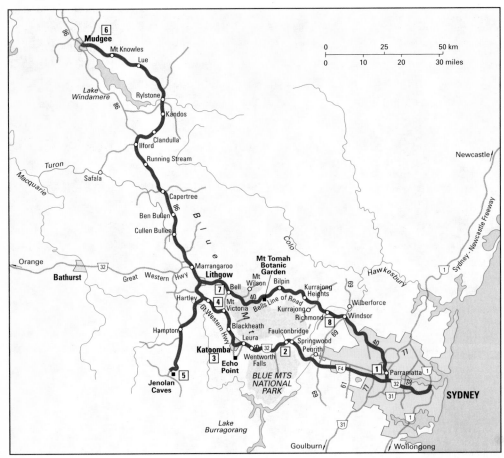

to the Victorian country house, **Yester Grange**.

ⓘ Great Western Highway, Glenbrook

Continue along the Great Western Highway to Leura.

Leura and Katoomba

3 Leura contains many antique shops and some lovely old houses. The main street is National Trust listed and you will also find the stately home, **Leuralla**, here. From Leura, take the Blue Mountains Scenic Drive to Katoomba, the Mountains' main town, which has long been a popular tourist destination. The town itself offers craft shops and cafés, but the magnificent scenery is the highlight. The best view is from Echo Point, just outside the town centre. From here, the famous **Three Sisters** sandstone rock formation stands like a guardian over the valley below. In the same area are the **Scenic Skyway** and the **Scenic Railway**.

ⓘ Echo Point, Katoomba

Continue on the Great Western Highway to Blackheath.

Upper Blue Mountains

4 This region contains the towns of Blackheath, Mount Victoria and Hartley. Blackheath offers excellent views of the forested **Grose Valley** from **Evans Lookout** and **Govetts Leap**, and is famous for its lovely gardens. The settlement of **Mount Victoria** is classified as an urban conservation area and contains many historic buildings; while Hartley is a well-preserved 'ghost town'.

From Mount Victoria, continue on the Great Western Highway and turn left to Jenolan Caves 1km (½ mile) out of Hartley.

Jenolan Caves

5 The winding road to Jenolan Caves is an experience in itself and on arrival you are greeted by the Grand Arch which spans the road. The caves are part of a large wildlife reserve and contain many stalagmites, stalactites and other curious formations. **Jenolan Caves House** offers excellent accommodation and is, in fact, the only place to stay in the area.

Return to Hartley and take the Great Western Highway (Route 32) west, turning off at the Mudgee sign outside Lithgow.

Mudgee

6 Mudgee is one of NSW's most interesting wine-growing regions: the first vines were planted here in 1855 and there are now around 20 boutique-style wineries that produce excellent wines. Names to look out for include **Craigmoor**, **Seldom Seen** and **Montrose**. The town contains some interesting buildings, such as the 1862 **Post Office**, the **Railway Station** (1884), and National Trust classified **Market Street**.

Return to the Great Western Highway near Lithgow. At Lithgow, turn off to Bell and the Bells Line of Road (Route 40).

The Three Sisters, in the cool Blue Mountains: the haze is actually an oily vapour given off by gum trees

Bells Line of Road

7 This alternative route to Sydney was built by convicts in 1841 and is far more scenic than the highway to the south. There are several attractions *en route* – the small villages of **Bell** and **Mount Wilson**, with its lovely English-style gardens; **Mount Tomah Botanic Garden**; and the apple growing settlements of **Bilpin** and **Kurrajong**.

Continue to Richmond.

Richmond and Windsor

8 These historic towns were founded in 1810, although the area was farmed as early as the 1790s. Both lie near the Hawkesbury River, one of Sydney's most popular boating waterways. Richmond has many buildings from the mid 1800s, while Windsor's structures are somewhat older, including the lovely 1820 **St Matthew's Church**.

ⓘ Tourism Hawkesbury, Richmond Road, Clarendon

From Windsor, take Route 40 to Parramatta, the Great Western Highway and Sydney.

Sydney – Parramatta 22 (14)
Parramatta – Faulconbridge (Lower Mountains) 54 (34)
Faulconbridge – Katoomba 28 (17)
Katoomba – Mount Victoria (Upper Mountains) 18 (11)
Mount Victoria – Jenolan Caves 58 (36)
Jenolan Caves – Mudgee 182 (113)
Mudgee – Bell 143 (89)
Bell – Richmond 61 (38)
Richmond – Windsor 6 (4)
Windsor – Sydney 57 (35)

SPECIAL TO ...

6 Lithgow is the home of the famous **Zig Zag Railway**, a remarkable, winding line that was constructed between 1866 and 1869. By 1910 the line had been superseded by another route, but today the restored railway and its steam trains operate as an exciting tourist attraction.

RECOMMENDED WALK

4 A short walk from Blackheath to Govetts Leap is highly recommended. The view from this lookout into the forested **Grose Valley** is nothing less than spectacular. If you are suitably equipped, there are several challenging bushwalks through the valley.

FOR CHILDREN

8 The Australiana Pioneer Village, at Wilberforce, to the northeast of Windsor, is a faithful reconstruction of an early 19th-century pioneer settlement. Children will enjoy the entertaining and easily absorbed history lesson that the village provides.

3 days – 585km (364 miles)

WOLLONGONG & THE SOUTH COAST

Sydney • Botany Bay • Royal National Park
Wollongong • Kiama • Nowra–Bomaderry
Jervis Bay and St Georges Basin • Ulladulla
Batemans Bay • Sydney

This tour to the south of Sydney takes in historic Botany Bay – the landing place of Captain Cook in 1770 – and the the lovely Royal National Park. Once out of the Sydney metropolitan area there are long stretches of wonderfully unspoilt coastline, historic towns and villages and the major city of Wollongong to explore. The route takes you as far south as the resort of Batemans Bay and returns along the same route, or you can link up with Tour 9, Sydney to Canberra.

SPECIAL TO ...

1 Kurnell, on the southern side of Botany Bay, is the spot where Captain James Cook landed in 1770. Modern Kurnell is an industrial area, but at the peninsula's northern end there is a visitor centre and museum, and the **Captain Cook's Landing Place Historic Site**.

SCENIC ROUTES

The drive into Wollongong along the coast from Stanwell Tops, south of the Royal National Park, is superb. From this high point there are wonderful views of the beaches and headlands stretching down the coast.

From the Sydney Town Hall on George Street take Park, Elizabeth and Oxford streets, then Anzac Parade and Bunnerong Road (Route 70) out of the city to La Perouse.

Botany Bay

1 Named by James Cook in 1770 when he moored the *Endeavour* here, Botany Bay is now a port area that has changed dramatically since Cook's time. At **La Perouse**, however, there are a number of historical sites. The La Perouse Monument marks the arrival of French explorers in 1788 while offshore, **Bare Island** was once a fort and military barracks.

Bateman's Bay, a fishing port popular with tourists, Canberra residents and penguins

Monument at Botany Bay, where Cook first dropped anchor

Return along Bunnerong Road, turn left into Botany Road, then follow the signs to join the Princes Highway (Highway 1). Turn off the highway at the Royal National Park sign at Loftus.

Royal National Park

2 The Royal, Australia's first and the world's second-oldest national park, dates from 1879 and provides Sydneysiders with a wonderful playground at their southern gateway. The Royal's beaches are superb – particularly wave-pounded **Garie Beach** – and you can also go boating or canoeing at Audley, where there is a visitor centre. The Royal offers some wonderful walks, varying from one hour to two days!

Return to Highway 1 and continue south, taking the Stanwell Park turn-off to join the coast road to Wollongong.

Wollongong

3 The state's third largest city, with a population of around 230,000, is primarily a port and industrial centre, but the area has retained much of its natural beauty. Located at the foot of the steep **Illawarra Escarpment** and fringed by wonderful surf beaches, Wollongong provides its residents with a stunning location. To the south, **Lake Illawarra** is popular for water sports, while the **Illawarra State Recreation Area** offers excellent bushwalking.

This university city also offers the **Wollongong City Art Gallery** and the interesting **Illawarra Historical Society Museum**. The nearby **Mount Kembla Historic Village** contains several 1890s buildings with antiques and teashops at weekends.

[i] 93 Crown Street, Wollongong East

Leave Wollongong on Highway 1 and continue south, turning off at the Kiama exit.

Kiama

4 The site of Kiama was first discovered in 1797 and the town has long been a fishing port and holiday centre. Kiama contains many old

buildings, including the National Trust timber cottages in Collins Street, and there are good beaches in the area. A famous attraction here is the **Blowhole**, through which the spray rushes noisily – the town is named after an Aboriginal word for 'where the sea makes a noise'. South of Kiama, picturesque **Gerringong** and the lovely sandy stretch of **Seven Mile Beach National Park** are easily accessible via the coast road.

i Visitor Centre, Blowhole Point

Continue south on Highway 1.

Nowra–Bomaderry

5 The Shoalhaven District's main town is actually two settlements, linked by a bridge over the Shoalhaven River. This region was explored as early as 1805 and became the centre of a timber industry. Today, Nowra–Bomaderry is a thriving holiday centre, providing access to wonderful beaches and other local attractions. The National Trust 1885 homestead, **Meerogal**, is worth visiting, as are the **Nowra Museum**, the **Naval Aviation Museum** and the **Nowra Animal Park**. The Shoalhaven River is great for boating and fishing, and river cruises are available.

i Shoalhaven Tourist Centre, 254 Princes Highway, Bomaderry

Continue on the Princes Highway and take the Huskisson turn-off.

Jervis Bay and St Georges Basin

6 The area south of Nowra is one of the state's loveliest coastal regions. The gem here is Jervis Bay – a vast, almost circular, indentation in the coast with wonderful beaches. The sands at modest resort villages such as **Hyams Beach** are reputed be the world's whitest. The bay's waters are crystal clear and the area is excellent for diving. **Huskisson**, the main town, has all the normal facilities and a variety of accommodation.

The next inlet to the south is St Georges Basin – a large coastal lagoon which is a popular boating and fishing spot. There are a number of tranquil holiday villages here, such as **St Georges Basin**, **Sanctuary Point** and **Sussex Inlet**.

Continue south on Highway 1.

Ulladulla

7 The major holiday resort of Ulladulla is not the most exciting town, but is the centre of a region of lovely beaches, lakes and lagoons. The best surfing and fishing is at **Mollymook Beach**, while there is good swimming around **Burrill Lake** and **Lake Tabourie**, to the south of town. Ulladulla itself has an interesting port with a large fishing fleet, and the charming **Ulladulla Wildflower Reserve**.

Milton, on the highway just before Ulladulla, dates back to 1860 and is full of old buildings and interesting shops. You can also take a detour to **Bawley Point**, off the Ulladulla–Batemans Bay road – this tranquil beach resort offers good swimming,

lakes and fine cuisine at the **Bawley Point Guest House**.

Drive south on Highway 1.

Batemans Bay

8 Batemans Bay is an important fishing centre, specialising in oysters and crayfish. The area is popular with landlocked Canberra residents, who can drive here in a couple of hours. The best beaches are to the north of town, at the low-key resorts of **Pebbly Beach** and **Durras** or you can take an interesting river cruise from Batemans Bay.

i Corner of Princes Highway and Beach Road

Return to Sydney via Highway 1, or you can link up with part of Tour 9 by leaving the highway at Nowra and driving to Kangaroo Valley.

Sydney – La Perouse (Botany Bay) 18 (11)
Botany Bay – Loftus (Royal National Park) 32 (20)
Loftus – Wollongong 40 (25)
Wollongong – Kiama 35 (22)
Kiama – Nowra–Bomaderry 45 (28)
Nowra–Bomaderry – Jervis Bay 25 (16)
Jervis Bay – Ulladulla 55 (34)
Ulladulla – Batemans Bay 53 (33)
Batemans Bay – Sydney 282 (175)

RECOMMENDED WALK

5 Bens Walk, Nowra, follows the banks of the Shoalhaven River and passes a number of historic sites. The easy 5km walk takes you through unspoilt bushland and to the unusual formation of Hanging Rock.

FOR HISTORY BUFFS

5 On the way to Nowra, Berry is a delightful historic town dating back to the 1820s – attractions here include the History Museum, the 1891 Court House, antiques shops and other colonial buildings.

BACK TO NATURE

8 Murramarang National Park, north of Batemans Bay, offers fine beaches, backed by tall eucalypts and rainforest. The local kangaroos and wallabies are practically tame and are frequently seen at campsites and on the beaches.

7 days – 1,077km (669 miles)

SYDNEY
TO BRISBANE

Sydney • Gosford and the Central Coast
Newcastle • Myall Lakes National Park
Forster–Tuncurry • Taree • Port Macquarie
Kempsey • Bellingen and Dorrigo National Park
Coffs Harbour • Grafton • Ballina • Byron Bay
Murwillumbah • Tweed Heads–Coolangatta
Surfers Paradise and the Gold Coast • Brisbane

This tour takes you from Sydney to Brisbane, so that you can explore southern Queensland, but there are many delightful places to visit *en route*. You travel along the northern New South Wales coastline, with its national parks, lovely beaches and pleasant coastal resorts, then cross into Queensland to visit the famous, ritzy Gold Coast before arriving in Brisbane, Queensland's capital city. You will also visit the historic town of Bellingen and nearby World Heritage-listed Dorrigo National Park, and there is a highly recommended optional trip to the famous Hunter Valley wine district.

As you head north up the Pacific Highway, the terrain becomes more tropical – in the far north of the state crops such as sugar cane, macadamia nuts, bananas and avocados are grown – and the temperature rises, especially close to the Queensland border. For this reason, the area is one of New South Wales's most popular holiday spots.

FOR CHILDREN

1 Old Sydney Town, a few kilometres off the highway near Gosford, makes an entertaining and educational excursion for children and adults alike. The 'town' is a faithful re-creation of the colony's early days, with costumed settlers, troops and convicts, 'floggings' and other pieces of street theatre, and reconstructed houses and public buildings.

*From Sydney Town Hall on George Street, turn into Druitt Street and follow the Harbour Bridge signs. Once over the bridge, take **Highway 1** (the Pacific Highway), joining the Sydney–Newcastle Freeway on the outskirts of the city. Leave the Freeway at the Gosford turn-off.*

Gosford and the Central Coast

1 North of the Sydney metropolitan region, and south of Newcastle, the Central Coast is an area of attractive coastline, meandering waterways, national parks and, increasingly, homes for workers commuting to Sydney and Newcastle. Gosford, at the head of Brisbane Water, is the region's main town and dates back to the 1820s. The main attractions of this area are natural ones, but there are several

---

Hands of ripening bananas point to Coffs Harbour's major industry

interesting ventures around Gosford: the **Australian Reptile Park and Wildlife Sanctuary**; **Askania Park**, with its rainforest species; and **The Ferneries** – a tree- and fern-filled reserve that also offers entertainment for children – are all worth a visit. You can also take a pleasant cruise on Brisbane Water from Gosford.

To the southwest, the sandstone plateau of **Brisbane Water National Park** contains Aboriginal engravings and many lovely unspoilt beaches, and is home to a wide variety of birds, including kookaburras and lyrebirds. The headlands here provide wonderful views south over the Hawkesbury River and Broken Bay to Sydney's northern outskirts. On the other side of Brisbane Water, **Bouddi National Park** (pronounced Boody) is a region of small beaches, cliffs and steep hillsides and rainforest. The nearby quiet beachside villages of **Killcare**, **McMasters Beach** and **Avoca Beach** are popular holiday destinations.

East of Gosford lies **Terrigal** – an attractive seaside town with excellent beaches and surfing, and good facilities and accommodation. Further up the coast, the **Tuggerah Lakes** region forms an area of inland waterways that are perfect for boating, while the nearby coastal beaches offer great surfing and swimming. The small resorts of **The Entrance** and **Toukley** are the main centres for this delightful region.

[i] 200 Mann Street, Gosford

*From Toukley, return to the Pacific Highway (**Route 1**) and continue north.*

Newcastle

2 Coal was discovered here as long ago as 1791 and Newcastle has long been an industrial and port city, located at the mouth of the Hunter River. Despite this mining and industrial background, the state's second largest city has some marvellous surfing and bathing beaches, and a number of historical and cultural attractions. The **Newcastle Maritime and Military Museum**, housed in 1880s Fort Scratchley, is one of the city's most imposing landmarks, while the **Newcastle Regional Art Gallery** is worth a visit. Many grand Victorian buildings still stand, including the **Trades Hall Building** (1895) and the **Longworth Institute**. You can also take a cruise on the harbour, or go on the guided **Heritage Walk** which takes in the most important historic sites.

To the south, the growing residential region of **Lake Macquarie** forms another wonderful recreation site for 'Novocastrians'. This is Australia's largest saltwater lake, with over 150km of foreshore, and there are plenty of opportunities for boating, fishing and picnicking. From Newcastle you can take a detour 50km or so up the coast to the 24km-long waterway of **Port Stephens**. This popular but unspoilt

holiday destination, based around the small resort of **Nelson Bay**, offers white sandy beaches, clear blue waters, boating, fishing and cruises.

ⓘ Queens Wharf, Newcastle

From Newcastle, continue on **Highway 1** *and turn off at the Tea Gardens exit.*

Myall Lakes National Park

3 Myall Lakes is one of the state's most attractive and unspoilt national parks – an enchanting blend of ocean beaches and surf, a chain of freshwater lakes, and bushland that is great for walking. Camping, houseboating, fishing, canoeing, birdwatching, scuba diving and surfing are all popular here, and accommodation is available at **Tea Gardens**, **Hawks Nest** and **Bulahdelah**. The lakes are a haven for pelicans, black swans and other water birds, while the eucalypt forests and heathland are home to grey kangaroos, wallabies, echidnas and possums.

The national park can be reached from the highway via the Tea Gardens turn-off, or from Bulahdelah. South of the park, Tea Gardens and the neighbouring village of Hawks Nest are attractive fishing and resort centres, separated by a bridge, on the banks of the Myall River. Boat trips up the river and on to the lakes are available. **Seal Rocks**, at the northeastern end of the park, is a particularly pretty spot for those seeking an ocean beach.

Leave the national park from Seal Rocks and take the scenic Lakes Way to Forster.

See Newcastle's harbour from the deck of a tour boat, then enjoy its museums, parks and beaches

Forster–Tuncurry

4 The twin towns of Forster and Tuncurry, joined by bridge over Wallis Lake, are best known for their fishing industry and tourism. The area is popular with scuba divers and recreational fishermen, and full of good beaches (both to the north and south) and scenic drives. Lake cruises are available and you could also visit the **Forster Art and Craft Centre**, or take in the view from the scenic platform at **Bennetts Head**.

ⓘ Little Street, Forster

Continue north on the Lakes Way road and join **Highway 1** *south of Taree.*

Taree

5 Taree was first settled in 1829 and grew up around the timber and dairying industries. Today, this town of some 16,000 people is the base for tourists visiting the area's excellent beaches and inland attractions. You can take a cruise on the Manning River, and there are some pleasant forest drives in the area. The English-style town of **Wingham**, 20km to the northwest, dates back to the 1840s and contains many historic buildings, and the National Trust listed **Town Common**. You can also visit coastal **Crowdy Bay National Park**, to the northeast of Taree.

ⓘ Pacific Highway, Taree North

Continue north on **Highway 1** *(the Pacific Highway), turning off for Port Macquarie.*

SCENIC ROUTES

3 The scenic **Lakes Way** route between Myall Lakes and Forster passes through some wonderful coastal scenery, including the **Booti Booti State Recreation Area**. This protected region encloses the long sweep of Seven Mile beach, with its clear swimming and surfing waters, several other beaches, a lake and magnificent headlands. The reserve is well known for its varied birdlife and there are a number of walking tracks and lookouts that provide wonderful views over the coast and inland.

FOR HISTORY BUFFS

6 At **Wauchope**, just 20km from Port Macquarie, the village of **Timbertown** is one of the more faithful re-creations of the old days. Illustrating the life of the early pioneers who were mostly involved in forestry industries, this complex offers demonstrations of timber working and other crafts, furnished houses, traditional Australian food and the opportunity to join in with some bush songs.

Port Macquarie

6 This major fishing port and popular holiday centre was first discovered in 1818 and named after the governor of the time – Port Macquarie later became a penal colony and military base. Historical highlights are the award-winning **Hastings Historical Museum**, housed in a restored 1830s building and displaying pioneer relics; and a visit to convict-built **St Thomas's Church** (1824). The **Macquarie Nature Reserve** provides attractions of another kind – there are many birds here and the reserve is famous for its koalas.

The area is well known for its fishing and beaches, and you can take a scenic cruise on the Hastings River. Children are well catered for with **Kingfisher Park** and its native animals, a **shell museum**, the **House of Dolls**, **Sea Acres Wildlife Refuge**, and the performing dolphins and sea-lions at **King Neptune's Park**. A few kilometres to the west, the family-run **Cassegrain Winery** produces good wines and is worth a visit.

ⓘ Corner of Hay and Clarence streets

Rejoin and continue driving on Highway 1.

Kempsey

7 The inland pastoral town of Kempsey, on the Macleay River, has its own attractions but is best known as the base for some lovely nearby coastal scenery. In Kempsey itself you can visit the **Historical Museum** and the many 1880s buildings in the western part of town. The town is also home to the world-famous **Akubra** hat.

To the southeast, the little village of **Crescent Head** is surrounded by an unspoilt 20km beach and bushland and is a popular holiday spot with those who enjoy being close to nature. The area is also well known for its good fishing, surfing and hang-gliding.

Four thousand-hectare **Hat Head National Park** contains impressive sand dunes, a 15km (9-mile) stretch of golden beach, swamps, lagoons, forest and a great variety of bird life. A drive to **Smoky Cape** (named by Captain Cook) is a must – from this 140m (460-foot) high vantage point, with its accompanying 1891 lighthouse, there is a wonderful view of the coastline.

North of the park, the small town of **South West Rocks**, located on Trial Bay, is another popular holiday spot. The interesting and now roofless **Trial Bay Gaol**, dating from the 1880s, is a major tourist attraction here. The gaol site is included in the **Arakoon State Recreation Area**, which also offers lovely beaches, pockets of rainforest and walking tracks.

ⓘ South Kempsey Park, Pacific Highway

Continue north on the highway, but take the Bellingen turn-off about 25km before Coffs Harbour.

Bellingen and Dorrigo National Park

8 A slight detour to the picturesque inland town of Bellingen, just 12km off the highway, is worthwhile. Bellingen dates back to the timber-felling days of the 1840s and is now an outstandingly well-preserved Heritage Commission town. You can tour the historic sites on the **Bellingen Omnibus**, pulled by Clydesdale horses, visit alternative lifestyle craft shops and galleries, or take one of the area's many lovely drives, including a particularly scenic route to the rainforested and World Heritage-listed Dorrigo National Park. This outstanding upland park contains a section of the Great Dividing Range escarpment, numerous waterfalls, rivers and some superb subtropical rainforest.

The nearby timber and farming town of **Dorrigo** is a great base for forest drives and there is a small historical museum here, as well a large collection of steam locomotives, carriages and other railway *memorabilia* in the **Dorrigo Steam Railway Museum**.

Return to the highway and continue to Coffs Harbour.

Dangar Falls in World Heritage-listed Dorrigo National Park

Coffs Harbour

9 One of the largest holiday centres on the coast, the sub-tropical city of Coffs Harbour is much more commercialised than its neighbours, but offers a wide variety of attractions. In town, the **Coffs Harbour Historical Museum** has a good collection of Aboriginal, pioneer and shipping relics, and a stroll around the harbour is also interesting, to view the fishing fleet and large number of pleasure craft moored here. From the jetty you can walk out to **Muttonbird Island**, a breeding ground for these birds between September and May. There is also the **North Coast Regional Botanic Garden**, and the **Porpoise Pool**, with its performing porpoises and sea-lions.

However, sand and surf are what Coffs Harbour is all about and there are many fine beaches, both around the city and to the north. This is also the home of the rather kitsch, but much visited, **Big Banana**. This huge, bright yellow symbol of one of the area's major industries also has an educational purpose, and contains interesting displays on almost every aspect of bananas.

i Pacific Highway

Continue on Highway 1.

Grafton

10 The 'garden city' of Grafton, particularly famous for its glorious lilac-flowered jacaranda trees, is an attractive inland settlement on the Clarence River that thrives on the sugar cane, dairying, sheep and cattle industries. There are several National Trust buildings in town, including **Christ Church Cathedral** (1884), the **Court House** and **Police Station** (1881), and **Schaeffer House** (1900), now the local historical museum. Take a cruise on the river, visit one of the many parks, or just enjoy walking the broad tree-lined streets – there are over 7,000 trees in this pleasant city. October–November is a great time to visit Grafton, when the blooming trees are the focus for the annual **Jacaranda Festival**.

Just north of Coffs Harbour, this concrete landmark welcomes you to the world of bananas: see them grow, sample them in food, or buy banana-shaped souvenirs

SPECIAL TO ...

The **Hunter Valley**, reached via the Pacific Highway and Kurri Kurri from Newcastle, is NSW's premier vine-growing region. Wine has been produced here since the 1830s and the 40 or so wineries release some excellent vintages. Located around **Cessnock** and the small towns of **Pokolbin**, **Rothbury** and **Broke**, some of the recommended wineries are **Lindemans Hunter River**, **Tyrrells**, **McWilliams Mount Pleasant** and **Rothbury Estate**. Also worth a visit is the large **Hungerford Hill Wine Village**.

Byron Bay: a powerful lighthouse has been guiding seafarers round the cliffs since 1901

You can also take a number of scenic drives from here – the routes via a ferry to picturesque **Maclean** (90km/56 miles return) and **Ulmarra** (28km/17 miles return) are recommended. The entire riverside village of Ulmarra is National Trust classified and well worth a visit. To the northeast, the old fishing town of **Yamba** has excellent beaches and is particularly popular with the surfing fraternity. Further up the coast, **Bundjalung National Park** offers 38km (24 miles) of beaches, and fishing, canoeing and boating.

[i] 49 Victoria Street

Continue on **Highway 1**.

Ballina

11 On the estuary of the Richmond River, Ballina is a holiday town with good nearby beaches, excellent fishing and a sub-tropical climate. Although the town itself is not terribly exciting, there is an interesting **Maritime Museum** in the Tourist Information Centre; you can take a cruise on the river; or enjoy great views of the coastline from **Lighthouse Hill Lookout** and its 1879 lighthouse. The **South Ballina Wildlife Sanctuary** is worth visiting for the local fauna, and a scenic inland drive to the small village of **Teven** (24km/15 miles return) – along quiet backroads – is recommended.

[i] Norton Street

Take the coast road via Lennox Head to Byron Bay.

Byron Bay

12 This small town, with its magnificent beaches and understated tourist facilities, is truly the gem of the northern New South Wales coast. Originally a timber town, port and whaling station, Byron Bay is now a very popular, sensitively developed, holiday resort that is famous for its alternative lifestyle appeal. The many kilometres of sandy beaches here (Wategos, Tallow, Main, Clarks and Belongil) are wonderful for bathing and surfing, and the area is a renowned

snorkelling and scuba diving spot. **Cape Byron** is the Australian mainland's most easterly point and there is an excellent walking track to the cape and 1901 lighthouse (see **Recommended Walk**). Despite its size, Byron is a very cosmopolitan town and offers city-standard cafés, restaurants and bars.

A drive into the hills west of town is well worthwhile for a wonderful view of the sweeping coastline around Byron Bay. Take the Bangalow route and, once you've admired the views, spend some time in this charming old village. Further out in these lush sub-tropical hills, the towns of **Mullumbimby** (40km/25 miles return) and **Nimbin** (120km/75 miles return) are picturesque centres of the local hippy and alternative lifestyle communities, although Nimbin has become somewhat seedy. If you do get as far as Nimbin, be sure to visit **Nightcap National Park** – a small rainforested reserve which is World Heritage listed.

[i] 69 Jonson Street

From Byron Bay, return to **Highway 1** *and continue north.*

Murwillumbah

13 North of Byron Bay, the highway curves inland and brings you to an incredibly scenic area. Murwillumbah, on the Tweed River, dates back to the 1860s and is at the centre of a highly fertile sugar cane growing region. You can visit the **Condong Sugar Mill** during the crushing season (July to December), or tour the **Madura Tea Estates**, Australia's first commercial tea-

BACK TO NATURE

5 **Crowdy Bay National Park**, off the highway 25km to the northeast of Taree, is a lovely coastal area of beaches, cliffs, wetlands and a profusion of flowers. Birdlife is prolific – over 100 species visit or inhabit the park – and there are some excellent walks, particularly to 113m-high **Diamond Head**, from where there is a magnificent panorama of the coastline.

growing enterprise. **Avocado Land**, to the north, is another interesting agricultural venture that is open to visitors.

The town and surrounding area is dominated by dramatic **Mount Warning**, in the national park of the same name. This strangely shaped peak was named by Captain James Cook in 1770 as a reminder of the dangers to ships off the nearby coast, and is the core of what was once a vast volcano. The World Heritage listed national park is a short drive from Murwillumbah and is a must. The energetic can undertake the steep walk (four hours return) to the summit and be rewarded by truly fantastic views.

ⓘ Corner of Alma Street and Pacific Highway

*Continue on **Highway 1**, crossing into Queensland at Coolangatta.*

Tweed Heads–Coolangatta

14 These twin towns span an invisible border – Tweed Heads is the most northerly town in NSW, while Coolangatta is in Queensland. They form a much frequented holiday destination which is an extension, albeit a little less commercialised, of the nearby Gold Coast. The beaches here are excellent and fishing is a popular activity. An interesting attraction is the **Minjungbal Cultural Centre** – an Aboriginal enterprise which features a museum, an ancient ceremonial site and a nature reserve. You can also take a cruise on the Tweed River, or drive down the peninsula south of Tweed Heads to the attractive fishing village of **Fingal Head**. The lighthouse

here dates from 1872 and overlooks the curious basalt formations of the Giants Causeway.

ⓘ Beach House Plaza, Marine Parade, Coolangatta

*Continue north on **Highway 1**.*

Surfers Paradise and the Gold Coast

15 The popular Queensland tourist mecca of the Gold Coast starts at Coolangatta, but it is at Surfers Paradise that this glitzy stretch reaches its peak. Although the beaches here are excellent, the commercialisation may not suit everyone – see **The Gold Coast** (page 26) for details.

ⓘ The Mall, Cavill Avenue, Surfers Paradise

*Continue on **Highway 1** towards Brisbane.*

Sydney – Gosford 88 (55)
Gosford – Newcastle 87 (54)
Newcastle – Tea Gardens (Myall Lakes NP) 72 (45)
Tea Gardens (Myall Lakes NP) – Forster 95 (59)
Forster – Taree 34 (21)
Taree – Port Macquarie 82 (51)
Port Macquarie – Kempsey 52 (33)
Kempsey – Bellingen 107 (66)
Bellingen – Coffs Harbour 36 (22)
Coffs Harbour – Grafton 82 (51)
Grafton – Ballina 131 (81)
Ballina – Byron Bay 30 (19)
Byron Bay – Murwillumbah 50 (31)
Murwillumbah – Coolangatta 31 (19)
Coolangatta – Surfers Paradise 20 (12)
Surfers Paradise – Brisbane 80 (50)

Surfers Pardise it may be, but calm waters suit these vessels anchored near by

RECOMMENDED WALK

12 The walk from Byron Bay to Cape Byron is highly recommended. From the eastern end of Clarks Beach follow the walking track through Palm Valley, then up and around the cliffs to Australia's most easterly point and the lighthouse. The views are spectacular and from high on the point you can often see dolphins and stingrays in the waters below. During the winter migration season this is a popular location for whale watching.

THE GOLD COAST

This very commercialised but incredibly popular holiday destination will not appeal to everyone, but there is a veritable host of attractions here, with children particularly well catered for. For adults there is a casino, plenty of nightlife and several glamorous shopping precincts, but, in addition to all this glitz and highrise, the beaches and natural attractions – especially those inland – are excellent. There are numerous settlements along this warm and sunny stretch of coast, but most of the action centres around Surfers Paradise and Southport. The Gold Coast offers accommodation of all kinds – from backpackers' hostels and camping grounds to self-catering units and international standard resorts. There are also some 500 restaurants and cafés here, providing almost every kind of food imaginable.

Beaches, cruises and sporting activities

The Gold Coast, from Coolangatta in the south to Sanctuary Cove in the north, is a 45km (28-mile) stretch of golden beaches and surf. Surfing is very popular here, and, while the beaches become very crowded at peak holiday times, you can always find a spot off the beaten track. A maze of canals and rivers backs the coast and there are numerous boat cruises available – on the Nerang River and the Broadwater, and to South Stradbroke Island. This virtual-

Jupiter's Casino, its Gold Coast glamour enhanced by shimmering reflections of a thousand lights

ly uninhabited island can be reached by launch from the Runaway Bay Marina, north of Southport, and offers good fishing and walking, and a complete contrast to the busy Gold Coast – there are no cars on the island, for example.

In addition to swimming and surfing, scuba diving, waterskiing, fishing and boating of all kinds are popular here. Golfers are well catered for at the championship The Palms course; you can parasail, go bungee jumping or tandem skydiving, and visit the horse races.

Theme parks

There is an almost bewildering array of theme parks and entertainment centres on and around the Gold Coast, and this is the perfect place to visit if you have children. The most popular attraction has to be Sea World at Main Beach, the largest marine park in the southern hemisphere. Dolphins, sea-lions and whales are the stars here, and there are also water slides and various funfair rides.

Dreamworld at Coomera (inland on the Pacific Highway) bills itself as 'Australia's answer to Disneyland' and offers various themed areas, some 27 rides and the opportunity to cuddle a koala. Also at Coomera is the Le Mans Grand Prix, a 700m go-kart circuit. At nearby Oxenford the attractions are Warner Bros Movie World, 'where the movies come alive', and Wet 'n' Wild – a large water park with exciting slides, toboggan rides and a wave pool.

In the heart of Surfers Paradise, two attractions for children are Ripleys Believe it or Not, based on the popular TV show, and Grundys Entertainment Centre – a large indoor complex with rides, dodgems and electronic games.

For adults

Glossy Jupiter's Casino, at Broadbeach Island, is one of the Gold Coast's major adult attractions. This vast centre includes a 605-room hotel, five bars, five restaurants, a nightclub, sophisticated live stage shows, and, of course, the well-

patronised 24-hour casino facilities where you can play blackjack, roulette and many other games.

The Spit is the home of the waterfront shopping, browsing and eating meccas of Marina Mirage (close to the Sheraton Mirage hotel), Mariners Cove and Fishermans Wharf. There are many boat hire outlets here and you can also try waterskiing or jet-skiing. In addition to its excellent golf course, The Palms, the residential area of Sanctuary Cove (north of Southport) offers world-class accommodation, shopping and recreation facilities.

Wildlife and natural attractions

In complete contrast to all this noisy, man-made entertainment, there is a gentler side to the Gold Coast. There are several bird and animal refuges in the area, the favourite of which is Currumbin Sanctuary. Located at the southern end of the coast, this 68-hectare park features koalas, kangaroos, pelicans, an animal orphanage and many colourful Australian birds – children will love feeding the bright green, yellow and blue lorikeets here. Further up the coast, Fleays Fauna Centre, at Burleigh Heads, is an educational enterprise where you can learn about wombats, koalas, possums, crocodiles and other Australian creatures in a lovely natural setting of forest and wetlands. Also in this area is the small Burleigh Heads National Park, a great place for a nature walk and coastal strolls.

Inland, Olsons Currumbin Valley Bird Gardens is a tranquil botanic garden, set in sub-tropical rainforest, which features exotic birds from all

Beyond the portals of Movie World they reveal how Tinsel Town works

over the world in a huge landscaped aviary. The entire Currumbin Valley, with its forests, streams, waterfalls and lush greenery, is worth exploring while you are in the area.

A visit to Lamington National Park is the highlight of any excursion away from the coast. Lamington, with its 20,000 hectares (49,420 acres) of superb sub-tropical rainforest, the McPherson Range and excellent views, became a protected area in 1915 and is one of Queensland's most popular national parks. There are two mountain resorts here, both reached via the small town of Nerang–Binna. Burra and O'Reillys Guesthouse are wonderful places to stay if you have the time. On shorter visits, however, there is still much to do and there are many walking tracks of just a couple of hours duration. Wildlife spotting may reward you with views of goannas, possums, bandicoots, crimson rosellas and brush-turkeys.

Museums

The Gold Coast isn't big on historical attractions but the Surf Museum in Cavill Mall at Surfers Paradise, and the Gold Coast War Museum at inland Mudgeeraba, are worth visiting. The Pioneer House at Nerang, *en route* to Lamington National Park, is an interesting reconstruction of a typical pioneer's home – the rough wooden slab hut and its handmade furniture are a reminder of the harshness of the early Queensland days.

BRISBANE

Riverside Centre • Queen Street • Southeast City Centre • South Bank • Adelaide Street Wickham Terrace • Riverside Centre

Founded as a penal settlement in 1824, Brisbane was initially a remote outpost, far from Sydney and the relatively civilised towns to the south. By the 1840s, however, free settlers were moving into the region and Brisbane became a port for the rich agricultural lands to the west.

This once sleepy, sub-tropical riverside city has undergone a great deal of development in the past two decades and, unfortunately, few historic buildings remain in a sea of modern glass and concrete. Pockets of old Brisbane exist, however, particularly in the southeast of the city, while the South Bank complex – across the Brisbane River – is a new and exciting development of museums, galleries, parkland and a multitude of entertainments. One of the best ways to see Brisbane is from the river and you can choose from a variety of cruises.

Reflecting sea and sky, Brisbane's skyscrapers abut the busy port with tour vessels cruising the river

ⓘ Information booths at Queen Street Mall and Brisbane City Hall (King George Square)

Start the tour at the Riverside Centre on Eagle Street.

Riverside Centre

1 This office and shopping centre is a great place to start and finish your walk. There are excellent views of the Brisbane River from the cafés and bars here, and from nearby **Waterfront Place**. On Sundays this area is also the setting for a large and colourful market. Boat and ferry trips depart from here, and you can cruise the river on vessels such as the *Kookaburra Queen* paddle-wheeler, or take a trip upstream to **Lone Pine Koala Sanctuary** (see For Children).

From Eagle Street, cross over to Creek Street, then turn right to reach Queen Street. Turn left here.

Queen Street

2 The city's main shopping thoroughfare, Queen Street is part pedestrian mall with some wonderful outdoor cafés and eating places. There is also an information booth here and many shopping arcades and department stores. On the left before reaching the Mall is the grand **General Post Office**, dating from 1871, while Post Office Square is to the right.

FOR CHILDREN

If children aren't excited by the **Lone Pine Koala Sanctuary**, 11km from the city at **Fig Tree Pocket**, via the Western Freeway (**Route 32**) or by boat from the city centre, there's something wrong with them! This famous fauna sanctuary is Australia's largest koala haven but also includes kangaroos, wombats, emus, cockatoos and many other native birds.

BACK TO NATURE

Just 8km from the city centre, the 57-hectare **Mount Coot-tha Reserve** is an attractive environment of forest, lookouts, waterfalls, walking trails, and the lovely **Mount Coot-tha Botanic Gardens**. Apart from their natural attractions the gardens feature the fascinating Planetarium and Cosmic Skydome, and there is a wonderful panorama of the city from the lookout here.

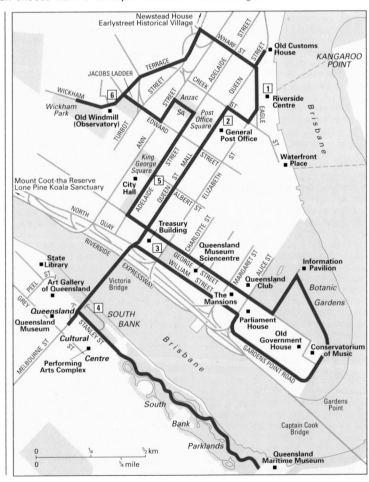

Brisbane, capital of Queensland and home to over a million people, is no more considered a sleepy backwater. Its civic pride is well served by its colossal City Hall

Turn left at the junction of Queen Street and George Street.

Southeast City Centre

3 The important thoroughfare of George Street contains some of Brisbane's most historic buildings. On the right is the imposing Italian Renaissance-style **Treasury Building**, dating from 1885, which is being converted into Brisbane's casino, while further along is the excellent **Queensland Museum Sciencentre** with over 160 hands-on exhibits that will delight both adults and kids. At 40 George Street, the lovely old terrace of **The Mansions** dates from 1890 and is now a shopping arcade. The **Queensland Club**, on Alice Street opposite the **Botanic Gardens**, is a fine example of 1880s colonial architecture; while French Renaissance style 1868 **Parliament House**, also on Alice Street, can be visited on weekdays.

Brisbane's sub-tropical Botanic Gardens were established in the 1850s and have a great location beside the Brisbane River. This is an excellent spot to rest, or you can take a guided tour. Within the gardens area are the **Conservatorium of Music** and 1862 **Old Government House**. Walking back towards Victoria Bridge along William Street, you pass the historic **Commissariat Stores**, built by convicts.

Continue walking on William Street, crossing the Brisbane River on Victoria Bridge.

South Bank

4 This vast area on the south side of the Brisbane River was the location for World Expo in 1988 and has been totally revitalised to create Brisbane's most tourist attractive district. Earlier work here saw the creation of the **Queensland Cultural Centre**, a large development which includes the **Art Gallery of Queensland**, the **Queensland Museum**, **Performing Arts Complex**, **State Library** and a riverside park. The Art Gallery contains a surprisingly good collection of European, Australian and Asian art, while the interesting Queensland Museum concentrates on natural history and anthropology.

The new $150 million South Bank developments lie further to the south. Here you will find the landscaped **Parklands**, complete with rainforests and a waterway; the **Gondwana Rainforest Sanctuary** – a tropical rainforest environment with koalas, turtles, fish and crocodiles; and the **Butterfly House**, with hundreds of butterflies in a natural forest setting. Also here is the **Queensland Maritime Museum** (Dock Street), incorporating the old South Brisbane dry dock, a couple of ships and an excellent collection of sailing and maritime *memorabilia*. The South Bank also features restaurants, a market, boat trips, a man-made beach and swim-

ming lagoon and plenty of entertainment.

Return to the city centre via Victoria Bridge, then turn left into George Street and right into Adelaide Street.

Adelaide Street

5 Off Adelaide Street, King George Square is a large and pleasant open space dominated by the imposing neo-classical 1920s **City Hall** – climb the 92m (300-foot) high Clock Tower for wonderful views of the city. City Hall also houses a civic museum and art gallery and provides information on Brisbane's various self-guided heritage trails. Further along Adelaide Street is Anzac Square, with its **Anzac War Memorial**.

Turn left into Ann Street, right into Edward Street and walk up towards Wickham Terrace.

Wickham Terrace

6 This pleasant avenue, flanked by parks, is the location of the **Old Windmill** (also known as the Observatory). This structure was built by convicts in 1829 and, although little remains, is Brisbane's oldest surviving building. On your way back to the waterfront, check out the grand 1880s **Old Customs House** at the northeastern end of Queen Street.

Walk along Wickham Terrace and return to the Riverside Centre via Wharf Street and Eagle Street.

RECOMMENDED WALK

1 A good way to view the city is to take a short ferry ride to **Kangaroo Point**, across the river from either the Riverside Centre or Waterfront Place, and walk a kilometre or so along the point. From the lookout on River Terrace you will have an excellent view of the Brisbane River, the Botanic Gardens and the rather impressive city skyline.

FOR HISTORY BUFFS

Brisbane's oldest residence is 1846 **Newstead House**, at Newstead (northeast of the city centre), on the banks of the Brisbane River. This charming old house contains period furniture and can be reached by driving via Fortitude Valley and Breakfast Creek Road. More commercialised, but also worth a visit is **Earlystreet Historical Village**, a reconstruction of a pioneer settlement, with a collection of early Queensland buildings and other historical attractions. The Village is at Norman Park, a 15-minute drive east of the city.

3 days – 511km (317 miles)

TOOWOOMBA & INLAND

Brisbane • Toowoomba • Allora • Warwick and the Darling Downs • Stanthorpe and the Granite Belt • Beaudesert • Brisbane

As a complete contrast to Brisbane and the Gold Coast, the inland region of the Darling Downs and the Granite Belt is a fertile agricultural area that was first developed by cattle farmers in the 1840s. Prosperity has been maintained through cattle, sheep and grain farming; dairying; fruit, vegetable and grape growing; and horse stud farms. There are many old settlements in this region, including Toowoomba, known as the 'Garden City of Australia', Allora, Warwick and Stanthorpe. You can also take in the often wild beauty of the Scenic Rim and the Granite Belt. These upland areas contain many national parks and nature reserves and are home to a wide range of animals and birds. You can visit the wineries here, and even cross the New South Wales border to see the historic town of Tenterfield.

From Brisbane City Centre, take Milton Road and the Western Freeway (Route 32), then the Cunningham Highway (Route 15) and turn off on to the Warrego Highway (Route 54) via Ipswich.

Toowoomba

1 Toowoomba, Queensland's largest inland city, with its many parks and

The area around Stanthorpe, at the heart of the Granite Belt, is well-known for wine production

a fantastic location high on the Great Dividing Range, is indeed an attractive place. Toowoomba owes much of its prosperity to the fertile Darling Downs and many fine buildings were constructed on this wealth. The city is an architectural gem – the **Old Town Hall, Court House** and **Post Office** are good examples of colonial 1880s building, while the **Cobb & Co Museum,** commemorating the days of horse-powered transport, is a must. Also of historic and cultural interest are 1880s **Vacy Hall,** now a private hotel; the **Toowoomba Art Gallery;** and the many craft and antique outlets. Natural attractions here include the **Bicentennial Waterbird Habitat,** a breeding and nesting ground for many bird species.

i Regional Tourist Association, 541 Ruthven Street

Drive south on the New England Highway (Route 42).

Allora

2 One of Queensland's oldest towns, picturesque Allora makes a good stopping place on the highway. Dating from the 1850s, the town's main street is full of well-preserved shops and houses. National Trust 1869 **Talgai Homestead** is open to the public, and you can also visit 1898 **Richmond Homestead,** with its spacious gardens. Both of these properties take overnight guests if you are looking for somewhere unusual to stay.

Continue south on the New England Highway (Route 42).

Warwick and the Darling Downs

3 Warwick, the central and oldest settlement of the Southern Downs region, was established in 1840 and is a pleasant agricultural

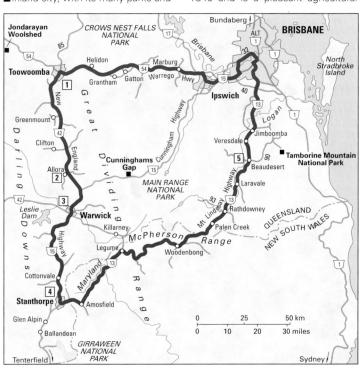

city with some lovely old buildings, such as the 1886 **Court House**, 1891 **Post Office**, and the impressive **Town Hall**. Also of interest are the **Warwick Regional Art Gallery** and 1870 **Pringle Cottage**, a museum of old photographs and vehicles. You can take scenic joyflights over the Southern Downs from Warwick, while a good time to visit is during the annual rodeo in October.

Nearby attractions include **Leslie Dam**, a popular watersports, fishing and picnic spot. Thirty kilometres to the east of Warwick, **Main Range National Park** is part of the Scenic Rim, the mountainous area that forms an arc around Brisbane and the Gold Coast. The peaks, ridges, and forest here contain many birds and animals, including a rare variety of lyrebird. Within the park, **Cunninghams Gap** is an excellent area for bushwalks and scenic lookouts.

i Albion Street (New England Highway)

Continue south on the New England Highway (Route 15).

when you visit nearby **Girraween National Park**. Massive granite outcrops dominate the landscape here – **Sphinx Rocks** is a particularly striking formation. Fauna in the area includes wallabies, kangaroos, wombats, possums and a wide variety of birds.

i Marsh Street

From Stanthorpe, drive east to Amosfield in NSW to join the Mount Lindesay Highway (Route 13). Continue on this road to Beaudesert.

Beaudesert

5 Now a prosperous market town, Beaudesert was first settled by pastoralists in the early 1840s and the **Historical Museum** includes an 1875 wooden hut as a reminder of these early days. Also worth visiting is the timber **St Mary's Church**, believed to be the largest such church in Australia. To the east, lush **Tamborine Mountain National Park** contains protected areas of upland rainforest and eucalypt forest. There are many easy walks in

FOR HISTORY BUFFS

Over the NSW border, 53km (33 miles) from Stanthorpe, the town of **Tenterfield** has an interesting history. Known as the 'birthplace of Federation', it was here in October 1889 that Sir Henry Parkes began his campaign for the federation of the Australian colonies, which finally occurred in 1901. Tenterfield has many historic buildings, including the 1876 **School of Arts**, where the federation speech was delivered, and the National Trust **Court House, Gaol** and **Police Station**.

View from Toowoomba, looking east over the Great Dividing Range to Brisbane

Stanthorpe and the Granite Belt

4 Virtually on the New South Wales border, Stanthorpe is at the heart of the 'Granite Belt', a vast rock outcrop which intrudes into both states. At an altitude of 811m (2,660 feet), this is one of Queensland's coldest towns and snow sometimes falls here in winter. However, the cooler climate has given rise to thriving fruit (apples, pears, plums and peaches) and grape growing industries. In town the attractions include the museum, with its pioneer relics, and many old verandahed buildings. There are numerous wineries in the area, particularly around **Glen Aplin** and **Ballandean**.

The reason for the name the 'Granite Belt' becomes obvious

the area and you are likely to spot orchids, palm-like cycads and bowerbirds among the forest.

i Historical Museum, Jane Street

Return to Brisbane via the Mount Lindesay Highway and Beaudesert Road (Route 13).

Brisbane – Toowoomba 128 (79)
Toowoomba – Allora 60 (37)
Allora – Warwick 25 (16)
Warwick – Stanthorpe 60 (37)
Stanthorpe – Beaudesert 171 (106)
Beaudesert – Brisbane 67 (42)

RECOMMENDED WALK

4 In Girraween National Park, take the 35-minute round-trip **Granite Arch Discovery Walk** to learn about the background to this fascinating area of granite outcrops and unusual vegetation. Girraween is Aboriginal for 'place of flowers' and there is a wonderful display of wildflowers here between July and October.

5–7 days – 671km (416 miles)

THE SUNSHINE COAST & FRASER ISLAND

Brisbane • Caboolture • Caloundra
Mooloolaba and Maroochydore • Noosa Heads
and the Sunshine Coast Hinterland • Tin Can
Bay and Rainbow Beach • Maryborough
Hervey Bay • Fraser Island • Brisbane or Cairns

Known as the Sunshine Coast, the resort area to the north of
Brisbane has wonderful beaches, a warm sunny climate and
the laid-back towns of Mooloolaba, Maroochydore and Noosa
Heads. This lovely region is great for swimming, surfing and
fishing; boating and river cruising; and the chance to explore
coastal national parks. Behind the coast lies the fertile Blackall
Range region – where macadamias, avocados, pineapples and
citrus fruits are grown, and where you will find picturesque
towns and villages, arts and crafts centres and national parks.

One of the region's highlights is Fraser Island – the world's
largest sand island, which is mostly national park and offers
wonderful opportunities for walking, eco-touring and simply
getting back to nature. Moreton and Bribie, two other islands
off this coast, are just as unspoilt and worth a short detour
from the main route. You will also visit the historic city of
Maryborough, one of Queensland's oldest settlements.

SPECIAL TO . . .

The city of **Bundaberg**, north
of Maryborough, is famous
for its rum – a byproduct of
the sugar industry. The
legendary Bundaberg Rum –
universally known as 'Bundy'
and available in both under-
proof and the extremely
potent overproof varieties –
can be sampled on a tour of
the Bundaberg Rum Distillery.
Bundaberg is also the access
point for Lady Elliott (by boat)
and Lady Musgrave (by air)
islands.

*Inside the Big Pineapple, a 15m-
high fibreglass fruit that promotes
Nambour's agricultural produce*

*From Brisbane City Centre, take
Lutwyche Road (**Highway 1**)
north out of the city and then
join the Bruce Highway.*

Caboolture

1 Just off the highway before you
reach the Sunshine Coast, the
small town of Caboolture has long
been renowned for its dairy products. The main attraction here is the
Caboolture Historical Village, a
restored open-air museum with over
60 buildings relocated from the
neighbouring area.

From Caboolture it is a 25km (15-
mile) drive to **Bribie Island**, linked to
the mainland by a bridge over
Pumicestone Passage. This island
is a popular and mostly undeveloped
holiday destination, with good fishing, boating and swimming off white
beaches. On the way to Bribie
Island, the interesting **Abbey
Museum of Art and Archaeology**
traces the history of civilisation.

*Continue north on the Bruce
Highway (**Highway 1**), turning
off at the Caloundra exit.*

Caloundra

2 From Caloundra the Sunshine
Coast stretches north in the form
of 65km of beautiful beaches.
Caloundra itself has plenty of beaches for swimming or surfing and
Pumicestone Passage is an excellent fishing ground. The **Queens-**

*A quietly curving stretch of the
Sunshine Coast, known for its
craggy headlands and river inlets*

land Air Museum contains an extensive collection of aircraft, while other worthwhile attractions include the **Old Lighthouse** (1896) and the *Endeavour* replica – a two-thirds scale model, complete with fully operational rigging, of Captain Cook's famous ship.

[i] Caloundra Road

Drive north to Mooloolaba on the coast road.

Mooloolaba and Maroochydore

3 These tourist towns provide good beaches and other attractions, while Mooloolaba is also an important fishing, prawning and yachting town, and Maroochydore is the Sunshine Coast's commercial and business centre. The strange names are Aboriginal – Mooloolaba means place of the snapper fish, while Maroochy comes from the word for a black swan.

You can cruise on the Maroochy River, the habitat of pelicans and swans, visit inland **Mooloolah River National Park**, just south of Mooloolaba and the domain of the rare ground parrot, or take a short

dwelling that belonged to one of the earliest settlers.

[i] Alexandra Parade, Alexandra Headland

Continue to Noosa Heads on the coast road.

Noosa Heads and the Sunshine Coast Hinterland

4 The resort town of Noosa Heads is a good example of restrained tourist development that complements, rather than dominates, the natural attractions. Noosa offers superb beaches and clear waters, high quality accommodation and facilities and a village-like atmosphere, especially on lively **Hastings Street**. Meandering behind the town, the Noosa Sound and Noosa River form another lovely playground, which can be explored on a cruise. **Noosa National Park**, 432 hectares of rainforest, heathland, eucalypt forest, rocky headlands and sandy coves, surrounds Noosa Head – the views from the lookouts here are superb and there are many good walking tracks and picnic spots. Other Noosa attractions, if you've

drive south to **Point Cartwright** and its wonderful coastal views. The Wharf at Mooloolaba takes the form of a 19th-century fishing village, and contains a marina, restaurants, specialty shops and an amusement centre. The excellent walk-through **Underwater World** with its oceanarium is nearby, while **Alexandra Headland** boasts a fine surfing beach. From Maroochydore, wonderful beaches and small resorts stretch all the way to Noosa Heads – **Mudjimba**, **Marcoola**, **Coolum**, **Peregian**, **Marcus** and **Sunshine** beaches are all deservedly popular. **Buderim**, a few kilometres inland, is a lovely old town with a long history of cane growing and sugar production. Ginger has been grown here since the 1920s and the crop is processed at the nearby Yandina factory. The town is known for its lovely bougainvillaea and other flowering trees and contains the 1876 **Pioneer Cottage** – a restored timber

A bird's-eye view of the chic resort of Noosa Heads in its unspoilt setting at the north end of the Sunshine Coast

had enough of the beach, include the **Montville Art Gallery** at the Sheraton Noosa Resort, taking a biplane joyflight, and just browsing around the many craft shops and cafés. The commercial centres of **Noosaville** and **Tewantin**, to the west, are also holiday resorts and provide one of the access points for the superb **Cooloola National Park**. You can take a cruise through the lakes into the national park's 'Everglades' area or, with a 4WD vehicle, you could drive from here to **Teewah Beach** (and on to Cooloola Beach).

There are also many delights to be discovered inland in the Sunshine Coast Hinterland. The **Blackall Range** runs parallel to the coast and is full of attractive villages, scenic

Eumundi's famed Saturday market: bright and breezy to compete with the sunshine at the north end of the Sunshine Coast

SCENIC ROUTES

4 The area's most scenic route is the 50km or so Range Drive from Landsborough (west of Caloundra) through the Blackall Range to Nambour. This upland region is full of picturesque villages such as Maleny, Montville, Flaxton and Mapleton, and you can also visit Mapleton Falls and Kondalilla national parks and Mary Cairncross Park – just south of Maleny and providing fine views of the Glass House Mountains.

lookouts and natural wonders (see Scenic Routes). **Nambour**, west of Maroochydore, is the centre of an agricultural area which specialises in growing sugar cane and fruits such as pineapples. The 'Big Pineapple' marks the entrance to the **Sunshine Plantation**, which cultivates tropical fruits and is open to the public. Further north, the historic town of **Eumundi** holds a colourful Saturday morning market.

ⓘ Hastings Street

From Tewantin, you can drive (if you have a 4WD vehicle) through the Cooloola National Park to Tin Can Bay and Rainbow Beach. Alternatively, drive to Cooroy and join the Bruce Highway to Gympie, then take the Tin Can Bay road.

Tin Can Bay and Rainbow Beach

5 These small resort towns are alternative access points to Cooloola National Park. The marina at Tin Can Bay is a great place to hire a boat to cruise or fish on Tin Can Inlet, while the quiet coastal town of Rainbow Beach lies in the middle of the 20km (12-mile) long beach of **Wide Bay**. The **Cooloola National Park**, a wilderness of heathland, forest, swamps and the world's largest intact dune system, is famous for its coloured sand cliffs – around 40,000 years old and similar to those found on Fraser Island. Much of the park can be reached only by 4WD vehicles or walking tracks.

ⓘ 8 Rainbow Beach Road, Rainbow Beach

Take the Cooloola Coast Road from Tin Can Bay or Rainbow Beach.

Maryborough

6 Dating back to 1843, the agricultural centre of Maryborough is one of Queensland's oldest cities. Historical attractions include the **Wharf Street Heritage Precinct** – the location of many of Maryborough's oldest buildings, **Baddow House** (1883), National Trust **Brennan & Geraghty's Store**, the **Court House** and the **Royal Hotel**. The best way to see all this is

BACK TO NATURE

Moreton Island, reached by vehicular ferry from Redcliffe (off the Bruce Highway south of Caboolture), is a large sand island, second only in size to Fraser Island. Most of Moreton is wilderness national park, with long sandy beaches, sand dunes, heaths and freshwater lagoons to enjoy. There is an abundance of birdlife here and huge shell middens, reminders of the Aboriginal people who long inhabited the island. The unsealed roads are suitable only for 4WD vehicles.

on the local Heritage Trail – details from the tourist office. An open-air market is held each Thursday and nearby **Ululah Lagoon**, the town's original water supply, is now a bird and wildlife sanctuary.

ⓘ Maryborough Promotions Bureau, 30 Ferry Street

Take the Hervey Bay road from Maryborough.

Hervey Bay

7 Thirty kilometres to the north of Maryborough, Hervey Bay is the main departure point for **Fraser Island**, but also a holiday town in its own right. There are good (surf-free) beaches, fine fishing and diving here, and the town is a popular whale-watching spot during the August to October migration season. From Hervey Bay, vehicle ferries and flights depart frequently for Fraser Island, and you can also fly to **Lady Elliott Island**, a popular holiday and scuba diving resort on the Great Barrier Reef, from here.

ⓘ 63 Old Maryborough Road, Pialba

Take the vehicular ferry to Fraser Island.

Fraser Island

8 The world's largest sand island, Fraser is 123km (76 miles) long and covers an area of 184,000 hectares (454,660 acres) – the island was first recorded by James Cook in 1770 and later named after the unfortunate Eliza Fraser who was shipwrecked here. This World Heritage listed island is composed mainly of sand, but there are areas of volcanic rock, crystal clear streams, rainforest, wildflowers and over 40 freshwater lakes. Sand-blows are another feature of the island – these often giant dunes change shape and move in the

FOR HISTORY BUFFS

Gympie, on the Bruce Highway inland from Noosa Heads, dates back to 1867, when the town became the centre of one of Queensland's major gold rushes. Once the gold ran out in the 1920s Gympie reverted to agricultural pursuits and is now an elegant provincial centre with some fine old buildings. Other attractions here are the Deep Creek Gold Fossicking Park, where you can pan for gold; the excellent Historical and Mining Museum; and the Woodworks Museum, focusing on the timber and forestry industries.

direction of the prevailing winds. The northern half is covered by **Great Sandy National Park**, while Cathedral Beach on the east coast is the home of the famous coloured 'teewah' sand cliffs – ancient sand deposits which have been coloured ochre and yellow by minerals.

There is, thankfully, little development on Fraser Island, but there are several low-key resorts and camping is permitted at various locations. Sailing, fishing, walking on deserted beaches, bushwalking and just relaxing are the main activities here. You may spot dingoes and wild brumby horses, and humpback whales pass through the **Great Sandy Strait** between August and October each year. Fraser's birdlife is prolific – there are over 200 species here, including peregrine falcons, kingfishers and white-breasted sea eagles.

Access to the island is by vehicular ferry from Hervey Bay (Urangan Boat Harbour), or from Inskip Point to the north of Rainbow Beach. You can also fly in from Hervey Bay and Maryborough. To see anything of the island (there are no roads as such) you will need a 4WD vehicle, which can be hired in Hervey Bay, Rainbow Beach or Noosa.

To return directly to Brisbane, drive south from Maryborough on the Bruce Highway. Alternatively, you can fly north to Cairns from Maryborough or Bundaberg to link up with Tour 8.

Brisbane – Caboolture 50 (31)
Caboolture – Caloundra 47 (29)
Caloundra – Maroochydore 21 (13)
Maroochydore – Noosa Heads 40 (25)
Noosa Heads – Tin Can Bay (via Gympie) 118 (73)
Tin Can Bay – Maryborough 65 (40)
Maryborough – Hervey Bay 30 (19)
Hervey Bay – Brisbane 300 (186)

All aboard! There's room for crowds of the curious on the plantation train at the Big Pineapple

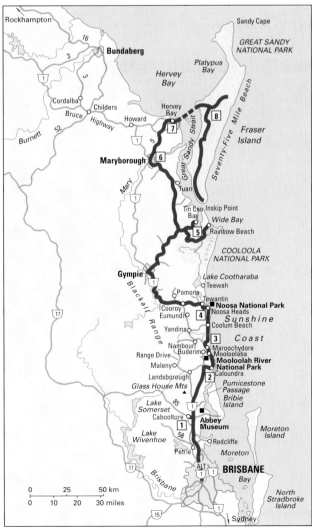

CAIRNS & AREA

Cairns City • Green Island • The Low Isles
Fitzroy Island • Kuranda • Adventure Activities
The Marlin Coast

The once rather sleepy tropical city of Cairns has been transformed in the past decade into northern Australia's tourist capital. It is blessed with a wonderful location – at the edge of the aquamarine Coral Sea, close to the Great Barrier Reef and tropical rainforests and backed by high, forested peaks. You will need several days (at least three) to see the sights of Cairns and the Marlin coast, visit the islands and take the train trip to Kuranda.

Aboriginal performer of the Tjapukai Dance Theatre, Kuranda: daily presentations are a 'must-see' attraction of this village

ℹ️ Far North Queensland Promotion Bureau, corner of Sheridan and Aplin streets

Cairns City

1 Most of the interest in this relaxed city centres around the waterfront. Trinity Wharf and the Marlin Jetty are the busy embarkation points for trips to the Great Barrier Reef and some idyllic island destinations. Fronting Trinity Bay, the long **Esplanade** is great for an evening stroll and watching the prolific birdlife, including herons, pelicans and spoonbills. Wandering the wide, tree-lined streets of Cairns is another favourite occupation – there are many good cafés to enjoy and plenty of places to shop – **Pier Marketplace** and the exotic **Conservatory** are some suggestions. Walking is also a good way to see some of the city's tropical-style houses, often raised above the ground for cooling purposes.

The **Cairns Museum and Art Gallery** is worth visiting to discover something of the area's interesting history. The **Flecker Botanic Gardens** and **Centenary Lakes**, in the northern suburb of Edge Hill, are a lovely collection of tropical plants, lakes and palm forests, and a visit to the **Royal Flying Doctor Service** base is highly recommended.

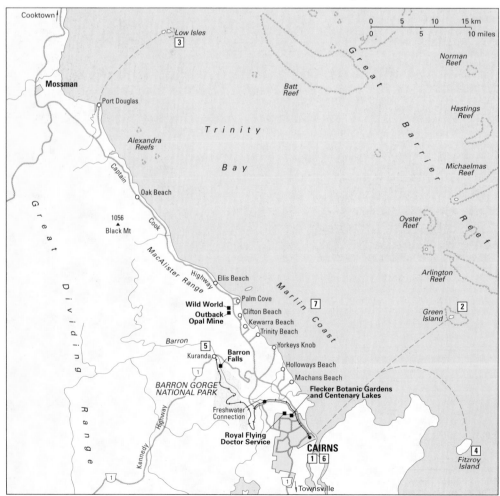

Green Island

2 One of the most popular destinations from Cairns, Green Island is a lovely coral cay with a resort and white beaches, surrounded by protected reefs. At the famous **Underwater Observatory** you can walk beneath the sea and observe thousands of colourful fish. Green Island also offers **Marineland Melanesia**, with its coral gardens, crocodiles and a display of Melanesian art.

The Low Isles

3 Like Green Island, these are coral cays where you can swim, snorkel, take an introductory scuba dive or go for a beach walk in the company of a marine biologist. Access to the Low Isles is usually via a coach ride to nearby Port Douglas, from where the boat trip departs.

Fitzroy Island

4 The lovely beaches and rainforest of Fitzroy Island have made it another favourite day trip from Cairns. You can fish, snorkel or dive here, and there is also a resort which permits day visitors to use its pool.

Kuranda

5 This small village, high in the hills 34km from Cairns, is the destination for the famous **Cairns–Kuranda Railway** trip. This historic rail line dates from the 1880s and is a remarkable feat of engineering. The one and a half hour trip, on board

kets and tropical plants. You can visit the **Australian Butterfly Sanctuary** (the largest in Australia), the **Kuranda Wildlife Noctarium**, or browse around the colourful village markets, held from Wednesday to Saturday. Another big attraction is the dance, song and storytelling show by an internationally famous Aboriginal dance group at the **Tjapukai Dance Theatre**. Just outside Kuranda, **Rainforestation** is billed as an 'Aboriginal experience' and includes a 'Dreamtime Walk', boomerang throwing and a performance by the Pamagirri Aboriginal Dancers.

Adventure Activities

6 Cairns is the base for a bewildering array of outdoor activities. Some of the adventures on offer are whitewater rafting on the Barron and Tully rivers, canoeing, scuba diving, tandem parachuting, bungee jumping, hot-air ballooning and a variety of joyflights. There are numerous tour operators in Cairns through which these sometimes wild adventures can be booked.

Drive north of Cairns on the Captain Cook Highway.

The Marlin Coast

7 To the north of Cairns the mangroves and mudflats give way to a superb piece of coastline with lovely sandy beaches. This is the Marlin Coast (named after the proliferation of this large game fish in the local waters), which stretches for over

restored old carriages, takes in the spectacular zig-zag climb up the range and passes through 15 tunnels – the train climbs 300m (985 feet) in 20km (12 miles). You have excellent views of the **Barron Gorge National Park** and **Barron Falls**, which tumble 240m to the valley below. The trip departs from Cairns Railway Station but you can also join the train at **Freshwater Connection**, just outside the city. This historic railway station has an interesting restaurant and there is also a **Railway Museum** here.

There is much to see and do in picturesque Kuranda, known as the 'village in the rainforest'. Firstly, admire the delightful old **Railway Station**, with its hanging fern bas-

The exclusive resort of Palm Cove, on the Marlin Coast

30km towards Port Douglas. **Holloways**, **Yorkeys Knob**, **Trinity**, **Kewarra**, **Clifton** and **Palm Cove** beaches all compensate for the lack of a strip of sand in Cairns itself. Note that swimming in the sea here from October to April is often restricted due to the presence of jellyfish and other marine stingers, but most of these beaches provide special swimming enclosures. There are other attractions too – at Holloways Beach you can visit the **Vic Hislop Shark Show**, while the Palm Cove area offers **Wild World** and the **Outback Opal Mine**.

6/7 days – 1,004km (624 miles)

NORTH & INLAND FROM CAIRNS

Cairns • Port Douglas • Mossman and Daintree National Park • Cape Tribulation National Park Cooktown • Mareeba • Chillagoe–Mungana Caves National Park • Ravenshoe • Malanda and Yungaburra • Atherton • Kuranda • Cairns

The varied region to the north and inland from Cairns is the setting for this fascinating nature-based tour. You travel from picturesque Port Douglas to the World Heritage listed rainforests of Daintreee and Cape Tribulation national parks, and on to isolated Cooktown. North and west of here, the scenery becomes dry and rugged, but you eventually reach the fertile farming lands of the high Atherton Tableland. The region is also famous for its caves system at Chillagoe, and a treasure house of ancient Aboriginal art near the outback hamlet of Laura.

A 4WD vehicle is necessary for parts of this tour – certainly from Mossman to Cooktown – and the best time to visit is during the drier May to November period. You are likely to encounter marine stingers in the ocean between October and April and beware of crocodiles north of the Mossman area.

Four Mile Beach: most visitors go no further south as roads become impassable except for 4WD

SPECIAL TO ...

The tiny bush settlement of **Laura**, off the Cooktown/Mareeba road, is your base for viewing the incredible Aboriginal rock art galleries of the **Quinkan Reserve**, one of the world's most extensive areas of prehistoric art, and Australia's most important Aboriginal art site. The sandstone caves and overhangs here were only 'discovered' in the 1960s and are full of primitive paintings of men, the eerie Quinkan and Imjim spirits, a horse and many other animals. Some of the sites are open for inspection, in the company of local Aboriginal rangers.

The Daintree rainforest has suffered from commercial logging, erosion and being split into 'development' parcels, but is now a protected area

Take the Captain Cook Highway north from Cairns, passing along the Marlin Coast (see City Tour 3).

Port Douglas

1 The days when Port Douglas was a quiet fishing village are long gone. Dating back to the 1870s, this picturesque town has experienced a rash of tourist development in recent years, but thankfully it has not lost its considerable charm. Wide, palm-fringed streets, excellent cafés, restaurants and boutiques and the well designed **Sheraton Mirage Resort**, just out of town, all help to create a destination with international flair.

The town's attractions include **Four Mile Beach**, with its white sands and clear waters; the **Shipwreck Museum**, with relics from Cook's *Endeavour* and many other ships; the **Marina Mirage** boating, shopping and entertainment complex; river boat trips on the *Lady Douglas* paddle-wheeler; and the **Rainforest Habitat**, with its lush tropical plants and native animals. The outer Great Barrier Reef is closer to the shore here than in most parts of Queensland and there are many diving, snorkelling or sightseeing cruises available to the reef. You can also cruise to the **Low Isles** and **Cooktown**, while safari tours into the surrounding rainforest are also available.

i 23 Macrossan Street

Return to the highway and continue north to Mossman.

Mossman and Daintree National Park

2 The small sugar milling town of Mossman dates back to 1876, but nowadays it is better known as the gateway to the unique Daintree National Park. In Mossman itself there are tours of the **Mossman**

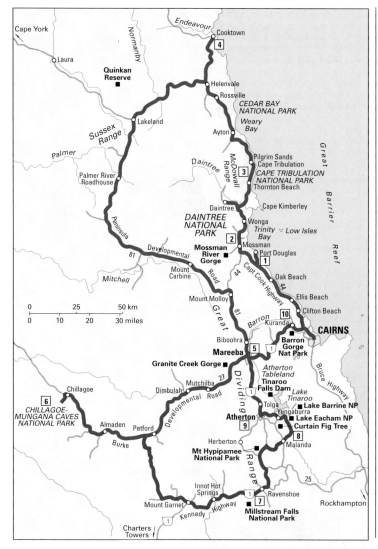

FOR CHILDREN

1 On the highway halfway between Cairns and Port Douglas, the **Hartleys Creek Crocodile Farm** is a great place to take children. There are over 200 saltwater and freshwater crocs, cassowaries, emus, dingoes and many other creatures here, and the farm features daily events such as cassowary feeding and a crocodile attack show!

RECOMMENDED WALKS

8 The well-marked walking tracks through the rainforest surrounding Lake Barrine and Lake Eacham are a great way to see more of the delightful environment, and to spot some of the abundant wildlife. There are many birds here, including colourful parrots, as well as turtles, goannas, water dragons, and the shy platypus, which can sometimes be seen in the lakes.

Central Mill from June to December, and rides on the **Bally Hooley Steam Express** train through the canefields to Port Douglas. North of Mossman and at the edge of the national park, the old timber-cutting town of **Daintree** marks the end of the sealed road. Cruises on the mangrove-lined Daintree River, inhabited by crocodiles, leave from here, while other local attractions include the **Timber Museum**, **Butterfly Farm**, and the interesting **Rainforest Environment Centre**.

This remarkable national park was placed on the UNESCO World Heritage list in 1989 to protect its dense tropical forests – some of the world's most magnificent lowland rainforest. Many creatures live within the huge park, including the rare Bennett's tree kangaroo, enormous birdwing butterflies and the flightless cassowary, while an incredible 35,000 orchid species are found here. Be sure to visit the lovely steep-sided Mossman River Gorge, with its waterfall and rockpools, at the southern end of the park and you can also call in at exclusive **Silky Oaks Wilderness Lodge** for a meal or coffee.

From Daintree, drive back towards Mossman, then turn off northeast to cross the Daintree River by ferry. Take the unsealed road to Cape Tribulation.

The banks of the Daintree River, renowned for its crocodiles

Cape Tribulation National Park

3 This exquisite national park takes in sandy beaches and rocky headlands, including Cape Tribulation (the name orginates from 1770 when Captain James Cook's ship, the *Endeavour*, was damaged on a nearby reef), lush rainforest and creeks, and the high lands of the McDowall Range. There are some good walks

SCENIC ROUTES

7 To the northeast of Ravenshoe the dairying and cheese-making hamlet of **Millaa Millaa** is famous for its 'Waterfall Circuit'. This short, unsealed route (impassable after heavy rain) leads to the spectacular Millaa Millaa, Zillie and Elinjaa waterfalls. The **McHugh Lookout**, west of Millaa Millaa, provides fantastic views of the Atherton Tableland, and you can also visit the village's **Eacham Historical Society Museum**.

along the coast and a few places to stay around the cape, if you would like to linger in this beautiful spot.

Although the rough and often steep **Bloomfield Track** through the park and on to Cooktown gives access to this special environment, its creation in the early 1980s gave rise to a great deal of controversy. Be aware that crocodiles inhabit the creeks and rivers in this area. Nearby **Cedar Bay National Park**, further north on the unsealed road, is a similar environment to Cape Tribulation, and you should also call in at the interesting Helenvale Hotel before reaching Cooktown.

Continue on the Cooktown road.

Cooktown

4 This frontier-style town on the Endeavour River has a most interesting history. Cooktown was first visited by Europeans when James Cook moored the holed *Endeavour* here for several weeks in 1770. It was another century before settlement, however, when Cooktown became the major port for the

Macho man in a macho land: an outback rodeo tests a man's courage and co-ordination

1870s Palmer River goldrush. The town grew rapidly and had a population of some 13,000 at one point – compared with the 1,000 or so of today!

Modern Cooktown is a charming, very relaxed place – full of old buildings and surrounded by lush forest and river scenery. Highlights include the **James Cook Historical Museum**, housed in an old convent; the **Cooktown Sea Museum**; the **Cemetery**, which contains the graves of many Chinese who worked on the goldfields; the **Botanical Gardens**; and the view from Grassy Hill.

ⓘ Cooktown Sea Museum, corner of Helen and Walker streets

Return towards Helenvale, then take the Lakeland road and drive via Mount Carbine and Mount Molloy to Mareeba.

Mareeba

5 At the centre of a rich tobacco, coffee and tropical fruit growing area, Mareeba is the Atherton Tableland's most substantial town, with a few attractions for tourists. You can tour local coffee and tobacco plantations; visit the Trainland complex, with its working locomotives and other railways *memorabilia*; and walk through nearby **Granite Creek Gorge**, a jumble of enormous granite boulders which were created by ancient volcanic activity.

ⓘ Shire Offices

From here take the Burke Developmental Road, via Dimbulah, to Chillagoe–Mungana caves. (Note that the 45km unsealed section of this road may be impassable during the December to March wet season.)

Chillagoe–Mungana Caves National Park

6 This dry and rugged limestone area, west of the fertile Atherton Tableland, contains unusual jagged ridges and an extraordinary underground cave system. The national park here protects over 1,800 hectares (4,450 acres) of this limestone belt, its caves, richly coloured stalactites, stalagmites, shawls and pendants, and a large bat population. There are ranger-guided tours of **Royal Arch Cave** and **Donna Cave**, while other caverns can be explored independently. There is a large bird population here and you may also spot wallabies and wallaroos. The small town of Chillagoe was once a thriving mining centre, with some of Queensland's richest gold, silver, lead, copper and tin deposits. Nowadays, the annual May rodeo and races draw large crowds, but otherwise it's a quiet backwater. The old copper smelters and the **Chillagoe Historical Museum**, with its mineral collection and Aboriginal artefacts, is of interest however.

Return along the same road towards Dimbulah, but turn right to Mount Garnet. At Mount Garnet turn east on to the Kennedy Highway to Ravenshoe.

Ravenshoe

7 The small settlement of Ravenshoe, one of Queensland's highest towns, is the base for short tours to various waterfalls and other natural wonders. You can take a ride on the **Historic Steam Railway**, a steam train and restored timber carriages which operate on a 14km track through the local forest country, while nearby **Millstream Falls National Park** contains the widest waterfall in Australia. The **Innot Hot Springs** and their steaming thermal waters are further west, on the way to Mount Garnet – you can take a mud bath or relax in a thermal spa. Mount Garnet was a copper and tin mining town – you can try your luck at panning for alluvial tin here.

Continue on the Kennedy Highway towards Atherton, but take the Malanda turn-off.

FOR HISTORY BUFFS

9 A short detour southwest from Atherton takes you to the historic 19th-century tin mining town of **Herberton**. There are some lovely old buildings here, including the School of Arts, National Bank and Loudon Mill, while the Historical Village contains the Tin Pannikin museum and 30 old re-sited structures, which date back to the 1870s and come from various parts of the region.

Malanda and Yungaburra

8 The small town of Malanda is at the heart of rich dairying country that supplies produce to far north Queensland and the Northern Territory, on the 'world's longest milk run'. Local attractions include the **Malanda Falls Environmental Park**, which encompasses the falls, a lovely swimming hole, walking tracks and rainforest.

The picturesque town of **Yungaburra** is the best access point for visits to the national parks of **Lake Barrine** and **Lake Eacham**. These clear volcanic lakes are surrounded by lush rainforest and there are many marsupials and 100 species of birds in the area. The **Lake Eacham Wildlife Museum** is also worth visiting for its native wildlife. Also nearby are **Lake Tinaroo**, the main water supply for the Atherton Tableland region, and the Curtain Fig Tree – a magnificent tree with aerial roots which cascade over 15m to the ground.

Take the Atherton road out of Yungaburra.

Atherton

9 Perched 760m (2,500-foot) high on the tableland, and offering a cool alternative to the heat and humidity of Cairns below, Atherton (population 4,600) is the region's main agricultural centre. Maize, potatoes, avocados and macadamia nuts are all grown here in abundance. **Hallorans Hill Environmental Park** is an extinct volcanic crater with excellent views over the tableland – take the walking track to the top. Other local attractions are the **Old Post Office Museum**; the **Chinese Joss House**, dating from 1900; a **minerals and gemstone museum**; and the **Homestead Tourist Park**, a working avocado plantation with a restaurant and a variety of entertainments.

South is the **Crater National Park**, centred around a sheer, 70m (230-foot) wide crater created by ancient volcanic activity and now containing a deep lake. This area contains some lovely sub-tropical rainforest. You can also head north to **Lake Tinaroo** and the **Tinaroo Falls Dam**, a great spot for a picnic and the start of a scenic forest drive, or visit the peanut growing town of **Tolga**, where it is possible to tour the **Peanut Marketing Board complex** from April to July.

i Atherton Promotion Bureau, Mabel Street

Continue on the Kennedy Highway (Highway 1), via Mareeba.

Kuranda

10 You may have already visited Kuranda on the recommended train trip from Cairns, but travelling by road gives another perspective. Apart from the village's attractions (see City Tour 3), the nearby **Barron Gorge National Park** is a spectacular area of tropical rainforest and rich flora and fauna, and the location of the 240m (785-foot) high Barron Falls. The energy of this waterfall has been harnessed under a hydro-

Taking the rainforest walk in Daintree National Park. The area escaped the volcanic eruptions over 100 million years ago that destroyed primitive forests elsewhere in the far-north jungles

electric scheme – you can visit the Barron Gorge Hydro Power Station by driving along the gorge. From Kuranda, there is a scenic drive down the escarpment to Cairns.

Return to Cairns on the Kennedy Highway.

Cairns – Port Douglas 67 (42)
Port Douglas – Mossman 20 (12)
Mossman – Cape Tribulation 59 (37)
Cape Tribulation – Cooktown 106 (66)
Cooktown – Mareeba 278 (173)
Mareeba – Chillagoe-Mungana Caves 142 (88)
Chillagoe-Mungana Caves – Ravenshoe 159 (99)
Ravenshoe – Malanda 45 (28)
Malanda – Atherton 31 (19)
Atherton – Kuranda 70 (43)
Kuranda – Cairns 27 (17

BACK TO NATURE

9 Mount Hypipamee National Park, a few kilometres south of Atherton, is an interesting volcanic environment. The mountain's summit contains a crater with steep walls which plunge over 60m to a pool below. You can follow the walking track through thick rainforest to the crater's rim.

6 days – 1,097km (680 miles)

CAIRNS TO ROCKHAMPTON

Cairns • Gordonvale • Innisfail • Tully and Mission Beach • Cardwell • Ingham Townsville • Bowen • Airlie Beach and Shute Harbour • Mackay • Rockhampton and Yeppoon Bundaberg or Brisbane

This extensive one-way tour takes in the tropical country to the south of Cairns, while further south is the major city of Townsville, with excellent access to the Great Barrier Reef, and the glorious Whitsunday islands. The tour also includes the nation's sugar capital, Mackay, and Rockhampton, just north of the Tropic of Capricorn.

Off the coast are the wonders of the Great Barrier Reef and countless islands. The beaches here are beautiful, but beware of marine stingers during the October to April period.

Be wary of wading where you see this sign

From Cairns, drive south on the Bruce Highway (Highway 1).

Gordonvale

1 The small town of Gordonvale is worth visiting for the **Edward River Crocodile Farm**. Operated by the local Aboriginal community, the farm also features a tropical bird sanctuary and you can watch the daily croc-feeding session. Also here is the **Mulgrave Settlers Museum**, concentrating on local history from the 1870s.

Lovely **Bellenden Ker National Park**, which stretches from here south alongside the highway, is a high region of peaks, waterfalls and dense rainforest containing Queensland's two highest mountains – Mount Bartle Frere (1,622m/5,321 feet)) and Mount Bellenden Ker (1,580m/5,184 feet). The park is largely undeveloped but there are good walking tracks, and you may see the large, flightless cassowary here.

Continue south on the Bruce Highway.

Innisfail

2 The high rainfall in this tropical region has created a lovely green environment in which sugar cane and many exotic fruits are grown. The small **Chinese Joss House** here is a reminder that many of the early pioneers of the region were Chinese. Other Innisfail attractions include the **Johnstone River Crocodile Farm**, and the delightful

SCENIC ROUTES

1 The Bruce Highway between Cairns and Innisfail passes through some spectacular lush country. To the right lie the mountains of Bellenden Ker National Park, with sugar cane fields between the road and peaks, while the Thompson and Graham ranges are to your left. Closer to Innisfail there is more sugar cane land and patches of green rainforest.

SPECIAL TO . . .

2 Tea is not widely cultivated in Australia, but the **Nerada Tea Plantation** near Innisfail has been operating successfully since the 1950s. The plantation conducts regular tours, on which you can sample the popular brew.

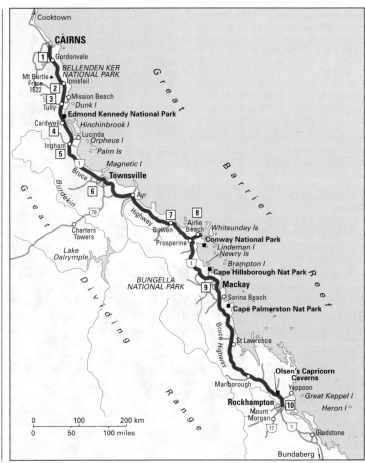

Turtles find an idyllic existence in the waters of the Great Barrier Reef

parkland and waterways of **Warrina Lakes**. Out of town, the interesting **Australian Sugar Industry Museum** (at Mourilyan to the south) and **Paronella Park** at nearby Mena Creek are worth visiting. This park contains the ruins of a Spanish-style castle which was built by a Spanish migrant early this century.

i Cassowary Coast Development Bureau, River Drive

Continue on the Bruce Highway.

Tully and Mission Beach

3 The sugar town of Tully and nearby Cardwell share the reputation of being Australia's wettest places, with an average rainfall of 4–500cm (150–200 inches) per annum. The area is famous for its excellent whitewater rafting on the Tully River and you can also tour the **Co-operative Sugar Mill**. To the northeast, the resort town of Mission Beach, named for the Aboriginal mission which was established here in 1912, is surrounded by rainforest and good sandy beaches. **Dunk Island**, just a few kilometres offshore, can be reached by boat from Clump Point, outside Mission Beach. From here you can also go on a fishing trip, or cruise to the Great Barrier Reef and various uninhabited islands. **Bedarra Island**, with its exclusive resorts, is also accessed from Clump Point but day visitors are not able to visit.

Drive south on the Bruce Highway.

Cardwell

4 Dating back to 1864, Cardwell is a popular holiday and fishing resort and the starting point for trips to **Hinchinbrook Island**. This remarkable place is Australia's largest island national park and a wonderland of rugged mountains, rainforest, waterfalls and sandy beaches. There is a resort on the island, and camping is allowed if you have a National Parks permit; alternatively, you can easily make a day trip.

From Cardwell you can take a scenic drive through the local forest, which includes creeks, waterfalls and the **Cardwell Lookout**, with

good views over the coast. To the north is the lush **Edmund Kennedy National Park**, part of the **Wet Tropics World Heritage Area**. There is a wide variety of bird and animal life here, including estuarine crocodiles.

i Tourist Association, 91 Victoria Street

Continue on the Bruce Highway.

Ingham

5 Yet another sugar town, Ingham is a pleasant settlement with many parks and gardens, such as the delightful tropical **Botanic Gardens**. You can tour **Victoria Sugar Mill** during the crushing season from mid-June to late November and discover just how cane is turned into sugar. Offshore, the Palm group of islands were named by Captain Cook in 1770. **Palm Island** is an Aboriginal homeland, but nearby **Orpheus Island** is a national park which can be visited by both day visitors and resort guests. The coral reefs attract snorkellers and scuba divers, and there are some excellent walks here. Access to the island is from Lucinda (northeast of Ingham).

i Corner of Bruce Highway and Lannercost Street

Continue south on the Bruce Highway.

Townsville

6 Australia's largest tropical city (population 96,000) was founded in 1864 and is now a busy port and commercial centre, as well as offering a great many attractions for visitors. Start at Townsville's main attraction – the **Great Barrier Reef Wonderland**. This complex includes a large living coral reef aquarium and explains a great deal about how the reef's ecosystem operates. Other highlights include the drive up 285m (935-foot) **Castle Hill**, which dominates the city and provides fine views; the **Townsville Museum**, housed in the 1877 Old Magistrates

FOR HISTORY BUFFS

An excursion to the city of **Charters Towers**, 135km (84 miles) southwest of Townsville, provides a fascinating trip into the past. Founded as a pastoral area, the town boomed when gold was discovered here in 1871, and vast amounts of the mineral were mined until 1911. Once referred to by its residents as 'The World', Charters Towers still contains many grand old verandahed buildings, including the city's very own stock exchange and several imposing banks.

FOR CHILDREN

8 The Whitsunday Wildlife Park at Cannonvale, near Airlie Beach, contains a comprehensive collection of native fauna and should be a great hit with children. This educational park offers everything from birdlife, crocodiles and snakes, to the more cuddly wallabies, kangaroos and koalas. Another great spot for kids is the **Whitsunday Aquarium** at Airlie Beach, with turtles and many colourful fish to admire.

BACK TO NATURE

Lovely **Heron Island**, off Gladstone (120km/75 miles south of Rockhampton), is one of Queensland's most natural resort islands. The main attraction is that the island is a coral cay right on the Great Barrier Reef, with marvellous snorkelling, diving and nature watching opportunities. The island is a nesting ground for turtles, which can be seen from November to April, while migrating whales pass by from June to October. The only hitch is that you must stay at the resort to experience all this natural beauty – day visitors are not allowed.

Court; Anderson Park Botanic Gardens; and the **Town Common Environmental Park**. This wetlands area is just a few minutes from the city centre and is a refuge for waterbirds and wallabies. For nightlife, check out the **Sheraton Breakwater Casino**, and if you want to shop aim for pedestrian **Flinders Mall**, at the heart of the city. Townsville also has some good beaches – a visit to **The Strand** is recommended.

Another very good reason to visit Townsville is the presence of **Magnetic Island**, 8km (5 miles) offshore. Although many people reside here, around half of the island is national park and there are many sandy beaches and walking tracks, as well as the opportunity to spot koalas, wallabies and goannas. You can also take a boat trip to the Great Barrier Reef from Townsville – pontoons on the reef provide good diving and snorkelling access, or you can do some reef fishing.

ⓘ Enterprise House, 3 The Strand; or Flinders Mall

Continue driving on the Bruce Highway, via the sugar town of Ayr.

Local resident of Heron Island, a small sand island that teems with interesting birds and other wildlife (access is by boat or helicopter)

Bowen

7 This is an attractive fishing and agricultural town that offers good beaches and access to several islands and the Great Barrier Reef. There are cruises to the little visited northern **Whitsunday Islands**, including **Middle** and **Gloucester**, as well as the reef. In town, the **Historical Society Museum** contains relics from old shipwrecks and Aboriginal artefacts. You can also drive to **Flagstaff Hill** for great views of the surrounding area, or visit **Mullers Lagoon** – a fantastic place for birdwatching.

Drive south on the Bruce Highway to Proserpine, then take the Airlie Beach turn-off.

Airlie Beach and Shute Harbour

8 The small towns of Airlie Beach and Shute Harbour, the gateway to the magnificent Whitsunday Islands, provide plenty of facilities for visitors. You can either stay on the mainland and take day trips, or base yourself at one of the many island resorts. Airlie Beach is the region's accommodation and nightlife centre, with bars, restaurants and live entertainment, while most boat trips depart from Shute Harbour. There are also a variety of outer Great Barrier Reef excursions, by boat, seaplane and helicopter.

The Whitsunday Islands and their waterways offer an incredible array of holiday pursuits and there are many excellent resorts here. The group is composed of some 74 hilly and often forested islands, many of which are national parks. Resort islands which welcome day visitors include the very commercial **Hamilton Island**; **Daydream Island**; **Long Island** (a national park, but with resorts); **Hook Island**, with its underwater observatory; and **South Molle**. Others, like **Hayman Island**, are only for resort guests; and you can also visit the uninhabited and protected Whitsunday Island.

The region is famous for its world-class scuba diving and snorkelling, with clear waters and beautiful coral formations, and there are many opportunities for boating, fishing and other watersports. In addition, you can go horseriding inland, tour the **Proserpine Sugar Mill**, or take a day trip to **Conway National Park**, a lovely region of unspoilt bushland and coast.

Enjoy Heron Island for its beach strolling – or its reef-walking!

ⓘ Whitsunday Tourism
Association, Airlie Beach

*Return to the Bruce Highway
and drive south to Mackay.*

Mackay

9 Australia's sugar capital is a pleasant riverside city with many historic buildings here which you can see on the self-guided heritage walk (details are available from the tourist centre). The area's beaches are excellent – **Sarina Beach** to the south is recommended, as are Bucasia and Blacks beaches north of town. Other Mackay attractions include the **Big Prawn**, a prawn farm which offers guided tours; the **Homebush Pottery**, located in an early 1900s store; and **Greenmount Homestead**, a 1915 house that contains a museum and memorial to a local pioneer family. You can also visit the Illawong **Fauna Sanctuary**, with its abundance of native fauna.

Mackay is the starting point for fishing and diving excursions, seaplane trips, or cruises to the lovely national park, **Brampton** and **Newry islands**. You can cruise to **Lindeman** and **Hamilton islands**, or take a trip to an underwater observatory on the Great Barrier Reef. There are several national parks in the area, including coastal **Cape Palmerston** and **Cape Hillsborough** with its friendly kangaroos and wallabies.

ⓘ The Mill, 320 Nebo Road

*Continue south on the Bruce
Highway.*

Rockhampton and Yeppoon

10 Rockhampton, the thriving commercial centre of the 'Capricorn Coast', is known as Australia's beef capital. This Fitzroy River settlement contains many National Trust buildings – take a walk along historic Quay Street to see some of the fine examples of architecture – and is home to the **Aboriginal Dreamtime Cultural Centre**, where you can experience Aboriginal dance, stories and culture.

Rockhampton's nearest beaches are located around the resort and harbour town of **Yeppoon**, 40km (25 miles) away. Other attractions here include the **Koorana Crocodile Farm** and **Cooberrie Park Flora and Fauna Sanctuary**, with its koalas and other native animals. From nearby **Rosslyn Bay** you can cruise to the resort island of **Great Keppel, Middle Island Underwater Observatory**, or the outer Great Barrier Reef. Inland attractions include the **Mount Morgan Historical Museum** (38km/24 miles to the south), which traces the area's gold and copper mining history; and **Olsen's Capricorn Caverns** – an unusual complex of above-ground dry limestone caves.

ⓘ Curtis Park, Gladstone Road

*From Rockhampton you can
drive south on the Bruce
Highway to undertake Tour 6 in
reverse order, or fly to Brisbane.*

Cairns – Gordonvale 22 (14)
Gordonvale – Innisfail 66 (41)
Innisfail – Tully 52 (32)
Tully – Cardwell 44 (27)
Cardwell – Ingham 52 (32)
Ingham – Townsville 110 (68)
Townsville – Bowen 202 (125)
Bowen – Airlie Beach 80 (50)
Airlie Beach – Mackay 144 (89)
Mackay – Rockhampton 325 (202)

RECOMMENDED WALKS

9 Eungella National Park, 80km (50 miles) northwest of Mackay, takes its name from an Aboriginal word meaning 'Land of Clouds'. This dramatic, misty upland area is well named – the 51,000-hectare (12,600-acre) park contains three high peaks, deep gorges and some splendid rainforest. There are good walking tracks in spectacular **Finch Hatton Gorge** and you may even encounter tortoises or a platypus in one of the streams or rock pools.

THE GREAT BARRIER REEF

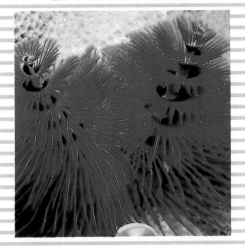

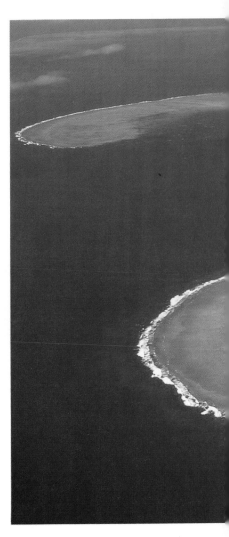

Queensland's status as the tourist mecca of Australia is most certainly due to the presence of the magnificent Great Barrier Reef, and the multitude of lovely islands which lie off the coast.

QUEENSLAND'S ISLANDS

Queensland's many lovely islands – from Lizard Island to the north of Cooktown, to South Stradbroke off the Gold Coast – offer a multitude of holiday opportunities, including diving, snorkelling, swimming, fishing and bushwalking.

THE GREAT BARRIER REEF

Often referred to as the eighth wonder of the world, the planet's largest living structure winds its way along the Queensland coast for 2,300km (1,430 miles) – from the Gulf of Papua to just south of the Tropic of Capricorn. The Great Barrier Reef is, in fact, a series of over 2,000 reefs which are linked together, along with some 700 islands and other fringing reefs. In the north the structure is only 15–20km (9 to 12 miles) wide, but this increases to as much as 300km (186 miles) further south. The reef is estimated to be around 2 million years old, and exploration has revealed that the coral extends as deep as 125m before the seabed is reached. The Great Barrier Reef was first recorded by Captain James Cook, who experienced great difficulty in finding a passage through this frustrating obstacle on his way up the east coast in 1770.

Reef life

The reef ecosystem is extraordinarily diverse. Reefs are 'built' by tiny coral polyps, which have a limestone skeleton that forms the basis of the structure, and algae, which bind the coral skeletons together. There are many different types of coral, but the most commonly seen are hard (stony) corals, such as staghorn formations, and soft corals – flexible formations, which come in an incredible variety of shapes and colours.

The reef has some 1,000 fish species – everything from the tiny, brightly-coloured parrot fish to huge potato cod and manta rays. Crustaceans, such as hermit crabs, lobsters and shrimps; brightly coloured sea stars; sponges; giant clams; and turtles – the green, loggerhead and hawksbill varieties are the most common – are other reef inhabitants. You may also see marine mammals such as whales or

Above: The reef drops steeply off into the abyss on its Pacific side
Top left: The coral reefs abound with colourful marine life

dolphins, and even the less common dugong, or sea-cow. Less appealing reef inhabitants – at least to humans – are sharks, box jellyfish and other marine 'stingers', stonefish and sea snakes. These are all dangerous or poisonous and are to be avoided, so take heed of any relevant advice from whoever is operating your excursion to the reef.

Seeing the reef

Tourism to the Great Barrier Reef comes in many forms. Scenic flights are a great way to view the overall layout; divers and snorkellers experience the best of the colourful corals and fish from close up; and those who take cruises and wish to stay dry can view this wonderful spectacle from a host of underwater observatories, semi-submersible vessels and glass-bottomed boats. There are dozens of diving schools along the Queensland coast for those who wish to learn to scuba dive while on holiday.

The best coastal access points for the outer reef are Port Douglas, Cairns and Townsville, and there is also good access (although this means a longer boat trip) from Shute Harbour and the Whitsunday islands. As far as resorts go, those on Green, Wilson, Heron and Lady

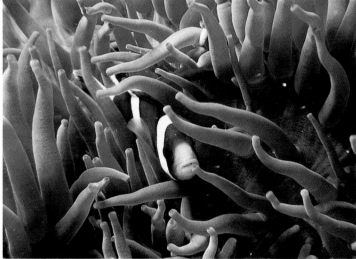

Elliott islands offer the best intro-
duction – these are all coral cays
directly on the reef, while most of
Queensland's other islands are of
the continental variety. There are, of
course, many other resort island
access points.

Conservation

Managed by the Great Barrier Reef
Marine Park Authority, the reef has
been on the UNESCO World
Heritage List since 1981 and is the
subject of much conservation con-
cern. The increase in tourism and
the development of new resorts

*Spot the clown fish, camouflaged
among the waving arms of
anemones, flower-like when
left undisturbed*

along the coast are threats, as are
pollution and the fear of oil spills
from the tankers which regularly
pass along the coastline. Another
recent problem is the proliferation of
the crown-of-thorns starfish – a
creature which feeds on the coral
polyp and has devastated large
areas of coral: there is currently no
satisfactory explanation for this
destructive phenomenon.

SOUTHEASTERN AUSTRALIA

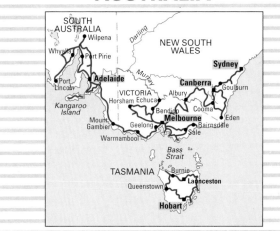

The very civilised southeastern corner of Australia has much to appeal to the visitor. A large proportion of the nation's population is clustered here, culture and the arts flourish in the cities of Canberra, Melbourne and Adelaide, there is a remarkable sense of history, and, with the exception of South Australia, the climate is generally far more temperate than in the northern regions.

The scenery here is very diverse, in a large area which covers Canberra and the Australian Capital Territory, Victoria, Tasmania, South Australia and the southern part of NSW. Attractions range from the picturesque Southern Highlands and quiet south coast of New South Wales, to modern Canberra, the nation's capital city. From Australia's highest peak – 2,228m-high Mount Koskiusko – and accompanying winter skifields to historic goldmining and agricultural towns, wineries and little country villages.

Explore the grand old city of Melbourne, from where you can drive along Victoria's scenic coastline, and fly or cruise across Bass Strait to the island of Tasmania – Australia's smallest state, but one that is famous for its gourmet foods, historic charm, an intriguing convict past, cooler weather and incomparable natural wonders. South Australia is a great place to see more of Australia's wildlife, sample some of her finest wines and visit the splendid Flinders Ranges, which mark the fringes of the state's vast outback region.

Canberra has a very recent history – the national capital was begun only in 1913, as an emphatic solution to the persistent rivalry between Sydney and Melbourne for the honour of being the nation's seat of government. In complete contrast, Hobart was founded in 1804 and is Australia's second-oldest major city. Tasmania was developed initially as a penal colony and has a fascinating but tragic convict and Aboriginal history. The fine cities of Melbourne and Adelaide date from 1835 and 1836 respectively, when settlers from the east coast and Tasmania began to search for new lands to farm and make their fortunes from. Victoria boomed as a result of a major gold rush during the 1850s, which attracted thousands of new settlers from Britain and other countries, while Adelaide and South Australia proudly became the only Australian colony to avoid the importation of convicts.

Tour 9
The highlight of this tour from Sydney to Canberra and the Australian Capital Territory is the Southern Highlands. Although there is rugged bush in the area, the highlands are also the state's little slice of England, where country houses, afternoon teas and cricket on the village green are the order of the day.

City Tour 4
The nation's capital, Canberra, is a modern, planned environment of hills, a large lake, important national buildings and pleasant, leafy suburbs that radiate from the city centre. Highlights here include Parliament House, important museums and galleries and the Australian War Memorial.

Tour 10
Landlocked Canberra residents flock to the quiet southern NSW holiday coast, which extends south to the Victorian border. From the historic towns of Bungendore and Braidwood you travel to the coast – an area of fine beaches, great angling, good walking and a tranquil environment.

Tour 11
This very scenic tour from Canberra to Melbourne travels through Australia's most mountainous region – the NSW Snowy Mountains, Victorian Alpine National Park and other sections of the Great Dividing Range. There are many national parks, winter ski fields and summer walking country here, as well as an interesting pioneer history. Closer to Melbourne, agricultural land takes over before you reach the Dandenong Ranges on the city's outskirts.

City Tour 5
Recently declared 'the world's most liveable city', Melbourne is indeed a pleasant environment. There are charming old buildings and avenues, a sense of European grandeur that is lacking elsewhere in Australia, fine dining, a multicultural population, and the beaches on Port Phillip Bay that add a touch of the outdoors to this rather cultured city.

Tour 12
The goldfields region that brought so much prosperity to Victoria contains the historic and still thriving towns of Ballarat, Bendigo and Maryborough, and much of this area now produces liquid gold – in the form of excellent wines. In the west lie the rugged peaks of the Grampians, while the northern edge of the state is marked by the nation's largest river, the Murray.

Tour 13
This wonderful southeast Victoria coastline of islands, peninsulas, lakes and beaches is, not surprisingly, the state's premier holiday playground. From the resorts on the Mornington Peninsula and the

famous fairy penguins of Phillip Island, to the uplands and beaches of Wilsons Promontory and the lakes of the Gippsland region, this is Victoria at its best.

City Tour 6

The capital of Tasmania, and Australia's most charming and unspoiled city, Hobart is a delightful place. The climate may be a little unpredictable, but the fine foods, historic streets and old sandstone buildings more than compensate. Cruises on the River Derwent and trips into the surrounding hills complete the picture.

Tour 14

The visual and gourmet treat that is Tasmania includes a large World Heritage area, old fishing villages, historic towns and cities, and the remarkable ex-convict settlement of Port Arthur. Tasmania is relatively small and the perfect place for motor touring, while the state's colonial-style accommodation is simply delightful.

Tour 15

From Melbourne's second city, Geelong, you travel to the lovely Bellarine Peninsula, then along the scenic Great Ocean Road, past the notorious shipwreck coast which has claimed dozens of vessels. After entering South Australia you reach the coastal Coorong National Park and continue through lower Murray River towns and the tranquil Adelaide Hills to the state's major city.

City Tour 7

The small but gracious city of Adelaide, South Australia's capital, is surrounded by parkland and crossed by the River Torrens – in this attractive environment you can enjoy broad avenues, grand old buildings and the city's fine reputation as a major centre of culture and the arts.

Tour 16

This southeastern South Australia itinerary takes in the nation's premier wine-growing area of the Barossa Valley, old Murray River ports, the agricultural Fleurieu Peninsula, and unspoilt Kangaroo Island with its superb wildlife and wild coastline.

Tour 17

A long and very varied trip, this tour around South Australia's Yorke and Eyre peninsulas and to the wild Flinders Ranges attempts to cover some of the remainder of this large and mostly desert state. You will encounter old mining towns, fishing settlements, ports and industrial centres and the grandeur of the outback fringe.

Canberra glories in its fine setting. Man-made Lake Burley Griffin is named for the American architect who planned the capital in 1911

2 days – 379km (234 miles)

SYDNEY TO CANBERRA

Sydney • Mittagong • Berrima • Moss Vale
Bowral • Kangaroo Valley • Bundanoon
Goulburn • Canberra

This tour reveals a different aspect of Australia. After passing through Sydney's southern suburbs you travel on to the Southern Highlands – an upland region that is one of the country's most 'English' areas. Towns here like Berrima and Moss Vale are the province of antique shops, afternoon teas and country pursuits. Nearby Kangaroo Valley is a pastoral haven that seems little touched by 170 years of settlement, while Morton National Park rivals the Blue Mountains for scenic grandeur. This southern area was opened up by farmers in the 1820s and 1830s. Nineteenth-century 'tourists' soon discovered the area, however, and the Highlands have long catered for Sydneysiders in search of fresh air and tranquillity.

From the Town Hall on George Street, drive west on Parramatta Road (Route 32), then take Route 31 (the Hume Highway and South Western Freeway) through Campbelltown. Take the Mittagong turn-off.

The giant 15m (50-foot) high Big Merino announces the speciality of Goulburn, the country's second-oldest inland city

Mittagong

1 It's worth stopping in Mittagong, the gateway to the Southern Highlands, for tourist information on the region and a look at some of the attractions – including the **Butterfly House**, and numerous art and craft outlets.

[i] Southern Highlands Visitor Information Centre, Winifred West Park, Hume Highway

Continue on the South Western Freeway to the Berrima turn-off.

Berrima

2 Australia's most well-preserved Georgian town dates back to 1830 and is packed with lovely old sandstone buildings, craft and antique shops, cafés and the **Surveyor-General Inn**, which has been serving drinks since 1834. Berrima's other notable buildings include the 1830s **Court House and Gaol**, 1835 **Berrima House**, and 1840s **Holy Trinity Church**, and you should also visit the **Berrima Historical Museum**.

Take the Moss Vale road from Berrima.

Moss Vale

3 The attractive town of Moss Vale is the centre for the surrounding pastoral district and a popular base for visitors to the region. There are some lovely parks here – take time out in **Leighton Gardens**, or visit nearby **Cecil Hoskins Nature Reserve**. To the east of Moss Vale, **Throsby Park Historic Site**, dating back to 1819, was the estate of the

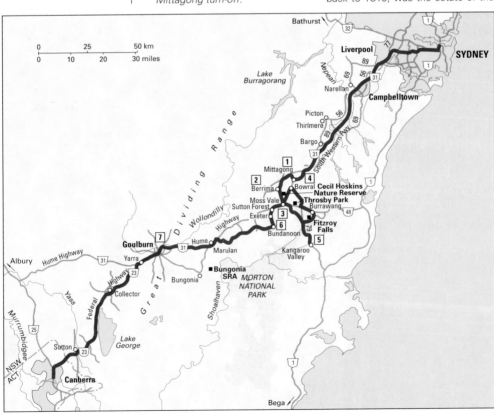

area's original pioneer family and is now under the protection of the National Parks and Wildlife Service.

At the nearby hamlet of **Sutton Forest** you can see **Hillview**, once the country residence of NSW governors, and many other grand homes from the 1880s. Another historic town in the area is **Exeter**, which contains numerous old buildings – including **St Aidan's Church**, with its pretty stained-glass windows.

Leave Moss Vale on the Bowral road.

Bowral

4 The region's most English of towns, tranquil, leafy Bowral is popular with retired people and those fleeing the madness of city living. The town is full of grand houses, parks and gardens, and a **Tulip Festival** is held here each October, when many private gardens are open to the public. November is the month for the **Bong Bong Picnic Races** – a famous weekend of horseracing and lots of country fun. You can also take in the **Bowral School House Museum**, play a round of golf, or visit the **Bradman Museum**.

Drive southeast from Bowral to the Illawarra Highway (Route 48), then take the Fitzroy Falls and Kangaroo Valley turn-off.

Kangaroo Valley

5 This green valley at the foot of a steep escarpment is so special that it is classified, in its entirety, by the National Trust. The picturesque township of Kangaroo Valley contains many old buildings and the rather grand 1898 **Hampden Bridge**.

The **Pioneer Settlement** here offers a museum, a blacksmith's shed and farm machinery and is an interesting excursion into the area's past. On the way to Kangaroo Valley don't miss **Fitzroy Falls**, a cascade of water tumbling over the Morton National Park escarpment. There is a picnic ground and a National Parks Visitor Centre here, as well as some pleasant walking tracks.

Return to the Illawarra Highway, driving through Moss Vale, then take the Bundanoon turn-off at Sutton Forest.

Bundanoon

6 The small highland town of Bundanoon has been a popular holiday destination since the 1890s, when city dwellers flocked here by train to enjoy bracing country air, spectacular views, horseriding and good walking. These attractions remain, and Bundanoon is a gateway to rugged **Morton National Park** – a pristine region of sandstone gorges, rivers and dense eucalypt forest. The area is popular with bushwalkers and birdwatchers and contains a wide variety of wildlife, including goannas and possums.

Continue on this minor road, rejoin the Hume Highway at Marulan and drive southwest.

The high sandstone plateau of Morton National Park has been deeply scored by rivers, and cliffs are laced with rushing waterfalls

Goulburn

7 The city of Goulburn (population 21,550) is one of the state's larger inland settlements and the centre of a rich wool, wheat and cattle district. The city's 19th century prosperity has resulted in many fine buildings – including the **Old Court House**, **St Saviour's Cathedral** (1874–84), and the **Town Hall**. Also of interest are the **Regional Art Gallery**, the 1848 **St Clair History Homestead** and **Rocky Hill War Memorial**, with its military museum. A more modern addition is the **Big Merino**, on the outskirts of town. This 15m (50-foot) high sheep is also an outlet for wool products and other items of Australiana.

ⓘ 6 Montague Street

Just outside Goulburn, turn off on to the Federal Highway (Route 23) which will take you to Canberra.

Sydney – Mittagong 110 (68)
Mittagong – Berrima 10 (6)
Berrima – Moss Vale 10 (6)
Moss Vale – Bowral 7 (4)
Bowral – Kangaroo Valley 46 (29)
Kangaroo Valley – Bundanoon 45 (28)
Bundanoon – Goulburn 62 (38)
Goulburn – Canberra 89 (55)

FOR CHILDREN

1 This town offers a couple of entertainments for children – the three-dimensional **Castle Maze** and **Butterfly House** with a collection of brightly coloured Australian butterflies.

BACK TO NATURE

3 The Cecil Hoskins Nature Reserve near Moss Vale offers easy walks around the lagoon and prolific bird life. Over 80 species of birds have been recorded here, and you may even spot a platypus.

SPECIAL TO ...

4 Bowral's main claim to fame is as the birthplace of the legendary cricketer, Sir Donald Bradman, who was born here in 1908 and captained the Australian team between 1936 and 1948. The excellent Bradman Museum, appropriately located in the village green's cricket pavilion, contains a fascinating collection of Australian cricketing *memorabilia* and photographs.

CANBERRA

City Centre • Regatta Point • Australian War Memorial • Kings Park • National Gallery of Australia • Parliament House • Yarralumla Australian National Botanic Gardens • City Centre

Australia's capital developed out of the long rivalry between Sydney and Melbourne for the right to become the nation's premier city. The site was selected in 1908 and construction began five years later. Designed by American Walter Burley Griffin, Canberra was planned to contain parks and gardens and to create a feeling of space.

The centre of this attractive city is located around the shores of Lake Burley Griffin, which was completed in 1964. A car is needed for this tour, and note that the roads system can be very confusing.

ⓘ Visitor Information Centres at Northbourne Avenue, Dickson and the Jolimont Centre, Northbourne Avenue, City Centre

Start the tour in Canberra's city centre.

SCENIC ROUTES

The most scenic route in Canberra is the flat and easy lakeside track. You can walk or pedal the entire 35km (21 miles) of shore, or just take in a short section – bicycles are available for hire from several sources including Acton Park, southwest of the city centre.

City Centre

1 The city centre, known as Civic, is a series of shopping malls, government offices and rather surburban looking streets – the centre's heart is at Civic Square. Canberra's nightlife is not renowned either, but **Casino Canberra** at the National Convention Centre has livened things up somewhat.

Australian flags stand to attention at New Parliament House

From the centre, drive along Commonwealth Avenue and take the Regatta Place turn-off.

Regatta Point

2 This lakeside spot is home to the **National Capital Exhibition** – the perfect place to start your Canberra tour. The various displays here relate the story of Canberra's development and give you a good perspective on the city. There is also a good view of the **Captain Cook Memorial Jet**, which sends a stream of water 140m into the air.

Return to Commonwealth Avenue, drive back towards the City Centre and turn on to Parkes Way. Turn left at Anzac Parade.

Australian War Memorial

3 The drive along the wide boulevard of Anzac Parade is dominated by the vast, domed Byzantine-style Australian War Memorial – a tribute to over 100,000 Australians who have perished in battle from World War I to Vietnam. The building also contains Australia's extensive national military museum and an art gallery.

Drive back along Anzac Parade, turn left on to Constitution Avenue and turn off right at Wendouree Drive.

Kings Park

4 From this point you have a good view of Lake Burley Griffin, appropriately named after Canberra's architect. With 35km (21 miles) of shoreline the lake is a wonderful aquatic playground for boating and sailboarding enthusiasts, while the surrounding parkland is popular with walkers and cyclists. In front of Kings Park, the **Carillon** was a gift from Britain. Also in the Kings Park area, **Blundells Farmhouse** dates from 1860 and is one of the few remaining old structures around Canberra.

Old Parliament House, reflecting on past glories: it lost its role when its ultra-modern replacement opened in 1988

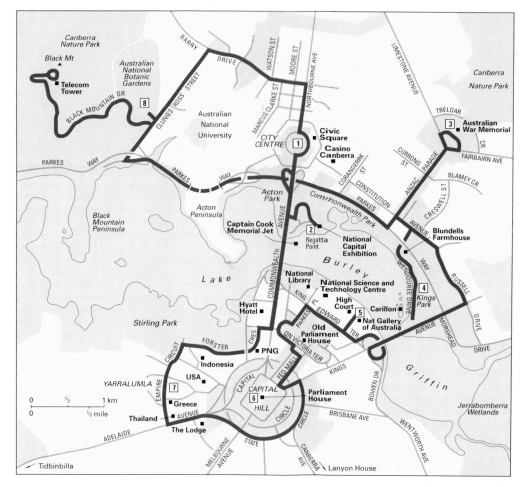

Return to and turn right on to Constitution Avenue, continue along Russell Drive and turn right on to Kings Avenue. Cross the bridge and take the King Edward Terrace turn-off.

National Gallery of Australia

5 The marvellous National Gallery was opened in 1982 and contains a large collection of Australian and European art. There are particularly good sections on post-war Australian artists and Aboriginal art, while the collections of Asian and Pacific art, photographs and decorative arts are also of a high quality.

Other important buildings on King Edward Terrace are the **High Court of Australia**, which can be toured; the **National Science and Technology Centre**; and the **National Library of Australia**.

Drive along Parkes Place and then follow the road to Queen Victoria Terrace. Head up Federation Mall.

Parliament House

6 This is the nerve centre of Australian politics, which cost the nation over $1,000 million. Opened in 1988 to celebrate Australia's bicentenary, this ambitious creation in glass, steel and granite definitely has its architectural merits. A tour of the interior includes the House of Representatives, the Senate, and the unusual foyer with its marble columns. Make sure you take in the view from the roof – from here you can see the 1927 Old Parliament House below, now a museum and art gallery.

Drive around Capital Circle and take the Adelaide Avenue exit.

Yarralumla

7 The suburb of Yarralumla contains the Prime Minister's residence, The Lodge, and most of the city's 70 or so diplomatic missions. A drive around the area (especially the streets enclosed by Empire Circuit and Forster Crescent) is very interesting, as many of the embassies are built in traditional styles. Look out for the exotic **Thai Embassy**, the neo-classical **Greek building** and the vast, stately **USA Consulate**. You are welcome to visit the cultural centres inside the **Indonesian Embassy** (Darwin Avenue) and the **Papua New Guinea High Commission** (Forster Crescent).

Return towards the city centre via Commonwealth Avenue Bridge and turn left on to Parkes Way. Turn right on to Clunies Ross Street.

Australian National Botanic Gardens

8 These lovely gardens focus on Australian native plants and contain everything from a rainforest environment to stands of eucalypts and an Aboriginal nature trail. Behind the gardens is 812m (2,664-foot) high **Black Mountain**, capped by the **Telecom Tower**. You can take in the splendid panorama from the tower's viewing gallery.

Return to the city centre via Clunies Ross Street, Barry Drive and Northbourne Avenue.

BACK TO NATURE

Tidbinbilla Nature Reserve, southwest of Canberra in the ACT, is a great spot for bird-watching and observing native animals in the large wildlife enclosures. You will see kangaroos, koalas and many native birds here and can take an informative nature walk around the reserve.

FOR CHILDREN

5 Also known as **Questacon**, the fascinating **National Science and Technology Centre** contains over 150 scientific exhibits in six themed galleries – the exhibits are mainly of the 'hands-on' variety and irresistible to children.

FOR HISTORY BUFFS

National Trust classifed **Lanyon House**, 30km (18 miles) to the south at Tharwa, is Canberra's most gracious old home. Dating from 1859, the homestead contains period furniture and an excellent collection of paintings by the prominent Australian artist Sidney Nolan.

3 days – 631km (391 miles)

NSW
FAR SOUTH COAST

Canberra • Bungendore • Braidwood • Mor
Narooma • Bermagui • Merimbula • Eden
Bega • Cooma • Canberra

This short tour from Canberra takes in the 1830s villages of Bungendore and Braidwood, and the beautiful NSW coastline from Moruya to Eden, almost at the Victorian border. South of Bermagui, the area known as the Sapphire Coast is a lovely region of beaches, inlets, small towns and fishing fleets. Inland lie the dairying towns of Bega and Cooma, the 'Gateway to the Snowy Mountains'.

Most of this region was first settled in the 1850s and the area today is far quieter than the coastline to the north of Sydney.

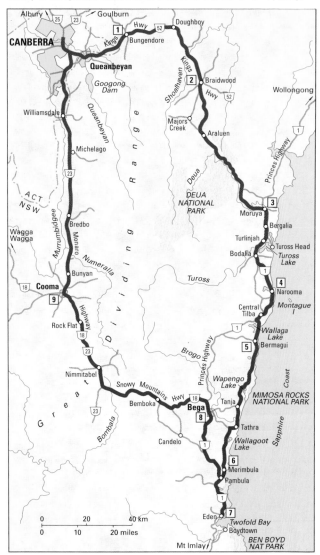

Game-fishing at Twofold Bay

Take the Kings Highway (Route 52), via Queanbeyan, from Canberra.

Bungendore

1 The village of Bungendore dates from the 1830s and has long been a stopping place for travellers at the junction of several important roads. There are a number of old buildings here, some containing antique and craft shops, while the 1885 **Carrington Hotel** is famous for its old-style accommodation and good food, and nearby **Lark Hill Vineyard** is open to the public for wine tastings.

Continue on Route 52.

Braidwood

2 This entire settlement, dating from the 1830s has been listed as a historic village by the National Trust. Braidwood is a classic, wide-thoroughfared country town and contains many interesting old verandahed buildings, craft and antique shops, and the **Braidwood Museum**, with its good collection of artefacts.

ⓘ Braidwood Museum, Wallace Street

From Braidwood, take the Moruya road.

Moruya

3 The river town of Moruya dates back to the 1850s, when it became the centre for the local goldmining industry. Granite is quarried in the area, which produced stone for the **Sydney General Post Office** and the Harbour Bridge pylons. Old buildings include the **Presbyterian Church** (1864) and the 1880 **Court House**. There is also a **Historical Museum** and several antique and bric-à-brac shops to explore. To the west, **Deua National Park** is a beautiful 81,000-hectare (200,150-acre) wilderness region of limestone outcrops and caves. Access is difficult, but the road from Braidwood to Moruya passes beside a section of the park.

Drive south on Highway 1 (the Princes Highway).

Narooma

4 Located on a headland at the mouth of the Wagonga Inlet, Narooma grew out of the sawmilling industry. The town is now a popular tourist resort, while oyster farming, fishing and timber are the main industries. You can take a cruise on the inlet, go big game fishing, or visit the nature reserve of Montague Island. Nearby **Central Tilba** is a National Trust 'living village' with 25 classified timber buildings, crafts shops and a cheese factory. The village has changed little since the 1880s and is a delightful spot for afternoon tea.

ⓘ Visitor Centre, Princes Highway

Continue south on Highway 1, then turn off on the coast road to Bermagui.

Bermagui

5 The south coast's fishing capital is a paradise for anglers, with excellent lake, coastal and game fishing (for marlin, tuna and kingfish). The beaches are good here too, especially **Horseshoe Bay**, while **Wallaga Lake** is a great spot for swimming, sailing or sailboarding. To the south, **Mimosa Rocks National Park** contains some good beaches, lakes for canoeing, and prolific birdlife.

Continue south on the coast road via Tathra.

Merimbula

6 This seaside town and oyster port, near the mouth of the Pambula River, is famous for its wide and often empty beaches and **Merimbula Lake**, a great spot for water pursuits. The **Old School**

at the park's southernmost tip is **Green Cape Lighthouse**, built in 1883.

Return to Pambula and drive north on Highway 1.

Bega

8 Bega is famous for its cheese making. Bega's location near the coast and the Snowy Mountains offers the possibility of skiing and swimming on the same day! Of interest in the town are the **Family Historical Museum**, and the **Grevillea Estate Winery**. To the southwest, the village of **Candelo** is a delightful reminder of the past with its teashops and rural museum, while the National Trust classified town of **Tathra** is Bega's nearest coastal resort.

ⓘ Zingle Place

Breakwaters extend protectively from Narooma's unspoilt coastline

Museum, built in 1874, has been transformed into an interesting museum of local history. Nearby **Pambula** has a good beach that is popular with surfers.

Drive to Pambula, then continue south on Highway 1.

Eden

7 Eden was once a whaling port but the major industries today are fishing and timber. The town has a wonderful natural harbour on **Twofold Bay** and a large fishing fleet is based here – tuna, snapper, abalone and salmon are caught nearby. South of town, the **Davidson Whaling Station Historic Site** is worth visiting for a reminder of the bloody days of the whaling industry.

Nearby **Ben Boyd National Park** contains beautiful beaches, heath and woodland, fascinating rock formations and is home to wombats and the rare ground parrot. Standing

Take Route 18, then Route 23 to Cooma.

Cooma

9 Cooma is a hive of activity in winter, as skiers make their way to the slopes. It was the centre for the 1950s and 1960s Snowy Mountains Hydroelectric Scheme, and the **Snowy Memorial** is a reminder of the 121 people who lost their lives while working on the project. Also of interest is **Lambie Street**, with its fine buildings. Skiing tours are available from here in winter, and whitewater rafting in spring and summer.

ⓘ 119 Sharp Street

Return to Canberra on the Monaro Highway.

Canberra – Bungendore 42 (26)
Bungendore – Braidwood 49 (30)
Braidwood – Moruya 86 (53)
Moruya – Narooma 44 (27)
Narooma – Bermagui 32 (20)
Bermagui – Merimbula 64 (40)
Merimbula – Eden 26 (16)
Eden – Bega 61 (38)
Bega – Cooma 112 (70)
Cooma – Canberra 115 (71)

CANBERRA TO MELBOURNE

Canberra • Jindabyne • Thredbo • Khancoban
Tumut • Albury–Wodonga • Mount Beauty and
Falls Creek • Bright • Myrtleford • Wangaratta
Benalla • Mansfield • Eildon • The Yarra Valley
The Dandenong Ranges • Melbourne

After leaving Canberra, you drive west to cross the Great Dividing Range. From the town of Jindabyne, the route winds up through Kosciusko National Park to the ski resort of Thredbo, then skirts the northern section of the park. Mount Kosciusko, Australia's highest point at 2,228m (7,310 feet), is located here. Many people are surprised at Australia's extensive skiing facilities, but the sport began at Kiandra in the Snowy Mountains as far back as the 1860s and the world's first ski club was formed here in 1870, long before skiing became fashionable in Europe.

From here it's down to the city of Albury–Wodonga on the Murray River, across the border into Victoria, and into the Alpine National Park. There are more ski resorts in this region and you can also visit the wine-growing areas around Rutherglen and Glenrowan, and picturesque old towns such as Beechworth and Mansfield. *En route* to Melbourne there are agricultural towns and gentle pastoral scenery, then a drive through the forests surrounding Victoria's largest man-made waterway, Lake Eildon. From here, it's up into the lovely Dandenong Ranges before arriving in Melbourne.

Delicate clusters of wattle (acacia) blossom by the roadside

From Canberra City Centre take Route 23 (the Monaro Highway) south to Cooma, then turn on to Route 18 and take the Alpine Way to Jindabyne.

Jindabyne

1 The original township lies under the waters of Lake Jindabyne, created in the 1960s as part of the Snowy Mountains Hydroelectric Scheme. Today, Jindabyne is a small resort town, on the shores of the picturesque lake, which offers good trout fishing, sailing and waterskiing. In winter, the town is packed with skiers heading for the nearby slopes.

Continue on the Alpine Way to Thredbo.

Thredbo

2 Although there are many ski resorts on the northern side of the mountain, Thredbo, to the south of Mount Kosciusko, is the most picturesque village and also offers a good range of summer activities. This attractive European-style alpine village lies at the foot of the mountain and the chairlift ride up Mount Kosciusko is a must. You can ski in winter, but at other times of the year tennis, horseriding, fishing, bush-walking and cycling are available.

In winter, the **Kosciusko National Park** become Australia's major downhill and cross-country skiing area, but at other times of year this region of streams, lakes, undulating hills, granite outcrops and snow gums is transformed by a magnificent display of wildflowers. The

Discover the wild, rugged beauty of Kosciusko National Park

SPECIAL TO ...

Northeastern Victoria is famous for its fortified wines – regarded as some of the world's finest. An excursion to **Rutherglen**, 50km (31 miles) west of Albury–Wodonga, allows you to sample some of these marvellous ports, muscats and tokays, as well as high quality red and white wines. Some of the best wineries around Rutherglen include **Fairfield Vineyard** (with its grand 1880s mansion), **Morris Wines, Bullers Calliope Vineyard** and **Campbells Winery**, which are all open for tastings and cellar-door sales.

park, the largest in New South Wales, is home to the rare pygmy possum, kangaroos, wallabies, wombats, echidnas and an amazing variety of birdlife.

[i] Kosciusko National Park Headquarters, Sawpit Creek

Continue on the Alpine Way.

Khancoban

3 The old village of Khancoban, at the end of the scenic Alpine Way to the west of the mountains, took on a new lease of life with the advent of the Snowy Mountains Scheme. The nearby **Murray 1 Power Station** can be inspected, and the area is also excellent for trout fishing, whitewater rafting and walking. To the north, you can visit the **Tumut power stations** and **Yarrangobilly Caves**. The caves, 7km (4 miles) off the highway, were first discovered by a European in 1834 and are now a major tourist attraction. Four caves, famous for their varied formations, are open to the public, while the surrounding limestone outcrops are an added highlight. You can also swim in the nearby thermal pool, with its year-round temperature of 27°C.

Continue on the Alpine Way, which joins the Snowy Mountains Highway (Route 18) beyond Cabramurra.

Tumut

4 Located in a valley on the Tumut River, beneath the slopes of the Great Dividing Range, Tumut is an attractive town of around 6,000 people. The settlement dates back to the 1840s and old buildings include the National Trust listed **All Saints Church** (1876), the **Court House** (1878), and 1874 **Police Station**. To the south of town are **Blowering Dam and Reservoir** and the **Blowering Trout Farm and Hatchery**, one of Australia's largest, which can be visited.

Paddle steamers pass banks of gum trees as they ply the Murray

Continue on Route 18, which joins the Hume Highway (Route 31) beyond Adelong. Drive southwest on Route 31.

Albury–Wodonga

5 The twin towns of Albury (NSW) and Wodonga (Victoria), on opposite sides of the Murray River, form one of NSW's largest cities and provide an excellent overnight stopping place for travellers. Albury is of far greater interest to the visitor than Wodonga, with many historic buildings, the **Albury Regional Museum**, **Albury Regional Art Centre** and the 1871 **Botanic Gardens**. The **Hovell Tree** marks the spot where explorers Hume and Hovell crossed the Murray River in 1824.

Nearby **Lake Hume**, several times the size of Sydney Harbour, forms one of Australia's largest man-made waterways, and a fantastic recreation facility for the locals. The dam here was completed in 1936 and the hydroelectric station provides power for both Victoria and New South Wales. The **Hume Weir Trout Farm** is open to the public – you can even catch your own trout here! Also in the area are the bizarre **Ettamogah Pub** and interesting **Ettamogah Wildlife Sanctuary**, with its variety of Australian fauna. You can also cruise on the Murray River on a replica paddle-steamer.

[i] 553 Kiewa Street, Albury

From Wodonga, take the Kiewa Valley Highway (Route 191).

Mount Beauty and Falls Creek

6 Its location just outside the Bogong High Plains section of the Alpine National Park makes Mount Beauty a magnet for skiers. This part of the park contains 1,986m (6,516-foot) high **Mount Bogong**, Victoria's highest point. At the end of a scenic

SCENIC ROUTES

7 The drive from Bright into the **Mount Buffalo National Park** provides excellent views of the surrounding area. From the small town of **Porepunkah** the road winds for 23km (14 miles) up the plateau and there is a fine view from **Bents Lookout**. Continue to **The Horn Lookout** (this section of road is closed in winter) for another magnificent panorama of the area's peaks, farming land and valleys.

FOR HISTORY BUFFS

8 A short detour to Beechworth, off the highway between Bright and Wangaratta, is highly recommended. Dating back to 1852, Beechworth is one of Victoria's best preserved old towns – declared a 'Notable Town' by the National Trust. The wide streets are flanked by many carefully restored buildings – examples are the 1857 **Police Station**, 1858 **Court House** and the 1859 **Gaol**, in which the notorious bushranger, Ned Kelly, was once held. During the goldrush era thousands of Chinese settlers came to the area and the cemetery contains many of their graves. **Beechworth Historic Park**, 5km (3 miles) north of town, preserves remnants of the old goldmining days.

drive up the hillsides from Mount Beauty, the small village of Falls Creek is the most picturesque of the Victorian ski resorts, and is perfect for summer walking – there are dozens of well-marked tracks here. The **Bogong High Plains** is a spectacular high plateau region, perfect for cross-country skiing. In summer, alpine wildflowers abound among the heath and grassland and the park contains a colony of rare pygmy possums, which were thought to be extinct until sighted here in the 1960s.

Drive west to Bright.

Bright

7 This small town in the Ovens Valley, at the foot of the Victorian Alps, is the perfect base for skiing and winter sports at **Mount Buffalo** and the **Alpine National Park**. At other times of year, the town is popular with walkers and trout anglers. Bright is famous for its trees – including Japanese maples and Himalayan cedars – that create a riot of colour in autumn. The **Bright Historical Museum**, located in the former railway station, explains the town's pastoral, goldmining and sawmilling history and is worth a visit. **Mount Buffalo National Park**, to the west, is great for skiing and walking. Australia's first ski lift was erected here in the 1940s and the area's relatively easy slopes make it very popular with families.

i Delaney Avenue

Drive northwest on the Ovens Highway (Route 156).

Myrtleford

8 This Ovens Valley town is the centre of a rich agricultural area, which specialises in growing tobacco and hops – these were first grown here in the 1850s to cater for

the gold prospectors who had flocked to the region. **The March Tobacco, Hops and Timber Festival** celebrates the town's crops, and tours of various farms are available. Beside the highway just outside town, the **Phoenix Tree** is a an old red gum which has been sculpted and carved to create the image of a phoenix bird. Restored Victorian **Merriang Homestead**, a few kilometres to the southwest, was built with handmade bricks and local granite – the house features 17

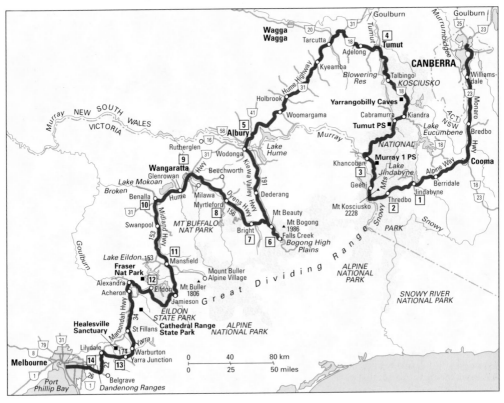

rooms and is also the studio of a local sculptor.

ⓘ Ponderosa Cabin, Clyde Street

Continue on the Ovens Highway.

Wangaratta

9 This substantial town is known for its gardens and churches, and is at the centre of an agricultural area – wool, wheat, dairying and beef cattle are the major pursuits. You can tour the **Wangaratta Woollen Mills**, and the **Wangaratta Museum** is worth a visit. The **Cathedral Church of the Holy Trinity** is a surprisingly grand 19th-century building, which was given cathedral status in 1902. The local cemetery contains the grave of Daniel 'Mad Dog' Morgan. This notorious bushranger, who killed over 70 people, was shot in the area in 1865.

Airworld Aviation Museum, south of town, contains the world's largest collection of antique aircraft, and the Wangaratta area is home to some excellent wineries. At nearby **Glenrowan** the winery to visit is Baileys (excellent ports, muscats and table wines), while **Milawa**, east of Wangaratta, is home to **Brown Brothers** – the producers of wonderful red and white wines. Glenrowan was the haunt of another famous bushranger, Ned Kelly, during the 1870s – the town has a good display on Kelly and his gang, and the **Ned Kelly Memorial Museum**.

ⓘ Corner of Handley Street and Hume Highway

Drive to Benalla on the Hume Highway (Route 31).

Benalla

10 Benalla, the 'City of Roses', has several points of interest. The **Benalla Art Gallery** contains a

Stunning view from a lookout in Mount Buffalo National Park, where high plateaus are skied in the winter

remarkable collection of paintings by some of Australia's most famous artists – Hans Heysen, Charles Conder, Arthur Streeton, Margaret Preston and many others are represented here. The **Benalla Gardens**, containing more than 2,000 rose varieties, are also worth a visit. There is another **Kelly Museum** here, and the **Costume and Pioneer Museum** contains Ned Kelly's prized cummerbund. Benalla is the headquarters of the **Gliding Club of Victoria** and joyflights are available from the aerodrome, as are hot-air balloon jaunts.

ⓘ 14 Mair Street

Take the Midland Highway (Route 153) south from Benalla.

Mansfield

11 This small resort town is also a timber and sawmilling centre and was the headquarters for the filming of the internationally-acclaimed *The Man from Snowy River*. The picturesque town contains several National Trust listed buildings from the 1880s, while the surrounding wooded high country is quite spectacular. From Mansfield it is a 50km (31-mile) drive to **Mount Buller Alpine Village**, Australia's largest ski resort, below **Mount Buller**. The area is also famous for its summer horseriding holidays, fishing and bushwalking opportunities.

From Mansfield, drive to Eildon around the eastern side of the lake, via Howqua and Jamieson.

RECOMMENDED WALK

11 From **Mount Buller Alpine Village**, east of Mansfield, a 3km (2-mile) return walk takes you to the summit of 1,806m (5,925-foot) high **Mount Buller**, one of Victoria's highest peaks. The walk can only be undertaken outside of the ski season, but this stroll through heath and grassland provides wonderful views of the surrounding countryside.

A stately forest of red gum trees beside Lake Mulwala at Yarrawonga, downstream of the twin towns of Albury (NSW) and Wodonga (Victoria). Thanks to the lake, fed by the Murray River, Yarrawonga has become a major inland water recreation area

The Yarra Valley

13 Between Warburton and Lilydale the small Yarra Valley towns of **Millgrove**, **Yarra Junction**, **Launching Place** and **Woori Yallock** form a riverside agricultural area with good fishing, horseriding and bushwalking. You can visit the **Upper Yarra Historical Museum** at Yarra Junction, while to the north of the Warburton Highway 1,275m (4,180-foot) **Mount Donna Buang** (which is often snow covered in winter) provides wonderful views of the Yarra Valley below.

ⓘ 109 Main Street, Yarra Junction

From Woori Yallock continue on Route 174 to Lilydale, then take Route 32 south, followed by Route 22 (the Mount Dandenong Tourist Road).

The Dandenong Ranges

14 This hilly region to the east of Melbourne is packed with appeal for the visitor. Gum forests, gardens, scenic drives and birdlife are some of the natural attractions. The scenic **Mount Dandenong Tourist Road** takes you to **Mount Dandenong**, **Olinda**, **Sassafras** and **Upper Ferntree Gully**, before heading into the city.

There are a number of small vineyards in the Lilydale area, then Mount Dandenong provides excellent views over the Melbourne suburbs. This is also the home of the **William Ricketts Sanctuary**, an unusual park that features sculptures of Aboriginal mythology. The **National Rhododendron Garden**, **Olinda State Forest** and **Edward Henty Cottage** at Olinda are all worth visiting. The cottage was the home of Victoria's first settler, who arrived in 1834. The recently created **Dandenong Ranges National Park**, between Olinda and Upper Ferntree Gully, is composed of three sections including the **Fern Tree Gully Forest**.

ⓘ Puffing Billy Railway, Old Monbulk Street, Belgrave

From Upper Ferntree Gully drive to Melbourne via the Burwood Highway (Route 26).

BACK TO NATURE

13 Considered to be Australia's top wildlife park, **Healesville Sanctuary**, north of the Yarra Valley, provides fascinating encounters with nature. All of the essential Australian animals are found in this natural bushland setting – koalas, kangaroos, emus, wallabies, wombats and platypuses are just some of the sanctuary's 200 species of mammals, reptiles and birds.

FOR CHILDREN

14 From Belgrave, the **Puffing Billy** antique steam train takes a 13km (8-mile) scenic journey to Lakeside. The narrow gauge track was constructed in 1900 and operated as a passenger service until 1958. Adults and children alike will love this journey into another era of transportation. At **Menzies Creek**, along the line, there is an interesting **steam train museum**.

Eildon

12 On the shores of the lake of the same name and surrounded by a stunning variety of natural attractions, the town of Eildon is the centre of the state's most popular inland boating and fishing area. Victoria's largest artificial waterway, **Lake Eildon**, was created as part of an irrigation system and is popular with fishermen, boating enthusiasts, canoeists and waterskiers. There are many houseboats moored here, providing an unusual form of accommodation. The southern section of the lake is surrounded by **Eildon State Park** – forested peaks and hills laced with tracks make this a wonderful environment for walking.

Forested **Fraser National Park**, on the western side of the lake, contains large numbers of kangaroos and wallabies and an amazing variety of birds – from pelicans to kookaburras and crimson rosellas. Gold was discovered here in the 1860s and there are still many remnants of this era in the park.

Cathedral Range State Park, to the south of Alexandra, offers more walking tracks and is the home of the beautiful lyrebird. Nearby Alexandra, a small farming centre, contains the National Trust listed **ANZ Bank and Post Office** and is home to the **Alexandra Timber Tramway and Museum**. Located in the old railway station, this attraction displays a vintage steam engine and other historical items.

From Alexandra, drive south on the Maroondah Highway (Route 34) to St Fillans, then take the scenic Acheron Way to Warburton and Yarra Junction.

Australia's answer to Royal Ascot – hats and all – is the Melbourne Cup, held on the first Tuesday of November. The whole country stops to watch the race

MELBOURNE

Southgate • Swanston, Collins and Bourke Streets • Museum of Victoria • Old Melbourne Gaol • Lygon Street • Chinatown • Spring Street Treasury and Fitzroy Gardens • Collins Street (East) • Victorian Arts Centre and National Gallery of Victoria • Royal Botanic Gardens South Yarra and Prahran • St Kilda • Southgate

ⓘ Tourist information booths at City Square and Bourke Street Mall

Begin the tour on the south bank of the River Yarra at the Southgate complex, across Princes Bridge.

Southgate

1 This shopping, eating and people-watching development on the south bank, opposite Flinders Street Station, has revitalised the southern limits of the central city. Apart from the centre's own attractions, there are good views of the Yarra and the city skyline from the Southbank Promenade in front of Southgate.

Cross Princes Bridge and walk up Swanston Street.

Swanston, Collins and Bourke Streets

2 These three streets enclose much of central Melbourne's main shopping area. On the right, Swanston Street's first major building is **St Pauls Cathedral**, dating from 1877 and featuring wonderful floor tiles and superb stonework; further along are **City Square**, with the 1865 statue of explorers Burke and Wills, and the large 1870 **Town Hall**. Turn left here into Collins Street and walk to the Block Arcade (corner of Collins and Elizabeth streets) – a fine example of 1890s architecture. Further along (at 376–392 Collins Street) is the marvellous Gothic-style **ANZ Bank**, dating from 1887. Turn right here into Queen Street, then right again into Bourke Street – the grand 1860s **General Post Office** is on the corner of Bourne and Elizabeth streets. This is the main shopping street, and apart from trams, is for pedestrians only.

Turn left into Swanston Street and continue walking north until you reach the modern **Melbourne**

W hile Sydney is glossy, sunny and mostly modern, Melbourne is undoubtedly Australia's most grand and gracious city – like an antipodean slice of Europe. Much of this is due to Melbourne's origins and subsequent development. The city was founded in 1835, long after Sydney, by John Batman who traded land from the local Aborigines and uttered the immortal words: 'This will be the place for a village'. The Victorian goldrush of the 1850s brought great wealth to the capital and by the 1880s the city had become known as 'Marvellous Melbourne'. Many fine buildings were erected during this era and a large number of these remain.

Although Melbourne does not have Sydney's spectacular location, its position beside the Yarra River and on vast Port Phillip Bay gives it a sense of space that is lacking in many cities. The multicultural population and proliferation of cafés, restaurants, markets and delicatessens adds to the city's European flavour and has helped to create Melbourne's reputation as the dining capital of Australia.

Trams – convenient and pollution-free – are the best way to get around the city and its suburbs

Central complex. This is not only a great place to shop and eat – the spectacular glass-roofed centre has been constructed around the historic **Shot Tower**, built in 1890 and originally part of the Coop's Shot Factory.

Take the Swanston Street exit from Melbourne Central.

Museum of Victoria

3 This large museum complex on Swanston Street contains the **Planetarium** and **Children's Museum**, as well as its natural and human history collections. Highlights of the main museum are the dinosaur exhibit, the legendary but now stuffed racehorse Phar Lap, and the excellent Koori (Aboriginal) displays. Adjoining the museum is the **State Library of Victoria** – it's worth having a look at the impressive Reading Room and the classical style Queen's Hall.

Walk up Russell Street, crossing La Trobe Street.

Old Melbourne Gaol

4 Despite its rather dull exterior, the National Trust listed Old Melbourne Gaol on Russell Street is

Unmistakably Oriental, this gateway leads to Chinatown

fascinating. This rather grim building dates from 1851–4 and was the scene of over 100 executions, including that of the notorious Ned Kelly. The gaol, with its three levels of cells and walkways ,was closed in 1923 and now contains gruesome reminders of Victoria's often violent past – death masks, a flogging triangle and a depiction of Ned Kelly's hanging in 1880.

Continue on Russell Street to Victoria Street and cross over into Lygon Street, Carlton.

Lygon Street

5 A walk through this street in the suburb of Carlton is well worthwhile. The original 19th-century buildings are interesting in themselves, but Lygon Street's post-war influx of Italians and other migrants, and more recent 'trendification', has turned it into an avenue of wonderful cafés, boutiques, bookshops, unusual food stores with a lively European-style atmosphere. There are also some fine houses in Drummond Street, parallel to Lygon Street.

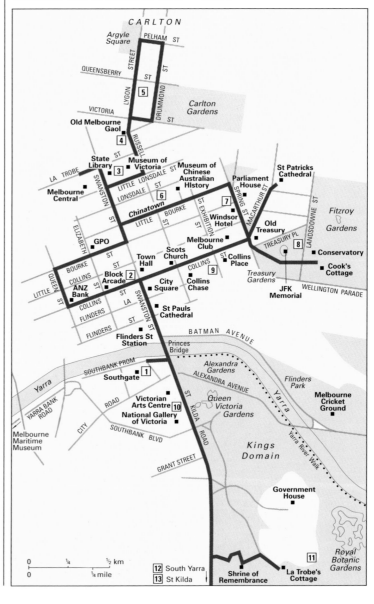

RECOMMENDED WALK

One of Melbourne's most pleasant walks is along the banks of the Yarra River from Princes Bridge and into the Royal Botanic Gardens. The river, especially at weekends, is a busy venue for rowing clubs. You can take a river- and garden-side walk as far as Anderson Street, then return to Princes Bridge by crossing the Botanic Gardens.

From here, you can either walk back to the city centre, or catch a tram – number 15 will take you from Lygon Street to Swanston Street. Alight near Little Bourke Street.

Chinatown

6 A walk along Little Bourke Street (from Swanston Street to Exhibition Street) takes you through Melbourne's thriving Chinatown. Chinese miners, prospectors and indentured labourers began arriving in Victoria in the 1840s and by 1880 there were 100,000 Chinese in Australia. Chinatown is naturally full of restaurants and interesting grocery shops, but also here, in Cohen Place, is the small **Museum of Chinese Australian History**. The museum features a remarkably long processional dragon and also offers interesting historical walking tours of Chinatown each morning.

Continue to the end of Little Bourke Street and turn right at Spring Street.

Spring Street

7 This grand avenue contains several government buildings – including the vast **State Parliament House**, begun in 1856 and Australia's most imposing secular building, which is opposite as you enter Spring Street. Further south is the smaller **Old Treasury Building**, dating from 1857 and built to contain gold from the Victorian mining towns. Behind these structures lies the impressive 1858 Gothic Revival **St Patricks Cathedral**, Melbourne's major Roman Catholic church. Opposite Parliament House is the beautifully restored 1880s **Windsor Hotel** – it is worth calling in here for tea or lunch just to experience a taste of grandeur that is more often associated with the Victorian age.

Ornate detailing on bijou terraces

Cross Treasury Place and enter the Treasury Gardens.

Treasury and Fitzroy Gardens

8 These adjacent gardens make up a quiet corner of the city, away from the bustle of Spring and Collins streets. The Treasury Gardens contain the modest **John F Kennedy Memorial**, while the larger Fitzroy Gardens have a lovely conservatory with spectacular floral displays. The main attraction here is **Cook's Cottage** – the one-time home of Captain James Cook, which was constructed in Yorkshire by Cook's father in 1755 and reassembled here in Melbourne in the 1930s. The old stable contains a small display on Cook's pioneering voyages.

Return to the Treasury and cross Spring Street, entering Collins Street.

Collins Street (East)

9 The eastern section of Collins Street is known as the 'Paris end' and it does indeed resemble a European boulevard. This is where Gucci, Cartier and other expensive

An unusual and mesmerising mythical form greets visitors to the National Gallery of Victoria

ments are easily accessible from St Kilda Road. The impressive **Shrine of Remembrance**, dedicated in 1934, is Victoria's most important war memorial and commemorates the 19,000 Victorians who died in World War I. You can take a guided tour of the main shrine and there are smaller monuments to those who died in other conflicts.

Charles La Trobe, Victoria's first governor from 1851 to 1854, brought a prefabricated house with him when he came out from England. Today, **La Trobe's Cottage** stands in the gardens and contains original furniture and many of the Governor's possessions. Nearby **Government House** dates from the 1870s and can be inspected only by pre-booking on a tour.

The remainder of this tour is outside of the city centre and is best done by car – or you can hop on one of the frequent trams. If driving, continue southeast on St Kilda Road, then turn left on to Toorak Road.

South Yarra and Prahran

12 Toorak Road leads you towards Melbourne's most expensive residential area, but also into South Yarra, with its boutiques, coffee shops, galleries and restaurants – most of which lie between Punt Road and Chapel Street. While in the area, do not miss **Como** at Como Avenue, South Yarra (east of Chapel Street and off Toorak Road). This gracious old mansion, with its original furnishings and fine gardens, dates from the 1840s and is National Trust listed.

Turn right off Toorak Road into Chapel Street and you are now in another shoppers' mecca which stretches all the way to High Street, Prahran. In addition to the colourful array of eateries and shops here, Greville Street (near High Street) has a Sunday market and is a wonderful spot for browsing among books and *objets d'art*.

Continue along Chapel Street then turn right into High Street, and left in to Punt Road, finally turning right along Fitzroy Street to reach St Kilda.

St Kilda

13 This once very seedy inner city area has recently been transformed to become one of Melbourne's most interesting suburbs. The attractions here are many – streets with innumerable cafés and sidewalk tables (especially Acland Street), lovely old houses, a Sunday street market, wonderful cake and pastry shops and the Port Phillip Bay beach. Although most Sydneysiders, for example, would consider this little more than a strip of sand, it does add greatly to St Kilda's appeal. You can also walk out along the **St Kilda Pier** with its restored kiosk café, visit **Luna Park** and take a boat trip across the bay to the historic maritime village and port of **Williamstown**.

Return to the city via Fitzroy Street and St Kilda Road.

designer shops are found, as well as the high-class department store, Georges, and a couple of five-star hotels with their shopping and eating arcades. Call in at Collins Place (25 Collins Street) which adjoins the Regent Hotel, and Collins Chase (no 123) below the Hyatt on Collins to sample some luxury. There are also many notable old buildings in this stretch, including the 1873 **Scots Church** (no 140) and the **Melbourne Club** (at 36–50 and dating from 1858).

Turn left into Swanston Street and return over Princes Bridge to St Kilda Road.

Victorian Arts Centre and National Gallery of Victoria

10 This modern complex on St Kilda Road, south of the river, houses most of Melbourne's cultural delights. In addition to the National Gallery, the **Melbourne Concert Hall**, impressive **State Theatre**, the **Playhouse**, **Studio Theatre** and **Performing Arts Museum** are all located here. The National Gallery of Victoria contains displays of porcelain, glass and silver as well as fine collections of European and Australian paintings and sculpture. There is also an Aboriginal art display and the gallery regularly hosts travelling exhibitions from overseas and other states.

Continue south on St Kilda Road.

Royal Botanic Gardens

11 A comprehensive walk around the Botanic Gardens and adjoining Kings Domain would take some time, but a couple of notable monu-

---

FOR CHILDREN

13 While adults are soaking up Melbourne's culture and history, **Luna Park** at St Kilda will be a bigger hit with children. This historic funfair, with its colourful gaping-mouth entrance, was first opened in 1912 and contains some exciting rides. Older children will enjoy roller blading along the seafront – skates can be hired from various local outlets.

5/6 days – 1,010km (627 miles)

The former gold town of Castlemaine: rich in old buildings

NORTHWESTERN VICTORIA

**Melbourne • Ballarat • Ararat • Stawell
Gariwerd (Grampians) National Park • Horsham
Avoca • Maryborough • Castlemaine
Bendigo • Echuca • Daylesford • Melbourne**

From Melbourne City Centre, take Elizabeth Street and Flemington Road (Route 8), then the Western Highway and Western Freeway (Route 8).

Ballarat

1 Australia's largest inland city (population 64,000), is an attractive place with many old buildings which date back to the 1850s. Located beside Lake Wendouree, Ballarat contains numerous parks and gardens and is famous for its begonias. Lydiard Street has many fine 19th-century buildings, including the **Mining Exchange** (now an antiques centre) and the grand 1875 **Her Majesty's Theatre**, where Dame Nellie Melba once performed. The **Fine Art Gallery** offers a large collection of Australian art, while the **Gold Museum** and the 1856 **Montrose Cottage** provide a good insight into the city's history.

The major attraction here, however, is **Sovereign Hill Historical Park** – Australia's most famous re-creation of a 19th-century town. The 1850s goldmining days come alive in this large open-air 'museum' which features mine diggings, a populated township with operating shops and facilities, and a mining museum. The Yellowglen winery, which specialises in high quality sparkling wines, is 20km (12 miles) southwest of Ballarat and well worth the drive.

This tour to northwestern Victoria is a fascinating journey into the past. Gold was first discovered in the region in the 1850s and cities and towns such as Ballarat, Ararat, Stawell, Avoca, Bendigo and Castlemaine profited greatly from this rich discovery. The goldmining industry brought many thousands of people to the fledgling colony of Victoria and ultimately led to the great prosperity which Melbourne enjoyed during the late 19th century. West of these towns, the magnificent Gariwerd National Park is a rugged region with an interesting Aboriginal history, while in the north of the state, the Murray River town of Echuca was once Australia's major inland port. There are many wineries in this western region, and at Daylesford you can sample the clear mineral waters or take a spa bath.

Gold fever: try your luck panning for nuggets at Sovereign Hill

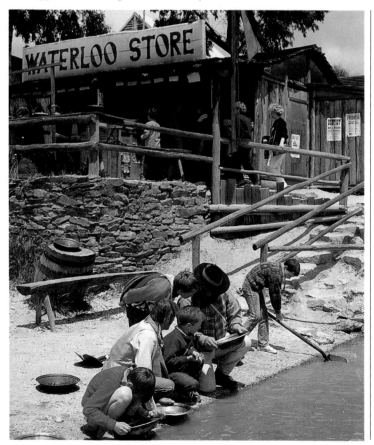

FOR CHILDREN

1 While adults are enjoying Ballarat's history and culture, the **Ballarat Wildlife and Reptile Park** is a great place for children. All of the favourite Australian mammals are here, including koalas, kangaroos and wombats, and the park also contains Tasmanian devils, a reptile house complete with salt-water crocodiles, and a vast open-air aviary.

SPECIAL TO . . .

3 The Stawell Gift 120m sprint race, held every Easter, dates back to 1878 and is one of the world's richest foot races – the prize money of some $100,000 attracts competitors from all over the world. The **Hall of Fame museum** in Stawell is dedicated to the athletes and organisers who have been involved in this famous race.

BACK TO NATURE

5 Although dry and sandy, the **Little Desert National Park**, northwest of Horsham, receives too much rain to be a true desert. This is the home of the rare mallee fowl and other threatened animals such as the southwestern pygmy possum. The park is also a haven for plants, and the spring wildflower display is spectacular. To the south of Little Desert, 369m (1,210-foot) high **Mount Arapiles** is known as the 'Ayers Rock of the Wimmera' – this is one of Australia's best rockclimbing areas and there are also some good walks here.

ⓘ 39 Sturt Street

Leave Ballarat on **Route 8** *(the Western Highway).*

Ararat

2 Originally an 1850s gold rush town, Ararat turned to grape planting and sheep farming in the 1860s and the town is now the centre of western Victoria's wine producing region. Nearby **Great Western** is the home of **Seppelts**, which is particularly famous for its sparkling wines. A tour of this winery, with its amazing underground wine storage tunnels, is a must. Also in the area and worth visiting are **Montara Wines**, **Mount Langi Ghiran Vineyards** and **Best's Great Western**. Other attractions include the **Ararat Gallery**, with its contemporary textiles, **Langi Morgala Museum** – a collection of mining and Aboriginal artefacts, and the pleasant **Alexandra Gardens**. The **Chinese Gold Discovery Memorial** honours the Chinese prospectors who discovered gold here in 1857.

ⓘ Barkly Street

Continue on **Route 8** *to Stawell.*

Stawell

3 This historic gold town still mines for the precious metal and you can watch the open-cut operations of the Stawell Joint Venture from a couple of viewing areas. Stawell is also an important wool producing region and the **North West Woollen Mill** is open to the public for tours and the purchase of quality items. The 1850s settlement of **Mount Pleasant Diggings** has retained several old buildings – the 1859 **Courthouse** is now a museum and you can also admire the 1872 **Town Hall** and **St Patrick's Church**. Stawell is an excellent base for exploring the nearby Grampians and

you can take scenic flights from the town. South of Stawell, **Bunjils Shelter** is an important Koori Aboriginal art site.

ⓘ Stawell and Grampians Information Centre, 54 Western Highway

From Stawell, take the Grampians Road to Halls Gap.

Gariwerd (Grampians) National Park

4 Famous for its rugged scenery, wildlife and abundant Aboriginal rock paintings, the Grampians is one of Victoria's largest and most spectacular national parks. First 'discovered' by explorer Major Thomas Mitchell in 1836, this area of sandstone ridges, waterfalls and lakes is the western extremity of the Great Dividing Range. Activities here include fishing for trout, canoeing and walking – there are over 50 walking tracks, offering everything from short strolls to challenging hikes. Over 200 bird species, including emus, wedge-tailed eagles and falcons, as well as kangaroos, possums, koalas and bandicoots are found in the Grampians. The wildflowers that bloom from August to November are spectacular and the nearby town of Halls Gap holds a wildflower exhibition each September and October.

The **Wonderland** area around **Halls Gap** is the most popular and accessible section of the Grampians. The Visitor Centre here offers displays on the park, tours of the rock art sites can be taken from here, and the **Brambuk Living Cultural Centre** focuses on the area's Koori history and culture. Also at Halls Gap, the **Grampians Wallaroo Wildlife Park** is a great place to meet the local wildlife – there are over 80 species of birds and animals here.

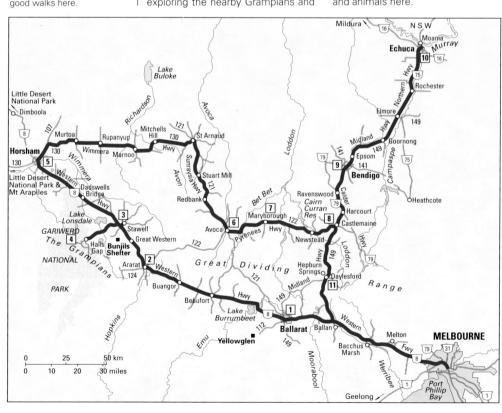

Return to Stawell and continue northwest on the Western Highway (Route 8).

Horsham

5 The unofficial capital of this area known as the Wimmera region, Horsham is an attractive riverside city at the heart of a wheat and wool growing belt. The fine **Art Gallery** contains works by several famous Australian artists and you can also visit the botanic gardens, the **Olde Horsham Village Museum**, fauna park and **antique market**, and the **Wimmera Wool Factory**, with its ultra-fine wool. The area is famous for its excellent fishing at **Wimmera Lakes**, to the south of town.

☐ 20 O'Callaghans Parade

Take the Wimmera Highway (Route 130) east to St Arnaud, then drive south on the Sunraysia Highway (Route 121).

Avoca

6 Situated near the Pyrenees Range, Avoca is another goldmining town that has turned to pastoral industries. There are many old buildings here, including the 1860s **Gaol and Courthouse**, the **Police Residence** and **Anglican Church**. You could also visit the **Avoca Rock Museum**, with its gemstones and meteorites. The Pyrenees vineyard area around Avoca and Redbank produces marvellous reds and good whites. Suggested wineries to visit are French-owned **Chateau Remy**, **Mount Avoca Vineyard** and **Taltarni Vineyards**. The **Avoca Wool and Wine Festival** is held each October.

☐ 199 High Street

Take Route 122 (the Pyrenees Highway) to Maryborough.

Maryborough

7 Maryborough was another gold era settlement, but today it is a rural centre with a variety of light industries such as knitting mills and printing. There are some delightful

The Grampians, a region of successive sandstone ridges, slope gently in the west, but to the east spectacular cliffs and unforgettable rock formations seize the imagination. Much Aboriginal rock art is found here. Above: Indian Head, Halls Gap Right: the jutting slabs known as the Balconies

old buildings here, including the 1892 **Railway Station**, with its 400m-long platform. American author Mark Twain described Maryborough as 'a railway station with a town attached'! The main square has a number of historic structures, such as the 1887 **Town Hall**, while bluestone **Worsley Cottage** dates from 1894 and is now a museum. There are good views of the town and surroundings from the Bristol Hill Lookout.

☐ Corner of Tuaggra and Alma streets

Continue east on the Pyrenees Highway.

Castlemaine

8 This old gold town is one of the region's most elegant settlements, with a great deal of fine 19th-century architecture. The remarkable, classical-style 1862 **Castlemaine Market** building is now a museum of local history, and one of Victoria's finest art collections is housed in the **Art Gallery and Historical Museum**. Also of interest are the impressive **Botanic Gardens**, and **Buda**, a late 19th-century residence with lovely gardens. Castlemaine also has a memorial to the 1860s explorers Burke and Wills – Robert O'Hara Burke was once a police superintendent here.

Castlemaine beer started life in the town in 1859 but now, under the famous label of Castlemaine XXXX, the beer comes from Queensland. The acclaimed **Castlemaine State Festival**, held every even-numbered

RECOMMENDED WALKS

The **Gariwerd National Park** offers many walking opportunities – everything from major hikes to short walks. The most easily accessed shorter strolls are in the **Wonderland** area, near Halls Gap. The local rangers will provide plenty of suggestions and advise on conditions.

SCENIC ROUTES

The **Goldfields Tourist Route**, marked by distinctive signs, links the old gold towns of Ballarat, Ararat, Stawell, Avoca, Maryborough, Castlemaine and Bendigo. Although this is primarily a historical trail, there are also plenty of scenic delights *en route*.

year, is a feast of classical music, dance, opera, jazz and theatre.

Take the Midland Highway (Route 149) north, then continue on the Calder Highway (Route 79).

Bendigo

9 Many towns in this region owe their development to the discovery of gold in the 1850s, but none fared better than the impressive city of Bendigo. The grand buildings here would be more appropriate in a major city – Pall Mall, the main thoroughfare, boasts the Italianate 1887 **Post Office**, 1896 **Law Courts**, 1881 Alexandra Fountain, 1897 **Shamrock Hotel**, and many others. View Street is another architecturally remarkable area, with many National Trust listed buildings.

The old **Central Deborah Mine** has been restored and is open for a fascinating tour. From the mine you can take a vintage tram ride around

FOR HISTORY BUFFS

1 Australia's most serious civil insurrection took place on the Ballarat goldfields on 3 December 1854. The **Eureka Stockade Rebellion** was mounted by miners protesting against licence fees and other grievances – a short but bloody battle with police and soldiers resulted in 35 men killed. The rebels were later charged with high treason, but were never convicted. Ballarat contains several historic sites relating to the rebellion, while the original Southern Cross flag, under which the rebels gathered, is on display in the **Fine Art Gallery**.

The grand old Shamrock Hotel in Bendigo, with its colonial-style architecture, speaks of a town that confidently saw a future for itself even as it developed out of the heady days of the 1850s gold rush

Bendigo's historic sites. Other reminders of the gold days are the 1860s **Chinese Joss House** and the **Golden Dragon Museum**, featuring 'Sun Loong' – at 100m (328 feet) this is believed to be the world's longest ceremonial Chinese dragon. The outstanding **Art Gallery**, with its large collection of Australian and European paintings, is a must, and there are many winemaking enterprises in the area. Recommended wineries at **Heathcote**, to the southeast, are the **Heathcote Winery** and **Jasper Hill Vineyard**. There are many other attractions, including the **Bendigo Mohair Farm** with its angora and Kashmir goats, and a recreation of the goldmining days at Sandhurst Town.

ℹ️ Charing Cross

Drive north on the Midland Highway, then the Northern Highway (Route 75).

Echuca

10 In contrast to the gold towns, Echuca's roots lie in the days of Murray River transportation. The town dates from 1854 and was once Australia's major inland port. Echuca (Aboriginal for 'meeting of the waters') is joined to its neighbour Moama, across the river in New South Wales, by a bridge. A visit to the Port of Echuca is a must. Only a portion of the 1860s 1km (½-mile) long wharf remains, but it is easy to imagine the bustle that once took place here. Two old steamers tied up at the wharf – the **PS** *Adelaide*, the world's second oldest operating paddle wheeler, and the 80-year-old **PS** *Pevensey* – are other attractions. Also in the port area are the **Bridge Hotel** (1858) and the **Port Visitors Centre**, in the 1867 **Star Hotel**.

Other highlights include the 1859 **Bond Store**, and what is perhaps the National Trust's most unusual building – the **Old Brothel**, constructed in 1875! The **Historical Society Museum**, housed in the 1867 police station, tells the town's interesting story, and you could also visit the **Kyabram Fauna Park**, with over 500 Australian birds, animals and reptiles. One of the main attractions here is cruising the Murray River on board a paddle-steamer – there are many cruises on offer, but the **PS** *Emmylou*, with its 1906 steam engine, provides something close to the original experience.

ℹ️ Corner of Leslie Street and Murray Esplanade

Return to Castlemaine, then continue south on the Midland Highway (Route 149).

Daylesford

11 The highland 'spa centre of Australia' began life as a gold-mining settlement, but natural springs were discovered here and by the 1880s the town had become an important health resort. There are 65 springs around Daylesford, but **Hepburn Springs** is the best known resort here – you can take various therapeutic baths and treatments, swim in the public pool or just drink the sparkling water. The excellent **Daylesford Historical Museum**, housed in the 1880s School of Mines, reveals much of the district's history. There are also many walking tracks in the area, and if you are here in early December you can join in with the colourful **Highland Gathering** – the largest such festival outside Scotland.

ℹ️ 49 Vincent Street

Drive south to join the Western Freeway (Route 8) at Ballan and return to Melbourne.

Melbourne – Ballarat 111 (69)
Ballarat – Ararat 92 (57)
Ararat – Stawell 32 (20)
Stawell – Halls Gap (Grampians NP) 24 (15)
Halls Gap – Horsham 88 (55)
Horsham – Avoca 172 (107)
Avoca – Maryborough 26 (16)
Maryborough – Castlemaine 47 (29)
Castlemaine – Bendigo 40 (25)
Bendigo – Echuca 94 (58)
Echuca – Daylesford 174 (108)
Daylesford – Melbourne 110 (68)

5 days – 1,044km (649 miles)

SOUTHEASTERN VICTORIA

Lighthouse at the entrance to Port Phillip Bay

From Melbourne City Centre, take St Kilda Road and the Nepean Highway (Route 3) to Frankston and continue to Portsea.

The Mornington Peninsula

1 With Port Phillip Bay on one side, and wild Bass Strait on the other, the holiday playground of the Mornington Peninsula offers both surf beaches and quiet bathing coves. **Frankston** is the main town, but drive on to the resorts of Mornington, Rosebud, Rye, Sorrento (the site of Victoria's first settlement in 1803) and Portsea. These towns all have good beaches, while **Point Nepean National Park** is the province of rugged cliffs and surf – you can also visit the 1850s **Cape Schanck Lighthouse** here. At **Dromana**, take the chairlift ride to 305m (1,000-foot) high **Arthur's Seat** – the views are quite spectacular. Near Dromana you can visit 1844 **McCrae Homestead**, while **Hastings** on the eastern side of the peninsula has a fauna sanctuary and interesting historical museum.

i 51 Playne Street, Frankston

From Hastings, follow Routes 67, 65 and 60 to join the South Gippsland Highway (Route 180) near Tooradin. Follow Route 180, then turn south on Route 181 and take the San Remo turn-off.

Phillip Island

2 Reached by bridge from San Remo, Phillip Island is a popular holiday spot that is renowned for its wildlife – especially the fairy penguins. The nightly **Penguin Parade** is not to be missed! Other wildlife highlights are the Australian fur seals in the island's southwest, koalas, and the kangaroos and wallabies at **Phillip Island Wildlife Park**. The north coast resort of Rhyll is the best place to see water birds like pelicans, and there is also a maritime museum here; while the picturesque main town of Cowes offers fine beaches and the Phillip Island Heritage Centre.

Melbourne • The Mornington Peninsula
Phillip Island • Wilsons Promontory National
Park • Sale and the Gippsland Lakes
Bairnsdale • Lakes Entrance and Metung
Moe and the La Trobe Valley • Melbourne

Victoria's southeast contains some of Melbourne's most popular coastal holiday areas – the Mornington Peninsula, Phillip Island, and the national park wilderness of Wilsons Promontory. Further east, the route heads inland to Central Gippsland – to the old town of Sale and the remarkable Gippsland Lakes region. From Bairnsdale you can explore the lakes, and drive on to the fishing and boating towns of Lakes Entrance and Metung.

The return to Melbourne is via the La Trobe Valley – an industrial region that holds some surprises for the visitor. Gippsland is famous for its excellent cheeses, which can be sampled here, and you can also take a detour north to the atmospheric old mining town of Walhalla.

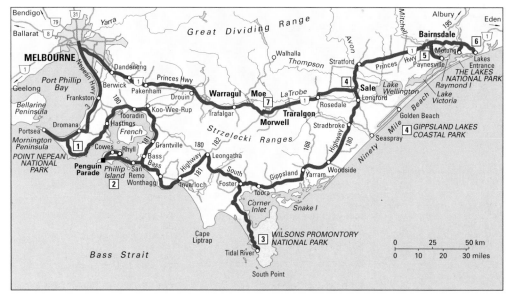

A breathtaking palette of blues and greens at Lakes Entrance

SPECIAL TO . . .

The dimensions of the giant **Gippsland worms** are astounding– they grow to lengths of 3m and around 2.5cm in diameter. You can see these unique creatures at **Wildlife Wonderland**, at **Bass** on the highway before *en route* to Phillip Island.

FOR HISTORY BUFFS

Forty-five kilometres north of Moe, **Walhalla** was once a town of around 5,000 people – gold was discovered here in 1862 and mined for 50 years. Today, Walhalla is a virtual ghost town but many old buildings remain: you can also visit the **Long Tunnel Extended Mine**, once one of Australia's richest gold sources.

FOR CHILDREN

2 For children, the highlight of this tour will be the **fairy penguins** of Phillip Island. Each night at the **'Penguin Parade'** these little creatures waddle up the beach to their sand burrows, providing much amusement and interest for everyone.

ⓘ Phillip Island Road, Newhaven

Return to San Remo and continue east on the Bass Highway (Route 181) to Wonthaggi. From here, take the scenic coastal road to Inverloch and join the South Gippsland Highway (Route 180) at Leongatha. Turn off south at Fraser.

Wilsons Promontory National Park

3 The Australian mainland's most southerly point is an extraordinary region of plains, mountains, magnificent coastal scenery and sandy beaches. Long inhabited by Aborigines, 'The Prom' became a national park in 1905 and this unspoiled 49,000-hectare (121,070-acre) region is home to kangaroos, koalas, wallabies, emus and wombats. Take the 15km (9-mile) **Nature Drive** from the park entrance and visit the Information Centre at Tidal River. The town of **Foster** is the main access point for Wilsons Promontory – there is accommodation here or in the national park.

Return to Foster and continue on Route 180 (the South Gippsland Highway).

Sale and the Gippsland Lakes

4 The town of Sale is the Gippsland region's administrative centre and a base for oil and natural gas exploration. Sale has many 19th-century buildings, including the 1863 **Sale Historical Museum**, the 1865

Criterion Hotel and **St Mary's Cathedral** (1870s). You can also visit the **Oil and Gas Display Centre** to discover more about the local industries.

The **Gippsland Lakes Coastal Park** is reached via the village of Seaspray – from here a road runs along the narrow spit of land to **Golden Beach**, a surfing and fishing resort. The coastal park takes in much of **Ninety Mile Beach**, a secluded stretch of dunes backed by a 400sq km chain of lakes – Australia's largest enclosed waterway system.

ⓘ Princes Highway

Take the Princes Highway (Highway 1) to Bairnsdale.

Bairnsdale

5 This agricultural centre is the gateway to the Gippsland Lakes region and an excellent base for exploring the area. Be sure to visit the National Trust classified 1893 **Bairnsdale Courthouse** and richly decorated **St Mary's Catholic Church**. The northeastern section of the **Gippsland Lakes** and **The Lakes National Park** can be accessed by boat from the resort of **Paynesville**, south of Bairnsdale.

ⓘ 240 Main Street

Continue east on Highway 1.

Lakes Entrance and Metung

6 Australia's largest fishing fleet is based in the town of Lakes Entrance, the site of an artificially created entry point into the lakes. The town is a popular holiday spot, with lake cruises and access to **Ninety Mile Beach**. You can also visit the **Riviera Marine Aquarium and Hatchery**, with its explanation of the local fishing industry. Metung, off the Bairnsdale – Lakes Entrance road, is a picturesque boating village from where you can hire boats to explore the waterways.

ⓘ Corner of Esplanade and Marine Parade, Lakes Entrance

Return to Bairnsdale and Sale, continuing west on Highway 1.

Moe and the La Trobe Valley

7 Much of the La Trobe Valley – particularly the Traralgon and Morwell area – is industrial, but the town of Moe is worth visiting for the **Old Gippstown Pioneer Township living museum** (also the Information Centre). This re-creation of a 19th-century township includes 30 authentic buildings which have been relocated here. At **Morwell**, stop to take a look at the excellent **La Trobe Regional Gallery**.

Return to Melbourne on Highway 1.

Melbourne – Portsea (Mornington Peninsula) 94 (58)
Portsea – Phillip Island 156 (97)
Phillip Island – Wilsons Promontory NP 188 (117)
Wilsons Promontory NP – Sale 185 (115)
Sale – Bairnsdale 69 (43)
Bairnsdale – Lakes Entrance 36 (23)
Lakes Entrance – Moe 186 (115)
Moe – Melbourne 130 (81)

Hobart's fishermen catch smaller fry than whales these days

HOBART

Sullivans Cove • Salamanca Place • Battery Point • City Centre • Tasmanian Museum and Art Gallery • Sandy Bay • Sullivans Cove

ⓘ Tasmanian Travel and Visitor Information Centre, corner of Davey and Elizabeth streets

Start the tour at Hunter Street, on the eastern side of Sullivans Cove.

Sullivans Cove

1 The Hobart waterfront area, known as Sullivans Cove, was the birthplace of Tasmania. On 21 February 1804 Lieutenant-Colonel David Collins stepped ashore here to found the fledgling colony of Van Diemen's Land. Hunter Street was once the city's main wharf and many of the old warehouses have been carefully renovated to contain restaurants and offices.

Victoria and Constitution docks have long been the mooring place for fishing boats and various craft – Constitution Dock marks the end of the annual Sydney to Hobart yacht race. **Mures Fish Centre** here is well known for its excellent seafood, while the impressive **Customs House** on Davey Street dates from 1902. Brooke Street Pier, is the departure point for river cruises. Before you reach Salamanca Place, have a look at the 1830s convict-built **Parliament House**.

Cross Parliament Square, which leads to Salamanca Place.

Salamanca Place

2 Salamanca Place – now one of Hobart's most appealing precincts – was originally a series of warehouses built between 1835 and 1860. Extensive restoration has created a picturesque street of cafés, galleries, arts and crafts shops and offices, and the area hosts a busy and colourful Saturday market. Behind Salamanca Place, the 1839 convict-built Kellys Steps lead up the hill to Battery Point.

At the top of the steps, turn left into McGregor Street.

Battery Point

3 Named after an 1818 battery of guns, this promontory is Hobart's most delightful suburb. Originally used as farming land, by the 1840s the suburb had become a desirable residential area. At the end of McGregor Street, **Lenna** is now a charming hotel, but was built as a home in the 1870s. Nearby **Princes Park** contains the 1818 **Signal Station**, Battery Point's oldest exisiting building. From here, walk down Runnymede Street to Arthur's Circus, a quaint circular street of 1840s and 1850s cottages.

A stroll along Colville, Trumpeter, Napoleon, Cromwell and De Witt streets and Hampden Road will reveal one of Australia's most charming urban landscapes. **St George's Anglican Church** dates from 1836–47 and is a fine example of colonial Georgian architecture,

Constitution Dock: catch the spirit of Hobart along its waterfront

Hobart is Australia's most unspoilt capital city. The River Derwent and the hilly surroundings provide plenty of natural attractions, while there are a remarkable amount of well-preserved 19th-century buildings here. Founded just 16 years after Sydney, Hobart is Australia's second oldest major city with a fascinating convict, maritime and colonial past. This is a small settlement of just 170,000 people and a walking tour is the best way to take in most of the sights, complemented by drives further afield. You can also take a river cruise to discover more about this peaceful, clean and friendly southern city.

There are a couple of ways to reach the island state – you can either fly from Melbourne, Sydney or other cities, or take the luxury ship, the *Spirit of Tasmania*, which sails from Melbourne three times a week.

while the elegant Georgian house **Narryna** (1833–6) contains the interesting **Van Diemen Folk Museum**.

From here, turn into Sandy Bay Road and return towards the city, through St David's Park.

City Centre

4 Originally Hobart's burial ground, St David's Park contains the grave of Lieutenant-Colonel Collins,

FOR CHILDREN

Hobart doesn't offer a great deal especially for children, but a cruise on the Derwent is probably a good way to amuse the kids for an hour or two. You can also take a boat trip from Brooke Street Pier to the **Cadbury's Chocolate Factory**, which will be popular with everyone!

SCENIC ROUTES

The best way to view Hobart, the river and surrounding countryside is from the summit of 1,270m (4,167-foot) **Mount Wellington**. The drive via Davey Street and the Huon Highway takes in the mountain's forested lower slopes, which are often snow-covered in winter. From the rugged summit the panorama is breathtaking.

FOR HISTORY BUFFS

3 The **Maritime Museum of Tasmania**, located in Secheron Road, displays a remarkable collection of model ships, photographs, paintings and many other relics of Tasmania's fascinating maritime history. The museum is housed in **Secheron House**, dating from 1831 and one of Hobart's finest examples of Georgian architecture.

BACK TO NATURE

In a superb location with good views of the River Derwent and Tasman Bridge, the **Queens Domain** and **Royal Tasmanian Botanic Gardens** provide a wonderful area of both natural and cultivated beauty. The gardens offer a conservatory, tropical house, fernery and a tranquil Japanese garden. Nearby **Government House** is the residence of Tasmania's governor, but is not normally open to the public.

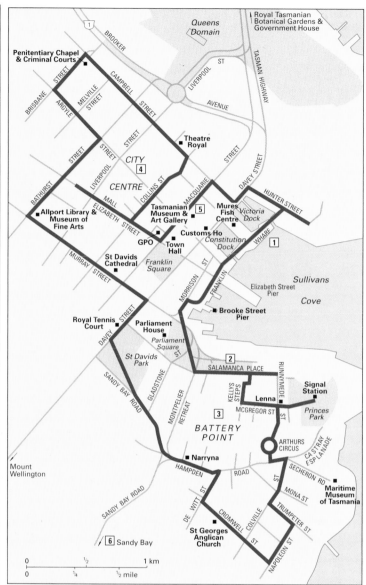

Built in 1837, the Theatre Royal's ornate interior has superb acoustics

Tasmania's first governor. Opposite the park is the **Royal Tennis Court** – dating back to 1875 and one of only two such courts in the southern hemisphere. From here, walk down Davey Street and turn left into Murray Street, the location of 1868 **St Davids Cathedral**. This lovely Gothic-style church is well worth inspecting for its stained glass, wooden ceiling and unusual parquetry floor. Further along Murray Street, the **State Library** contains the **Allport Library** and **Museum of Fine Arts**.

On Brisbane Street, the **Georgian Penitentiary Chapel and Criminal Courts** are now the National Trust headquarters. The buildings date from 1831 and contain cells and an execution yard. Walk back towards the waterfront along Campbell Street and past Australia's oldest theatre – the 1837 **Theatre Royal** with its ornate interior. From here, turn right into Collins Street to reach the Elizabeth Street Mall shops.

Turn left into Macquarie Street, passing the Town Hall.

Tasmanian Museum and Art Gallery

5 Located on Macquarie Street, the Tasmanian Museum and Art Gallery deserves a fairly lengthy visit. The Art Gallery contains some good colonial art, but the Museum is undoubtedly the main attraction. There are excellent displays on Australian mammals, including the Tasmanian devil and the extinct thylacine (Tasmanian tiger); the sad story of the Tasmanian Aborigines; and the state's fascinating convict past.

An option after the walking tour is to drive to Sandy Bay, via Sandy Bay Road.

Sandy Bay

6 Regarded as Hobart's most exclusive suburb, waterfront Sandy Bay contains lovely homes, a small beach, **Tudor Court** (a replica of an English village), and the **Wrest Point Hotel Casino**. There are good views of the River Derwent from Sandy Bay, while a visit to the casino's revolving restaurant at night is a good way to take in the panorama of water and hills.

Return to Sullivans Cove via Sandy Bay Road.

A burrowing carnivorous marsupial: the Tasmanian devil

AROUND TASMANIA

Hobart • New Norfolk • World Heritage Area Strahan and the West Coast • Wynyard and the Northwest Coast • Devonport • Deloraine Launceston and the Tamar Valley • St Helens and the East Coast • Freycinet National Park Richmond • Port Arthur • Hobart

From Hobart City Centre, take Brooker Avenue and the Lyell Highway (Route A10) via Berriedale and Granton.

New Norfolk

1 Your first stop is the National Trust listed town of New Norfolk in the Derwent Valley. First settled in the early 1800s, New Norfolk became the new home for several hundred evacuated Norfolk Islanders from 1807 onwards. The town is full of old buildings, including 1823 **St Matthew's Church** and the 1815 **Bush Inn** – two of Tasmania's oldest remaining structures. Other attractions here are jet boating on the Derwent River, the local **Historical Centre**, craft and antique shops and tours of the **Australian Newsprint Mills**.

ⓘ Council Offices, Circle Street

Continue on the Lyell Highway.

World Heritage Area

2 Tasmania's remarkable natural beauty has been internationally recognised by the UNESCO World Heritage status nomination of a large area of the southern and western part of the state. This area includes the remote **Southwest National Park** and the **Hartz Mountains**, the **Franklin–Gordon Wild Rivers National Park**, and the region to the north of the Lyell Highway – the **Cradle Mountain–Lake St Clair National Park** and **Walls of Jerusalem National Park**.

More than a superficial look at this vast area would take many days, but from Derwent Bridge on the highway it is possible to view the rugged beauty of the **Cradle Mountain–Lake St Clair** region. At Derwent Bridge, turn off to Cynthia Bay, where you

Although a small land mass by Australian standards, Tasmania offers more attractions per square kilometre than any other Australian state, while its size makes it the perfect venue for a leisurely motoring holiday. After Sydney, Hobart and Launceston are the nation's oldest cities and Tasmania has many old towns and historic buildings, and a fascinating convict past. There is also a host of natural attractions here – a large proportion of the state is classified as national park and reserves, while a vast region of 1.38 million hectares (3.4 million acres) is under UNESCO World Heritage protection. There are lovely beaches, intriguing islands, rainforest and a mild climate, which can turn to cold in winter. All of this is complemented by local gourmet foods, fine wines and quaint and historic houses which offer a special kind of accommodation.

The rugged peaks and plateaus of 1,545m (5,070-foot) high Cradle Mountain

SPECIAL TO ...

In recent years Tasmania has become famous as a gourmet's paradise. The food and wine here are extraordinary – everything from crayfish and smoked salmon, to delicious cheeses and thick cream, wonderful wines, handmade truffles and crisp apples. You can eat well in any major town, but some of the most interesting produce crops up in surprising places like small villages and seemingly remote islands.

a host of tours and attractions – cruising beautiful Macquarie Harbour and the Gordon River; taking a seaplane flight; or visiting **Sarah Island**, a notoriously brutal penal settlement from 1822 to 1833, where there are ruins of the harsh convict days. Don't miss the **Strahan Visitor Centre**, with its display on the local Aboriginal people, convicts and other history of this fascinating region.

Nearby **Zeehan**, on the Murchison Highway, is another mining town with many National Trust listed buildings – the town is the namesake of one of Abel Tasman's ships, which visited Tasmania in 1624. Spend some time at the **West Coast Pioneers' Memorial Museum**, stroll along Main Street and admire lovely old buildings like the **Gaiety Theatre**, and visit the steam locomotive and rail carriage display.

i The Esplanade, Strahan

> *From Strahan, drive to Zeehan and take the Murchison Highway (**Route A10**) through Rosebery to Somerset, then the **A2** west to Wynyard.*

Wynyard and the Northwest Coast

4 Tasmania's northwest is a region of fishing, farming and small port towns. Wynyard, the centre of a fertile dairying region, is dominated by the distinctive landmark of **Table Cape**. You can visit the lighthouse and lookout here for panoramic views of the north coast, or drive through the **Oldina Forest Reserve**, with its lovely Huon pine trees. Flights depart from Wynyard for **King Island**, out in Bass Strait. With its wildlife, lovely beaches, bushwalking and fishing, shipwreck history, the **Currie Museum** and a tradition of fine foods, the island is the perfect place for a relaxing stay.

To the west, **Boat Harbour** is a popular resort with a white sand beach and good scuba diving and fishing. Further along the coast lies **Rocky Cape National Park** – a small area of sheltered bays and beaches, woodland, and wildlife such as wallabies and wombats. To the west, the coastal village of **Stanley** contains many old buildings including the 1850s **Plough Inn** and **Highfield House**, dating from the 1830s. Also of interest here is the famous **'Nut'** – a distinctively shaped old lava plug which rises 150m above the town. You can take in the excellent coastal views by walking up, or riding on the chairlift.

East of Wynyard, **Burnie** is a manufacturing city and port with a few tourist attractions. You can tour the **Lactos Cheese Factory** and the **Associated Pulp and Paper Mills**; enjoy the history of the **Pioneer Village Museum** and 1840s **Burnie Inn**; and visit the **Burnie Art Gallery**. Further along the coast, the small town of **Penguin** is home to a fairy penguin colony, while **Ulverstone** is a popular summer holiday town with wonderful beaches and good fishing. The route between these two towns is particularly scenic.

Launceston's pleasant character is seen in its many fine old buildings, like this water mill. Built on the lovely Tanner river, the city rewards a stroll through its streets

can take a cruise on Lake St Clair. You can also go on a short nature walk here and pick up some information at the visitors' centre. Further west and just off the highway there is a picnic area above the Franklin River, also part of this special World Heritage region.

i Cynthia Bay

> *Continue towards Queenstown on the Lyell Highway.*

Strahan and the West Coast

3 The isolated west coast of Tasmania provides an interesting contrast between nature at its wildest and the marks of mining activities. **Queenstown**, the centre of a copper mining region, bears the scars of this activity in the treeless, 'moonscape' hills that surround the town. It's an interesting place though, with a 'Wild West' reputation and some historic buildings – you can tour the **Mount Lyell mine**, visit the **Mining Museum** and the **Galley Museum**, which tells the story of the West Coast region.

The tourist magnet of the area, however, is the port and fishing town of Strahan (pronounced 'Strawn'), located on the shores of Macquarie Harbour and the gateway to the World Heritage listed Wild Rivers National Park. Strahan offers

ⓘ Council Offices, Sanders Street, Wynyard

Continue on the Bass Highway (Route 1) to Devonport.

Devonport

5 The city of Devonport, at the mouth of the Mersey River, is a major point of entry to Tasmania – the luxury passenger/vehicle cruise ship, the *Spirit of Tasmania*, sails here from Melbourne three times a week. Attractions include the interesting **Tiagarra Aboriginal Cultural and Arts Centre**, where visitors can view ancient rock carvings; the **Maritime Museum**; and the **Don River Railway**, which takes you on a vintage train ride. The **Devonport Gallery and Arts Centre** and the tranquil **Tasmanian Arboretum**, a few kilometres out of town, are both worth visiting. National Trust listed 1916 **Home Hill** was the residence of former Australian Prime Minister, Joseph Lyons, and his wife Dame Enid Lyons – the first woman elected to the House of Representatives.

There are some excellent beaches in the area at **Port Sorell** and Hawley, and the **Asbetos Range National Park** is within easy reach. This park is home to 80 species of birds, Forester kangaroos, wombats and wallabies and contains superb stretches of sand such as Bakers Beach.

ⓘ 18 Rooke Street

Continue southeast on the Bass Highway.

Deloraine

6 The classified historic town of Deloraine, midway between Devonport and Launceston, is packed with old colonial buildings, galleries and craft centres and has great tourist appeal. You should see the **Folk Museum**, 1857 **St Mark's Church**, and take the self-guided heritage walk around town. Further afield, **Mole Creek** is the home of the state's famous leatherwood honey industry, and there are scenic drives south into the **Great Western Tiers** and to **Marakoopa Caves**. You could even head into the wild and dramatic **Walls of Jerusalem National Park** – part of Tasmania's World Heritage area.

Continue on the Bass Highway.

Launceston and the Tamar Valley

7 Tasmania's charming second city lies on the River Tamar and dates back to 1805. There are many well-preserved buildings here and an abundance of sights for the visitor. Take a self-guided walk along historic Cameron Street, dating from 1806, and visit the impressive **Queen Victoria Museum and Art Gallery**. Other historic buildings include the 1888 **Custom House** on

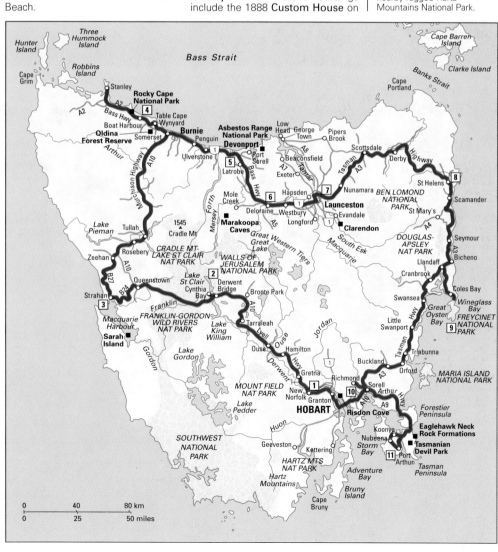

RECOMMENDED WALKS

1 Mount Field National Park, reached via New Norfolk, is one of Tasmania's most accessible national parks. This highland plateau region provides excellent bushwalking – from short nature strolls to challenging hikes – skiing in winter, and the opportunity to enjoy lakes, waterfalls and the famous Tasmanian trees, such as Huon pines, at close quarters.

the Esplanade, 1820 **Staffordshire House** (Charles Street), magnificent **Albert Hall** in City Park, and the 1860s **Old Umbrella Shop** on George Street – now a National Trust information centre and gift shop.

Cataract Gorge Reserve, just a few minutes from the city, is a pleasant area of gardens, bushland and walking tracks, crossed by the 1895 Alexandra Suspension Bridge. Also here are the re-created village of **Penny Royal World**, from where you can take a short cruise on the Tamar, and the **Ritchies Mill Art Centre** – a good place to buy local art and crafts. At night you can visit the **Country Club Casino**, and the shopping is excellent – a favourite

In the well-to-do market town of Launceston, an attractive windmill interests visitors

purchase being high-quality woollen goods from local knitting mills.

The fertile Tamar Valley, stretching north to Bass Strait, offers many attractions, including **George Town** on the eastern side of the river. This settlement dates back to 1804, and you can visit historic houses and the 1843 **Old Watchhouse**, also the start of a heritage walk. Low Head, a few kilometres away, has a maritime museum in the 1835 **Pilot Station** buildings. Some of Tasmania's best wineries are in this area – **Pipers Brook Vineyard** and **Heemskirk Vineyards** at **Pipers Brook** are particularly recommend-

ed. Across the river, the old goldmining town of **Beaconsfield** contains mining museums and other mine relics, while nearby **Exeter** is an excellent spot to sample more of the region's wines. **Asbestos Range National Park** (see Devonport) can also be accessed from here.

South and west of Launceston the villages of **Longford**, **Evandale** and **Hadspen** contain some special National Trust houses. Idyllic Longford is well worth a visit for its history and craft shops, while the magnificent mansion of **Clarendon**, near Evandale, is National Trust listed and dates from the 1830s. **Entally House** at Hadspen was built around 1820 and contains a wonderful collection of Regency furniture and silverware. Also within easy reach of Launceston, **Ben Lomond National Park** is Tasmania's premier skiing area in winter and a lovely alpine environment of wildflowers and wildlife at other times of the year.

[i] Corner of St John and Paterson Streets, Launceston

From Launceston, take the Tasman Highway (Route A3) to St Helens.

St Helens and the East Coast

8 Known as the Suncoast, this region is dotted with small resorts, fishing towns and good beaches. St Helens, the area's largest town and an old whaling port, is one of Tasmania's busiest fishing centres and offers scenic cruises, game fishing, and swimming and surf beaches. You should also visit the **St Helens History Room** for an insight into the area's past. To the south, **Scamander** has spectacular beaches and good fishing, while the port of **Bicheno** dates back to the early 1800s, when it was a sealing and whaling settlement. The freshly caught crayfish and scallops here are wonderful and there are many white sandy beaches to enjoy. A little to the north of Bicheno, the **Douglas-Apsley National Park** is a lovely area of eucalypt forest – there are some easy but scenic walks in the reserve.

[i] 20 Cecilia Street, St Helens

From Bicheno, continue on the A3 then take the Coles Bay turn-off.

Freycinet National Park

9 This is one of Tasmania's many natural highlights – with abundant bird and animal life, superb scenery and excellent beaches, Freycinet is nature at its best. The pretty resort and fishing town of **Coles Bay** is the gateway to the national park and offers a variety of accommodation. From here you can walk to the much-photographed white sands and azure waters of lovely **Wineglass Bay**, or visit one of the park's many quiet beaches.

Return to and continue south on the Tasman Highway from Swansea, then take the Richmond turn-off before reaching Sorell.

Richmond

10 Dating back to the 1820s, Richmond is one of Australia's most historic towns. The bridge here was constructed by convicts in 1823–5; **Richmond Gaol** dates back to 1825 and was used to house convicts; and the town is full of sandstone churches and 1830s buildings. Naturally, such an historic town contains many arts and crafts outlets, tea shops and other attractions – including a maze, the **Richmond Toy Museum**, and nearby 1830s **Prospect House**, where you can dine or stay overnight in old-fashioned style.

Return to the A3, then take the Arthur Highway (Route A9) at Sorell.

Port Arthur

11 Another Tasmanian highlight, Port Arthur – a penal settlement dating from 1830 – and the Tasman Peninsula are musts for every visitor. After passing through the Forestier Peninsula you will come to **Eaglehawk Neck**, a narrow strip of land that was once guarded by fierce watchdogs to prevent any escaped convicts from progressing further. South of here, take a short detour to the east coast's dramatic rock formations of **The Blowhole**, **Tasmans Arch**, the **Devils Kitchen** and **Patersons Arch**.

From 1831 to 1877 over 12,000 male convicts toiled under brutal conditions at Port Arthur, and many buildings remain from these rough

A reminder of the darker side of the British Empire: a survivor of Port Arthur's cruel penal history

and ready days. You can visit the restored **Model Prison and Church**, walk around other buildings and ruins, watch an audio-visual presentation, and learn more of the area's fascinating history at the **museum**. There are also cruises to the **Isle of the Dead**, where more than 1,700 convicts and other settlers are buried, and spooky night-time 'Ghost Tours' of the settlement.

Other Tasman Peninsula attractions include the **Tasmanian Devil Park**, with its devils and other native wildlife, and the narrow gauge **Bush Mill Steam Railway**. For a more comprehensive look at the peninsula you can return to Eaglehawk Neck and Hobart via the villages of **Nubeena** and **Koonya**.

Return to Hobart via the Arthur Highway and Tasman Highway (A3).

Hobart – New Norfolk	37 (23)
New Norfolk – Derwent Bridge	146 (91)
Derwent Bridge – Strahan	124 (77)
Strahan – Wynyard	212 (132)
Wynyard – Stanley	60 (37)
Stanley – Wynyard	60 (37)
Wynyard – Devonport	73 (45)
Devonport – Deloraine	50 (31)
Deloraine – Launceston	51 (32)
Launceston – St Helens	169 (105)
St Helens – Freycinet NP	120 (75)
Freycinet NP – Richmond	180 (112)
Richmond – Port Arthur	86 (53)
Port Arthur – Hobart	130 (80)

FOR HISTORY BUFFS

Off the east coast and reached via Triabunna, **Maria Island** is now a national park and animal sanctuary, but in 1825 it became the site of a penal settlement. The convict village at Darlington lasted only seven years, but today many of the old stone buildings remain and the 1825 former Commissariat Store is now an interesting museum and information centre.

More history is to be found at **Risdon Cove**, upriver from Hobart. This was the first site chosen for settlement in 1803, but it was superseded by Hobart in the following year. A reserve here contains ruins and other interesting historic sites.

6/7 days – 1,080km (669 miles)

MELBOURNE TO ADELAIDE

Melbourne • Geelong • Bellarine Peninsula
Torquay and Anglesea • Lorne • Apollo Bay and
Otway National Park • Port Campbell
Warrnambool • Port Fairy • Portland • Mount
Gambier • Millicent • Kingston SE • Coorong
National Park • Tailem Bend and Murray Bridge
Hahndorf and the Adelaide Hills • Adelaide

Following the western Victoria coastal road from Melbourne, this tour passes through the thriving city of Geelong and visits the historic Bellarine Peninsula. The itinerary then takes in some of Australia's most dramatic coastal scenery along the 300km-long Great Ocean Road – from Torquay to Port Fairy. This wild Bass Strait coast has claimed many shipwrecks and is dotted with fascinating small maritime towns.

Mount Gambier heralds your arrival in neighbouring South Australia, and the drive to the capital city of Adelaide includes the wonderful Coorong National Park and vast Lake Alexandrina, and the lower Murray River towns of Tailem Bend and Murray Bridge. Closer to Adelaide lie Hahndorf and the Adelaide Hills – one of Australia's most picturesque regions.

Koala country: these timid tree-dwelling creatures, with their cuddly-toy look, are hard to spot

From Melbourne City Centre, take St Kilda Road, the Westgate Freeway and the Princes Freeway (Highway 1) to Geelong.

Geelong

1 Victoria's second largest city dates back to 1838 – Geelong then boomed during the 1850s gold rush and has never looked back. The city is a thriving port and industrial centre that also contains much to interest the visitor. The fascinating **National Wool Museum** pays tribute to one of Australia's most important industries. The museum is housed in a 19th-century bluestone woolstore and high quality wool products are available in the shop. Geelong contains over 100 National Trust listed buildings – the 1838 **Customs House** (Victoria's oldest building), Corio Villa (1856), **Barwon Grange** (1855), and the **Church of Christ** (1864) are some of the architectural highlights. The **Maritime Museum** and the fine **Botanic Gardens** are also of interest.

i National Wool Museum, corner of Moorabool and Brougham streets

Leave Geelong by the Bellarine Highway (Route 91).

Bellarine Peninsula

2 This peninsula on the western side of Port Phillip Bay is a favourite holiday destination for the inhabitants of Melbourne and Geelong. The resorts of Portarlington, Ocean Grove and Barwon Heads are delightful, but **Queenscliff** is the peninsula's gem. Dating back to 1846, when it was a mere fishing village, Queenscliff is the region's most historic town.

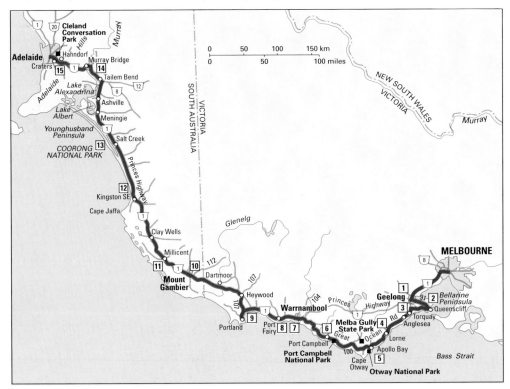

Attractions include the **Queenscliff Maritime Centre**, **Fort Queenscliff**, built during the Crimean War, the **Black Lighthouse** (1861) and several grand old 1880s hotels, such as the **Vue Grand** and the **Ozone**. The Bellarine Peninsula Steam Railway, which operates on a 16km (10-mile) track, is another popular attraction.

☐ Seaview House, Hesse Street, Queenscliff

From Queenscliff, drive to Ocean Grove and across the Peninsula south to Torquay.

Torquay and Anglesea

3 Torquay is one of the most popular resorts in the Geelong area. The beaches and surf here are excellent, and nearby **Bells Beach** is regarded as Australia's surfing capital, with an international competition each Easter. It is at Torquay that the 300km Great Ocean Road begins. Completed in 1932, the road winds through magnificent coastal and inland scenery, including the steep hills of the **Otway Ranges**. Your first stop is the quiet holiday village of **Anglesea** with its fine beaches. Surfing, fishing, boating and walking are all popular here, and the golf course is famous for its abundant friendly kangaroos.

☐ Mary Elliott Pottery, The Esplanade, Torquay

From Anglesea, continue on the Great Ocean Road (Route 100).

Lorne

4 The small fishing town of Lorne, dominated by the Otway Ranges, is one of Victoria's loveliest coastal resorts. The village was established in the 1860s and soon became a refined seaside resort. Lorne has retained many fine old buildings, including a number of guesthouses, and is perhaps the most charming of the Great Ocean Road destination. The beaches here are wonderful, surfing is popular and there is good walking in the **Angahook-Lorne State Park** and nearby **Cumberland River Valley**. Don't miss the coastal views from **Teddy's Lookout**, behind the town.

☐ 144 Mountjoy Parade

Continue driving on the Great Ocean Road.

Apollo Bay and Otway National Park

5 The port of Apollo Bay was first used by sealers and whalers, seeking shelter from the fierce Bass Strait storms. Fishing is a popular pursuit here and the wooded Otway Ranges are great for walks and scenic drives. In town, you can visit the **Bass Strait Shell Museum** and the **Historical Museum**.

Beginning just beyond Apollo Bay, the Otway National Park contains spectacular coastline, luxuriant forests and heathland. The park includes a section of the heavily forested Otway Ranges, which stretch from Anglesea in the east to Cape Otway. There are many walking trails here, while you can swim, fish, snorkel and surf along the coast. Within the park, Cape Otway

and its lighthouse mark the end of Bass Strait. The lighthouse was completed in 1848 and there is a cemetery here containing the graves of numerous shipwreck victims.

☐ 155 Great Ocean Road, Apollo Bay

Continue west on the Great Ocean Road.

Port Campbell

6 Port Campbell is yet another picturesque village and port, situated in the middle of a national park. The wharf, now used by the crayfishing fleet, was built in 1879 in the days when Port Campbell was the only safe anchorage in the region. The main attraction is the national park, but the town offers a **Historical Museum** and a self-guided **Discovery Walk**.

The Ocean Road's most spectacular coastal scenery is found within **Port Campbell National Park**. Dramatic formations such as the Twelve Apostles, Island Arch and

An icon of nostalgia: the sturdy old steam train at Queenscliff station harks back to the last century

London Bridge have been created by the erosive action of the stormy Southern Ocean on these friable limestone cliffs. The waters here have claimed many a shipwreck, including the *Loch Ard*, which went down in 1878 with just two survivors. A plaque at **Loch Ard Gorge** tells the story of this tragic event. The park has sheltered beaches and there is an excellent short 'Discovery Walk'. Fauna includes muttonbirds, fairy penguins, wallabies, echidnas and ringtail possums.

☐ National Park Information Centre, Tregea Street, Port Campbell

Continue on the Great Ocean Road.

Warrnambool

7 Originally a sealing and whaling port, this city of 22,000 people now thrives on tourism and a variety of industries. There are good beaches and several historical attractions. The Flagstaff Hill Maritime

RECOMMENDED WALKS

4 Part of the Otway Ranges, the Angahook-Lorne State Park offers a good range of walks from one to two hours, giving you the opportunity to see this lovely forested region close up. Major tracks start at the Sheoak picnic area and take in a variety of waterfalls.

BACK TO NATURE

5 Near the small settlement of **Lavers Hill**, northwest of Apollo Bay, **Melba Gully State Park** in the Otway Ranges is famous for its wildlife. The dense rainforest is home to wallaroos, ringtail possums and the rarely seen platypus, while at night rangers lead tours to see the park's glow-worms.

SCENIC ROUTES

The entire **Great Ocean Road** is one of Australia's most spectacular drives, and perhaps one of the world's most scenic. The road hugs the coastline for much of the route, revealing lovely coastal scenery, as well as the inland splendour of the Otway Ranges inland.

FOR HISTORY BUFFS

6 There have been at least 150 shipwrecks along the Great Ocean Road coast, particularly between Port Campbell and Warrnambool. The **Shipwreck Trail** links the sites of many of these wrecks. Road signs identify the trail, and information plaques overlooking the cliffs indicate where these 19th and early 20th-century wrecks occurred. Information sheets are available from local tourist centres.

Irregular erosion rates created Port Campbell's Twelve Apostles

Museum re-creates Warrnambool's 19th-century port days – the museum village is centred around the 1887 lighthouse and displays items from some of the area's 100 shipwrecks. Several ships are also moored here, including an old Tasmanian steamer.

Between late May and August each year, southern right whales come from the Antarctic to the area known as **Logans Beach Whale Nursery** to give birth. This wonderful event can be witnessed from a viewing platform on the cliff top.

ⓘ 600 Raglan Parade

Leave Warrnambool on the Princes Highway (Highway 1).

Port Fairy

8 Whitewashed cottages, historic bluestone buildings, and an interesting maritime past make Port Fairy one of Victoria's most picturesque coastal towns. There are over 50 National Trust classified buildings here, including the single-storey **Caledonian Inn** which has been operating since 1844, and the 1840s **Motts Cottage**. **Griffiths Island**, linked to the town by a causeway, was once a whaling station but is now frequented by muttonbirds during the October to April breeding season. Also on the island, solar-powered **Port Fairy Lighthouse** dates from 1859.

ⓘ Bank Street

Continue west on the Princes Highway.

Portland

9 The most westerly of Victoria's coastal towns, Portland was the

state's first permanent settlement, dating back to the early 1830s when whalers first visited the area. This is the only deep water port between Melbourne and Adelaide – a fact which has made Portland an important shipping and lobster fishing centre. There are many historic buildings here – the **Customs House** and 1842 **Steam Packet Hotel**, for example – and the region's beaches and fishing are popular with tourists.

ⓘ Cliff Street

Take Route 107 out of Portland, which links up with the Princes Highway (Highway 1) and continue west.

Mount Gambier

10 This gateway to South Australia is also the southeast region's most important town and the centre for pastoral and quarrying industries. Mount Gambier is an extinct volcano and the area is full of cones, craters, lakes and limestone caves. There are a number of old stone buildings in Mount Gambier, which are best seen on the local **Heritage Walk**. **Blue Lake**, in the volcano's main crater, is the area's major attraction. This 179m (587-foot) deep lake changes colour from grey to a brilliant blue each November and reverts to its normal tones in late March. The phenomenon is caused by calcite being activated by the warm weather.

ⓘ Jubilee Highway East

Continue towards Adelaide on the Princes Highway.

Millicent

11 Millicent, the next major Princes Highway town, was first settled in 1851 and named after the wife of an early resident. The swampy land here was drained and reclaimed in the 1870s and the fertile soil proved to be excellent for growing crops. The award-winning National Trust **Museum and Admella Gallery**, housed in the 1873 primary school, includes theme rooms, a craft gallery, horse-drawn vehicles and farm implements.

Continue on the Princes Highway.

Kingston SE

12 This town's curious name (SE means southeast) is designed to distinguish it from another South Australian settlement, Kingston-on-Murray. At the southern end of the **Coorong National Park**, Kingston is a seaside resort and fishing town. This is the beginning of 'lobster country', which explains the huge **Big Lobster** at the entrance to town. Fishing is popular and there is safe swimming at nearby **Wyomi** and **Pinks beaches**. **Cape Jaffa** dating from the 1860s, was re-erected at Kingston in the 1970s and is under the care of the National Trust.

Continue northwest on the Princes Highway and take the Salt Creek turn-off.

Coorong National Park

13 The Coorong is one of Australia's most unusual national parks. Squeezed in between the tall white sandhills of the Younghusband Peninsula and the highway, the Coorong is a 145km (90-mile) long stretch of water that provides a unique environment for 400 species of birds. The Coorong averages only 2km or 3km (1 to 2 miles) wide, but the waters are excellent for fishing, with plenty of bream, mullet and trout. This magical park contains many walking trails, and ranger-guided hikes are available from the Salt Creek headquarters.

The Southern Ocean beaches here are unspoilt and the surf is magnificent. Windsurfing, waterskiing and sailing are popular, and there are scenic drives along the shores of Lake Albert and Lake Alexandrina. The best access is from Meningie – also the ideal place to stay.

ⓘ Melaleuca Crafts, Main Road, Meningie

Drive north from Meningie on the Princes Highway.

Tailem Bend and Murray Bridge

14 Located on the Murray River and at the junction of two highways, Tailem Bend has always been an important transportation centre. The only major attraction here is the **Old Tailem Town Pioneer Village** – a collection of 50 restored buildings – 5km (3 miles) north of town.

Further upriver, Murray Bridge was just a ferry crossing in the 1850s – the first bridge was built in 1879, while the modern 734m (2,408-foot) long version dates from 1979. You can take a river cruise, tour the **Cottage Box chocolate factory**, and visit **Puzzle Park** and the **Butterfly House**, which features hundreds of colourful butterflies. The town's most historic building is

the **Captain's Cottage Museum** – a restored 1890s dwelling with relics and photographs of the region's early days.

ⓘ 15b Railway Terrace, Tailem Bend

*Continue on **Highway 1** and take the Hahndorf turn-off*

Hahndorf and the Adelaide Hills

15 Picturesque Hahndorf was founded by German Lutherans in 1839 and is distinctively European, with tree-lined streets, cafés and craft shops. The **Hahndorf Academy** contains 80 paintings by the town's most famous resident, the landscape artist Sir Hans Heysen (1877–1968), who lived here for 60 years. Other attractions include the **Beerenberg Strawberry Farm**, the **Hahndorf Antique Clock Museum**, and a **model train village**.

It's worth stopping off in some other Adelaide Hills towns, which are all off the Freeway *en route* to the city. **Bridgewater** contains the **Old Mill** with its 1860 water wheel

Blue Lake, at Mount Gambier, fills a crater created during the area's relatively recent volcanic era

– now part of the **Petaluma Winery**. At **Crafers**, the **Mount Lofty Botanic Garden** specialises in temperate climate plants and treess.

ⓘ 64 Main Street, Hahndorf

Return to the Freeway and continue to Adelaide.

Melbourne – Geelong 75 (47)
Geelong – Queenscliff (Bellarine
 Peninsula) 31 (19)
Queenscliff – Torquay 40 (25)
Torquay – Lorne 50 (31)
Lorne – Apollo Bay 45 (28)
Apollo Bay – Port Campbell 105 (65)
Port Campbell – Warrnambool 66 (41)
Warrnambool – Port Fairy 29 (18)
Port Fairy – Portland 71 (44)
Portland – Mount Gambier 116 (72)
Mount Gambier – Millicent 49 (30)
Millicent – Kingston SE 106 (66)
Kingston SE – Meningie (Coorong NP)
 145 (90)
Meningie – Tailem Bend 52 (32)
Tailem Bend – Hahndorf 70 (43)
Hahndorf – Adelaide 30 (18)

FOR CHILDREN

15 Cleland Conservation Park, at Mount Lofty in the Adelaide Hills, houses a collection of native animals and birds in natural bushland. The most popular feature – the adorable koalas – are shown at close quarters twice a day and will be a huge hit with children of all ages.

SPECIAL TO ...

15 Hahndorf's **Schutzenfest** is a special event that pays tribute to the region's German heritage. Held each January, this 'shooting festival' has its origins in the German provinces and German-style food, drinks, beer, music and entertainment abound.

ADELAIDE

The extraordinary intensity of Aboriginal patterns can be seen in the arts and crafts on show and for sale at the multi-arts Tandanya Aboriginal Cultural Institute

Victoria Square • King William Street • North Terrace (West) • Adelaide Festival Centre North Adelaide • Zoological and Botanic Gardens • North Terrace (East) • Central City Victoria Square

This lovely planned city, surrounded by parkland on all sides and crossed by the River Torrens, originated as the vision of Colonel William Light, the man charged with planning South Australia's capital in 1836. Adelaide has always been proud of the fact that it had no convict settlers and was the province of free immigrants. Known as the 'City of Churches', Adelaide once had a rather stuffy reputation, but today the city prides itself as a centre of culture, the arts and good living.

Adelaide has been far less reckless in terms of 'development' than most Australian cities and there is a proliferation of old buildings to admire. The combination of its small size, hectares of parkland, the river and a wonderful Mediterranean climate of warm dry summers and cool winters makes Adelaide the nation's most desirable address for its one million or so residents. The city is very compact and is best explored on foot – Light's neat grid of parallel streets makes it very easy to find your way around. There are also some optional excursions outside the city by tram and train ride.

SPECIAL TO ...

The world-famous **Adelaide Festival**, held every second year (even numbers) in late February and early March, is Australia's most acclaimed arts festival. The more traditional events are held at the **Adelaide Festival Centre,** while the Festival Fringe takes place at the **Living Arts Centre** (corner of Morphett Street and North Terrace). The centre houses arts and crafts studios and is worth visiting at non-festival times.

[i] Tourism South Australia Travel Centre, 1 King William Street

Start the tour at Victoria Square, the heart of the planned city area.

Victoria Square

1 Adelaide's central square, surrounded by old buildings and modern high-rise offices, is a good starting point for your walk. The square's fountain is based on three of South Australia's rivers and this is a pleasant spot to take a break from sightseeing or shopping. The terminal for the Glenelg tram is located in the park (see **For Children**).

Walk north along King William Street.

King William Street

2 Adelaide's broad, major north–south thoroughfare contains many interesting buildings. Immediately to the left is the 1867 **General Post Office** with its Victoria Clock Tower – once the tallest structure in the city, while on the right the **Old Treasury Building** dates back to 1839. The Treasury now contains a museum focusing on the history of land settlement in South Australia. Next door is the impressive 1866 Renaissance-style **Adelaide Town Hall**, which was modelled on Italian buildings. As a remarkable contrast, the 1989 33-level **State Bank Centre** (between Waymouth and Currie streets) is the city's tallest building. Renaissance-style **Edmund Wright House**, at no 57–63, was built for the Bank of South Australia in 1876 and is now the Registry Office.

Turn left at the junction of King William Street and North Terrace.

North Terrace (West)

3 This is the city's most gracious street, containing many of Adelaide's important buildings and museums. Immediately in front of you is the extremely grand marble and granite Parliament House, dating from 1883–1939 and the seat of the South Australian Government. Next door, the much more modest 1855 **Old Parliament House** has been turned into an interesting museum of South Australia's political and social history and features the original House of Assembly chamber. The nearby **Adelaide Casino** is housed in part of the 1927 Railway Station – a classic sandstone building which is now an elegant entertainment centre with dozens of gaming tables, restaurants and several bars.

Across North Terrace, the **Terrace Adelaide** is the city's premier hotel, while on the eastern side of King William Road the Regency-style **Government House** dates from 1838 and is one of Adelaide's most elegant buildings. This is the private residence of the governor of South Australia, but the lovely gardens are open to the public at certain times of the year.

Walk north on King William Road.

Adelaide Festival Centre

4 The left side of the road is dominated by the large, modern Adelaide Festival Centre – a complex of several theatres, a concert hall and restaurants which was completed in 1977. This is the focus of the acclaimed biannual Adelaide Festival and also South Australia's most important venue for performing arts. The **Festival Centre Gallery** holds changing exhibitions of paintings, sculpture and crafts. The centre is fronted by the tranquil environment of **Elder Park** and the River Torrens. The park features a lovely old rotunda dating from 1882 and you can take a river cruise from the landing stage here.

Continue on King William Road.

North Adelaide

5 After crossing the Adelaide Bridge, from which there are good views of the river, it's worth having a look at the **Adelaide Oval** (tours are available on Thursdays). Dating back to the 1870s, this is the city's international cricket stadium and is widely regarded as Australia's most attractive cricketing venue. A little further along King William Road is **St Peters Cathedral** – this magnificent church dates from 1869 but the towers and spires were added in 1902. The bells here are the heaviest in the southern hemisphre.

Walk along Pennington Terrace and you will reach Montefiore Hill and **Lights Vision** – a memorial to Colonel William Light, the city's founder and planner. It is appropriate that he is remembered by this statue facing towards the pleasing environment he created. Near by, on Strangways Terrace, is the 1897 Gothic-style **Carclew**, once a private house but now an arts centre. From here, you can take an enjoyable wander through the pleasant residential and shopping streets of North Adelaide – Melbourne Street is particularly worth visiting for its boutiques, shops and cafés.

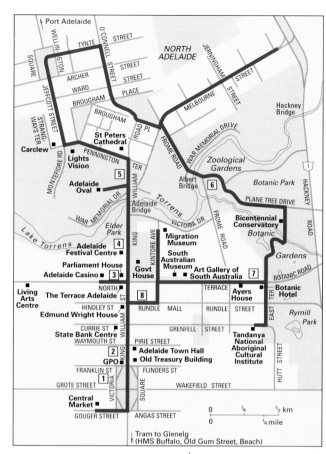

The focal point of Victoria Square is its fountain honouring three rivers in South Australia, the driest state in the driest country

A profusion of plants flourish in the Adelaide Botanic Gardens

FOR HISTORY BUFFS

A short train ride or drive away from the city centre, **Port Adelaide** is the city's old harbour town and contains many well preserved 19th-century buildings. The acclaimed **South Australian Maritime Museum** features the 1869 **Lighthouse**, which provides a spectacular view of the plains and hills, and two floating vessels. You can also take a variety of cruises from Port Adelaide, visit the **Historical Aviation Museum**, or a train buff's dream at the **Port Dock Station Railway Museum**.

FOR CHILDREN

A fun excursion for adults and children alike is the 30-minute tram trip to the seaside sub-urb of **Glenelg**, on board a 1929 vintage vehicle. Once at Glenelg there is a beach, shops and cafés to explore, and you can visit the **Old Gum Tree** – the spot where Governor Hindmarsh proclaimed the colony on 28 December 1836. You can also board **HMS** *Buffalo*, a replica of the original pioneers' ship which made the journey from Portsmouth, and visit the interesting naval museum.

From Melbourne Street, walk back towards the city on Frome Road, then cross the river on Albert Bridge.

Zoological and Botanic Gardens

6 The area of parkland to the north-east of the city centre contains the **Adelaide Botanic Gardens**, founded in 1855. The highlight here is the **Bicentennial Conservatory** – a large, futuristically shaped glass-house with a wide variety of rainforest trees and plants. Also in this area are the Zoological Gardens, home to the beautifully landscaped zoo. Rare species such as the Persian leopard and red panda are bred here, and you can see unusual Australian mammals like the yellow-footed rock wallaby.

Rejoin North Terrace.

North Terrace (East)

7 The eastern side of North Terrace contains many points of interest. One of the first buildings is the 1877 **Botanic Hotel** with its unusual tiered balconies, while elegant blue-stone **Ayers House** at no 288 dates from 1846 and was the home of Sir Henry Ayers (after whom Ayers Rock is named), seven times Premier of South Australia from 1855 to 1897. The house is now the headquarters of the state National Trust.

Although it means a short detour from North Terrace, don't miss the interesting **Tandanya National Aboriginal Cultural Institute** on Grenfell Street. The nation's only Aboriginal multi-arts complex, the institute is the home of performing arts such as dance and music, art and craft workshops, a museum and visual arts gallery. The shop here sells high quality Aboriginal-made products. Back on North Terrace, the **Art Gallery of South Australia** houses a good collection of Australian and European paintings and a wide variety of Asian and decorative arts. The nearby **South Australian Museum** offers the usual natural history and anthropological collections, but is most famous for its superb Aboriginal displays. The **Migration Museum** building on Kintore Avenue, just off North Terrace, dates from 1877 and was originally the Destitute Asylum. This innnovative establishment covers the social history of South Australian settlement and immigration and is highly recommended.

Return to North Terrace and cross into Gawler Place, entering Rundle Mall.

Central City

8 After so much history and culture, a visit to some of the city's shopping and eating areas makes a good change of pace. Rundle Mall contains Adelaide's major shops and department stores, including the large **City Cross Shopping Centre**. On the other side of King William Street, Hindley Street is Adelaide's nightlife centre, with clubs, pubs, restaurants and cinemas. From here you can walk back down King William Street to Victoria Square. The interesting **Central Market** on Gouger Street, just behind the square, has been selling an amazing array of fresh produce since 1870.

6 days – 481km (299 miles)

Open invitation to the Krondorf Winery, in the Barossa Valley, which welcomes visitors all week

From Adelaide City Centre take the Main North Road and **Highway 1** *north, then turn off at Enfield on to* **Route 20** *(the Sturt Highway). Leave the highway at the Gawler exit.*

Gawler

1 South Australia's oldest country town dates back to 1839 and contains many classic colonial buildings – the town was planned by Colonel William Light, the architect of Adelaide. The entire Church Hill district is a State Heritage Area and can be seen on a self-guided walking tour, while the **Folk Museum**, housed in the 1859 Telegraph Station, displays pioneer *memorabilia*.

i 61 Murray Street

Take the Lyndoch road.

Lyndoch and the Barossa Valley

2 The town of Lyndoch is the southern gateway to the Barossa Valley, which stretches for around 30km (18 miles) from here to Angaston. The first winery was developed around Lyndoch in 1896 and there are many wineries to visit – **Chateau Yaldara Wines** and **Orlando Wines** (at Rowland Flat) are your best bet.

The most German of the valley's towns, **Tanunda** developed from the original village of Langmeil, established in 1843. Parts of this old settlement still exist and much of Tanunda is National Trust classified. The **Barossa Historical Museum**, in the 1865 Post and Telegraph Office, specialises in German heritage items, and the extensive **Kev Rohrlach Museum** is also worth a visit.

There are numerous wineries around Tanunda, but **Hardy's Siegersdorf**, **Leo Buring Wines**, **Krondorf Wines** and **Peter Lehmann Wines** are recommended. South of Tanunda, **Bethany** is

Formal landscaping and staircase at the Chateau Yaldara Winery

BAROSSA, FLEURIEU & KANGAROO ISLAND

Adelaide • Gawler • Lyndoch and the Barossa Valley • Birdwood • Mannum • Strathalbyn Goolwa • Victor Harbor and the Fleurieu Peninsula • Kangaroo Island • McLaren Vale Adelaide

The Barossa Valley, Australia's premier wine-producing region, is an extremely picturesque area that was first settled by Lutherans from Silesia and Prussia in the late 1830s. Forty or so wineries produce over half of Australia's quality wines in a valley that is dotted with meticulously laid out vineyards, historic towns and beautiful old buildings. Further south are the National Motor Museum in the Mount Lofty Ranges town of Birdwood, and the Murray River ports of Mannum and Murray Bridge. From here you travel via the southern port towns of Goolwa and Victor Harbor to the rural Fleurieu Peninsula and the unspoilt haven of Kangaroo Island, famous for its wildlife and dramatic coastal scenery. You really need two days on the island to see the most important sights. The return journey to Adelaide is through another wine region, McLaren Vale, and the coastal resorts to the south of the city.

SPECIAL TO . . .

2 This area is famous for its festivals celebrating the joys of fine wine, food and music. The **Barossa Vintage Festival** is held in April (in odd numbered years); the **Barossa Classic Gourmet Weekend** takes place each August; while the **October Barossa Music Festival** features classical music performed by Australian and international musicians.

SCENIC ROUTES

2 The drive through the lovely Barossa Valley is particularly attractive. Neat rows of vines stretch up the green hillsides, the towns are clean and well tended and the entire scene is almost impossibly picturesque!

FOR HISTORY BUFFS

2 Seppelt and Sons, one of the Barossa's oldest vineyards, was established by a German migrant in 1851. North of Tanunda and reached via the hamlet of Marananga, Seppeltsfield is virtually a village in itself where the original bluestone Seppelt homestead still stands. The house has been restored and now offers accommodation.

FOR CHILDREN

2 While adults can enjoy wine-tasting here, children would probably prefer to be at Tanunda's Barossa Kiddypark – where train rides, dodgem cars and a super slide are provided, as well as a wildlife section with kangaroos, wallabies, emus, wombats and many native birds.

the valley's oldest settlement, founded in 1842.

The next main Barossa town is **Nuriootpa**, the curious name of which is believed to be Aboriginal for 'meeting place'. **Bluestone Coulthard House**, the home of one of the earliest settlers, is now the Barossa Information Centre, while **Luhrs Pioneer German Cottage**, a heritage listed 1848 dwelling, is also of interest. The wineries to visit here include **Penfolds Wines** and the **Wolf Blass winery**. On a ridge high above the valley, **Angaston** produces apricots and other dried fruits, as well as grapes. The **Yalumba Winery** here was founded in 1849, with **Saltram Wine Estates** established just 10 years later. Other Angaston attractions include the **Angas Park Dried Fruits Centre**, and National Trust **Collingrove Homestead**, the 1854 home of the Angas family. At nearby **Keyneton**, the **Henschke Wines** vineyard specialises in exceptional reds.

ⓘ Coulthard House, 66 Murray Street

From Angaston, drive south via Mount Pleasant to Birdwood.

Birdwood

3 The highlight of this attractive Mount Lofty Ranges town is the **National Motor Museum**, Australia's largest collection of veteran to modern-day cars and motorcycles. There are some 300 vehicles here, housed in the old **Birdwood Flour Mill** which dates from 1852.

Drive east, via Tungkillo, to Mannum.

Mannum

4 Mannum, one of the oldest Murray River towns, was founded in 1852 and became a major port – Australia's first steamboat, the *Mary Ann*, was built here in 1853. The

floating museum, the 1897 **PS** *Marion*, recalls the days of the paddle-steamers that plied the river. Cruises are available and houseboats can be hired here.

ⓘ Arnold Park, Randell Street

Take the Murray Bridge road out of Mannum, and from Murray Bridge (see page 81), drive on Highway 1 until you reach the Strathalbyn turn-off.

Strathalbyn

5 The eastern gateway to the Fleurieu Peninsula, agricultural Strathalbyn was founded in 1839 by predominantly Scottish settlers. The town contains many heritage listed buildings, and the National Trust **Museum**, housed in the 1850s old Police Station and the 1867 **Court House**. There are numerous craft and antique shops and a self-guided walking tour is the best way to experience this old-world charm.

ⓘ 12 Albyn Terrace

Take minor roads to Goolwa.

Goolwa

6 Located near the mouth of the Murray River and close to vast Lake Alexandrina, Goolwa was a thriving port and shipbuilding town in the riverboat days. It is popular with fishermen, boating enthusiasts and birdwatchers – a nearby bird sanctuary attracts many pelicans and other waterbirds. You can step back in time by cruising on the paddle-steamer *Mundoo*, or riding the historic steam **Cockle Train** to Victor Harbor. **Hindmarsh Island** is a quiet holiday retreat, while other attractions include the interesting National Trust **Museum**; the **Goolwa Barrage**, a manmade barrier to prevent salt water from entering Lake Alexandrina; and **Signal Point Interpretive Centre** – an excellent display on the history of the Murray.

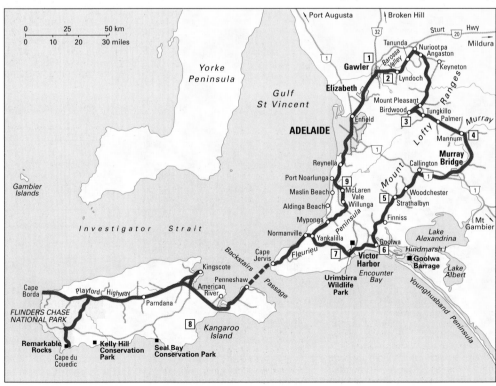

ⓘ Old Library Building, Cadell Street

Drive to Victor Harbor.

Victor Harbor and the Fleurieu Peninsula

7 Surrounded by Gulf St Vincent, the Southern Ocean and the River Murray Lakes System, the Fleurieu Peninsula is a favourite holiday playground. Inland, there are many historic towns, wildlife reserves, walking trails and wineries.

A major holiday resort and the area's largest town, Victor Harbor dates back to the 1830s. There are good beaches here and fishing is popular, while the town has a number of old buildings and the **Old Customs House** (1866) museum. **Granite Island**, linked to the mainland by a causeway, is home to a fairy penguin colony and seals and there are excellent views from the chairlift ride to the summit. A visit to nearby **Urimbirra Wildlife Park** reveals over 70 species of native birds and animals.

ⓘ Torrens Street, Victor Harbor

From Victor Harbor, drive across the peninsula and then via Normanville to Cape Jervis – the departure point for car ferries to Kangaroo Island.

Rocks, 1906 **Cape du Couedic Lighthouse** and, at **Cape Borda**, an 1858 lighthouse and a **Heritage Museum**. On the south coast, **Seal Bay Conservation Park** is the home of a colony of rare Australian sealions. At **Kelly Hill Conservation Park** there is an extensive system of caves which can be explored on guided tours, and you can see fairy penguins at Penneshaw.

ⓘ National Parks and Wildlife, Dauncey Street, Kingscote

Return to Cape Jervis and drive through Normanville, Yankalilla, Myponga and Willunga.

McLaren Vale

9 This little town is the centre of the McLaren Vale vine-growing area, which produces some excellent wines in over 40 (mostly small) wineries. **Hardys Wines** create excellent vintages in their 1838 **Reynella** winery and the 1876 **McLaren Vale** vineyard. Also recommended are **Ryecroft Vineyards** and the **Seaview Winery**. The best

Kangaroo Island is a wilderness-lover's paradise. Its Remarkable Rocks, below, are weirdly shaped granite 'sculptures' hewn by nature. At Seal Bay, right, the sealions seem indifferent to humans

RECOMMENDED WALKS

7 The 100m (328-foot) high **Bluff**, to the west of Victor Harbor, is a granite outcrop with good walking tracks. A walk to the summit will reveal wonderful views of the town, **Encounter Bay** and the surrounding countryside.

Kangaroo Island

8 Although there are several small settlements here, this rugged island is essentially a remarkable wilderness and wildlife reserve – the heathland and eucalypt forests are home to an incredible wildlife population. The island is surprisingly large, 145km (90 miles) long and 60km (37 miles) wide, and accommodation is available at **Penneshaw** (the ferry arrival point), **American River**, **Parndana** and **Kingscote**. This dates back to 1836 when it became South Australia's first official settlement – a memorial at Reeves Point commemorates the event.

Kangaroo Island's natural attractions are splendid. In the far west, **Flinders Chase National Park** is a haven for birds and wildlife, including koalas and friendly kangaroos. Also here are the **Remarkable**

time to visit the area is during the **Wine Bushing Festival**, held each October. On the way back to Adelaide you can visit the 'Wine Coast' resorts of **Aldinga Beach**, **Maslin Beach** and **Port Noarlunga** by making short detours from the main route.

Return to Adelaide via Reynella.

Adelaide – Gawler 40 (25)
Gawler – Lyndoch (Barossa Valley) 16 (10)
Angaston (Barossa Valley) – Birdwood 70 (43)
Birdwood – Mannum 37 (23)
Mannum – Strathalbyn (via Murray Bridge) 76 (47)
Strathalbyn – Goolwa 34 (21)
Goolwa – Victor Harbor 19 (12)
Victor Harbor – Cape Jervis (for Kangaroo Island) 72 (45)
Cape Jervis – McLaren Vale 75 (47)
McLaren Vale – Adelaide 42 (26)

BACK TO NATURE

7 Set in natural bushland north of Victor Harbor, the **Urimbirra Wildlife Park** features over 70 species of Australian animals and birds. Highlights are the nocturnal animal house and the crocodiles, and you can walk through the park to see the animals at close range.

AUSTRALIA'S FLORA & FAUNA

Visitors from the northern hemisphere are often struck by the strangeness of Australia – the bright sunshine, almost limitless outback horizons, peculiar eucalyptus trees with grey or even white trunks, unidentifiable flowers and shrubs and, of course, unusual birds and animals. Much of this uniqueness is due to the continent's 40–50 million years of isolation from the rest of the world – a fact which has also created a wonderful diversity and richness which will delight any nature lover.

Mammals

Australia, along with Papua New Guinea, is the only place in the world where three mammal groups – placentals, marsupials and monotremes exist together. A highlight for every visitor is seeing the unique marsupials: there are around 120 different types of these, and 46 members of the kangaroo and wallaby family, ranging from the large red kangaroo to the tiny quokka of Rottnest Island.

The lovable east coast koala tops everyone's list and, even if you don't see one in the wild, this generally placid creature can be observed and often handled in one of Australia's many wildlife sanctuaries. The list of fascinating marsupials is long – the lumbering wombat, the beautiful little endangered numbat, wallaby-like pademelons, many varieties of possums, and the ferocious-looking Tasmanian devil. Perhaps the most curious Australian mammals are the primitive egg-laying monotremes, represented by the rarely seen platypus and the echidna, or spiny anteater.

Placental mammals include the often maligned dingo, or native dog; the endangered Australian sea-lion, which can be seen on Kangaroo Island in South Australia; and the Australian fur seal. Offshore, the oceans are home to a variety of whales, including the southern right, humpback and minke species.

Birds

There are around 700 species of birds in Australia, many of which have developed in island isolation. The country's wide range of physical environments – from the central arid zone, to the snow-covered winter uplands of the southeast, and the long and extremely varied coastline – has also assisted in creating a diversity of birdlife.

Some of Australia's most distinctive birds are the members of the parrot family – galahs, sulphur-crested cockatoos and corellas, and the brightly coloured king parrot, crimson rosella and rainbow lorikeet. The much-loved budgerigar is another native Australian. The continent's largest bird is the flightless emu, which can reach 2m (6 feet) in height. Australia's second largest bird, the cassowary, is found only in the far north of Queensland.

Some other special Australian birds are the noisy kookaburra, the black swan, the delightful little fairy penguins – standing just 35cm (13 inches) tall and found in southern coastal regions, and the elegant brolgas (the crane family) and jabirus (a stork-like bird) of the northern and central regions. Another distinctive waterbird is the Australian pelican, while the magnificent wedge-tailed eagle, the country's largest bird of prey with a wingspan of up to 2.5m (8 feet), ranges far and wide.

Reptiles and amphibians

Australia contains some 600 species of reptiles. The most awesome of these is undoubtedly the maneating saltwater or estuarine crocodile, while the freshwater (Johnston's) variety is far more interested in fish and insects. Crocodiles are found only in the northern part of the continent – north of Broome in the west, to Rockhampton on the east coast. There are also 160 or so species of snakes, about two-thirds of which are venomous. Particularly dangerous are the taipan, copperhead and eastern brown snake, while members of the python family can reach up to 7m (23 feet) in length.

There are many lizards in Australia

Native wildflowers are often unique

and, although some look quite fearsome, they are generally harmless. The largest goannas (monitor lizards) can reach a length of 2m (6 feet), while the dragons, which include the strange looking thorny devil, and skinks like the blue-tongued lizard, are much smaller. Some other reptiles are sea turtles, such as the loggerhead, green and hawksbill

Goanna – one of many types of lizard in Australia

varieties; and tortoises. Australia's only amphibians are the 180 varieties of frogs – from the water-holding frogs to the bright green tree varieties of the northern rainforests.

Sharks, spiders and others

Another fearsome Australian creature is the shark, including the enormous white pointers which occasionally claim an unfortunate diver or swimmer. The spiders offer more dangers. Although many are harmless, the lethal funnel-web and the redback are very much to be avoided. Butterflies come in many types and colours, but the most spectacular are the huge birdwings (a wingspan of up to 19cm/7 inches) of far northern Queensland. The presence of another common insect, the termite, is very noticeable in the enormous mounds that they create throughout the outback.

Trees and plants

Australia's trees, plants and wildflowers have been the subject of much fascination since botanist Joseph Banks arrived on the continent in 1770. Like the fauna, the country's vegetation has evolved

Koala surrounded by its only food

A jewel-coloured lorikeet

totally independently from the species of other continents – almost 90 per cent of the plants found here are unique to Australia.

Virtually all of the indigenous trees are evergreens, with the 550 species of eucalypts being the most widespread. The tallest are the mountain ashes of Tasmania and Victoria – up to 98m (320 feet) high. Eucalypts have adapted to an incredible range of climates and are found

in such diverse regions as the snowy highlands of the southeast and the arid centre. Also widespread are the acacias and banksias – named after Joseph Banks and easily recognised by their flower spikes. Other tree species include magnificent, spreading Moreton Bay figs; strangely shaped xanthorrhoeas or grass trees; slow-growing Tasmanian pines; and the bulbous baobabs of the far north. Last but not least are the trees and plants of the lush tropical rainforests – palm trees, ferns and mosses.

There are around 15,000 species of flowering plants here. Most visitors will notice the wonderful wildflowers, many of which are unique to the continent. From orchids, native fuchsias, grevilleas and the magnificent red waratahs (the floral emblem of NSW), to the strangely shaped 'kangaroo paws' of Western Australia, all of these plants and flowers are quite magnificent. The best place to see wildflowers is undoubtedly in the south of Western Australia in springtime.

9 days – 1,937km (1,204 miles)

CENTRAL WESTERN SA & THE FLINDERS RANGES

Adelaide • Port Wakefield • The Yorke Peninsula • Port Pirie • Port Augusta • Whyalla Cowell • Tumby Bay • Port Lincoln • Quorn Hawker • Flinders Ranges National Park Peterborough • Burra • Clare • Adelaide

This extended tour attempts to cover some of the many wonders of the vast state of South Australia. The northern Yorke Peninsula was famous for its copper mining and retains a strong sense of history, while the Eyre Peninsula is a relatively sparsely populated region of rugged coastline, wheatfields and nature reserves. The wild and dramatic Flinders Ranges bring you to the edge of South Australia's vast and desolate outback region. This area of mountains, gorges, canyons, plains and superb wildlife is one of the highlights of any visit to Australia. Temperatures can be very high here in summer, while road conditions are often difficult – the best time to tour is from May to October. Visits to Port Pirie, Port Augusta and Whyalla provide a complete contrast to the state's less populated, scenic regions.

SPECIAL TO ...

2 The Kernewek Lowender (Cornish Festival) held at Kadina, Moonta and Wallaroo every second (odd numbered) year honours the area's distinctive Cornish background. Fairs, dances, Celtic games and a carnival are the highlights of this cheerful festival, as is sampling Cornish pasties and 'Swanky', the famous potent local beer.

From Adelaide City Centre, drive north on the Main North Road and Highway 1.

Port Wakefield

1 At the head of Gulf St Vincent, Port Wakefield developed as the major port for the mining area around Burra. The town is the gateway to the Yorke Peninsula and contains some well preserved 19th-century buildings. Some 26km (16 miles) to the east, the old town of Balaklava is full of history. The Terminus Hotel and Royal Hotel date from 1870 – the latter's visitors have included royalty; while Centenary Hall displays relics from the settlement's early pastoral days.

Take the Kulpara/Kadina road from Port Wakefield.

The Yorke Peninsula

2 The northern Yorke Peninsula contains a fascinating slice of history. This is the location of the famous mining region of 'Little Cornwall', or the Copper Triangle. Rich copper deposits were discovered in 1859 around Kadina, setting off a rush of

Among the hundred or so species of bird to be found in the Flinders Range are birds of prey like the proud wedge-tailed eagle

miners to the region. Most of these prospectors were from England's Cornwall, and they brought with them their distinctive customs and architecture.

Although the mines were worked out by 1923, this region contains fascinating remnants of the mining era, particularly at **Moonta**. This well-preserved town has a **mining museum**, the old **Methodist Church**, **miners' cottages** and many mining ruins. **Wallaroo**, on Spencer Gulf, offers a **Nautical Museum**, while the region's main town, Kadina, contains the **Kadina Museum** and the **Banking and Currency Museum**.

ⓘ Victoria Square, Kadina

Take the Port Broughton road from Wallaroo, continue to Merriton and then rejoin Highway 1 to Port Pirie.

Port Pirie

3 Located on Spencer Gulf, Port Pirie is an important industrial and commercial centre. The area was first settled by farmers in the 1840s but the main industries today are lead smelting (this is the world's largest lead smelting and refining plant), port activities and fishing. The National Trust **Museum** is a series of old buildings, including the **Customs House**, the elegant **Railway Station** and the old **Police Station**. This interesting complex includes re-created room settings and a rundown of Port Pirie's past. The stately National Trust home of **Carn Brae**, built in 1905, is furnished in late 19th-century style.

ⓘ Jubilee Place

Continue north on Highway 1.

Port Augusta

4 Although no longer a port, this modern city at the apex of Spencer Gulf is an important industrial and rail centre. The outback lies to the north, and Port Augusta is an important supply centre for this vast region: the **Royal Flying Doctor Service Base** and **School of the Air** operate from here and both centres can be visited. Other attractions are the fascinating **Wadlata Outback Centre**, which interprets the outback and Aboriginal heritage; **Homestead Park Pioneer Museum**, with its 130-year-old log homestead, pastoral and railway displays; and **McLellan Lookout**. There are excellent views of the gulf, Port Augusta and the Flinders Ranges from here.

ⓘ 41 Flinders Terrace

Continue southwest on Highway 1 for 26km (16 miles), then drive south on the Lincoln Highway (also Highway 1).

Whyalla

5 At the eastern gateway to the Eyre Peninsula, Whyalla is the state's largest provincial city and a steelmaking and shipbuilding centre. Visitors can tour the vast **BHP Steelworks** and visit the **Whyalla**

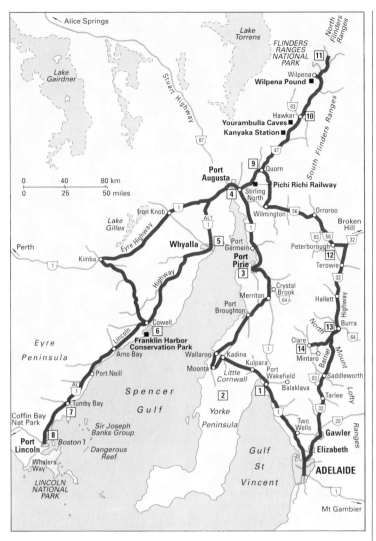

FOR CHILDREN

5 This tour does not offer a great deal especially for children, but the Whyalla Fauna and Reptile Park, where you can see native birds, free-ranging kangaroos and other reptiles and animals in a natural bushland setting, is probably the best bet.

Maritime Museum and Mount Laura Homestead, a National Trust museum housed in a former sheep station. There are excellent views from Hummock Hill and Flinders lookouts, and you can also visit the **Whyalla Fauna and Reptile Park**.

One of over 500 types of eucalyptus. The tallest is the karri, growing up to 85m (280 feet)

ⓘ Whyalla Maritime Museum, Lincoln Highway

Continue on the Lincoln Highway.

Cowell

6 This small settlement's claim to fame is as Australia's only commercial jade mining site. Rare black jade, the green variety and marble are all found in the area and you can see these being cut and carved at the **Jade Factory**. Franklin Harbor and the nearby coastline offer excellent beaches, surfing and boating, while **Franklin Harbor Conservation Park** protects this beautiful coastal environment.

Continue on the highway.

Tumby Bay

7 The small coastal resort and commercial fishing port of Tumby Bay has a magnificent white sandy beach and is a popular fishing area. Highlights here include the National Trust **Museum**, housed in an old wooden schoolroom; the 1871 **Police Station**; and, of course, swimming, fishing and boating. You

BACK TO NATURE

7 The islands and waters of the **Sir Joseph Banks Group Conservation Park** form a haven for dolphins, the rare Australian sea-lion and a range of birdlife. This is Australia's largest breeding ground for the Cape Barren goose, once an endangered species, while cormorants and terns are other regular visitors. Tours to these magical islands are available from Tumby Bay.

SCENIC ROUTES

8 **Whalers Way**, a privately owned clifftop drive from Port Lincoln to Cape Carnot at the very tip of the Eyre Peninsula, is a rare opportunity to view some of South Australia's most dramatic coastline. Beaches, cliffs, caves and blowholes abound and fur seals are often found in the area. Kangaroos and emus live on the heathland, and wildflowers put on a splendid show from May to November.

can also visit the offshore **Sir Joseph Banks Group** (see **Back to Nature**) to see sea-lions and birdlife.

Continue on the Lincoln Highway.

Port Lincoln

8 The home of Australia's largest tuna fishing fleet, Port Lincoln has a fantastic location on the vast natural harbour of Boston Bay, while the warm climate and the bay's aquatic wonderland make the town a popular tourist destination. There is also plenty of history here – **Mill Cottage**, owned by the National Trust, was built in 1866 and now houses a folk museum, while the town's first inn, the 1840 **Lincoln Hotel**, still stands on the waterfront. Offshore attractions include a visit to **Dangerous Reef**, where a viewing platform allows you to see the reef, a tuna farm and maybe even the white pointer sharks which inhabit these waters! **Boston Island** is an operating sheep station which can be toured, while shearing and other aspects of farm life can be witnessed at **Greenpatch Farm**.

The tip of the peninsula is almost entirely national park. **Lincoln NP**, to the southeast, is a wild region of cliffs, beaches and wildlife, while **Coffin Bay National Park**, on the northwestern side of the peninsula, has some spectacular lookouts and the fine Almonta surf beach.

ⓘ Eyre Travel, Tasman Terrace

*Return to Port Augusta via Cowell and the farming town of Kimba. From here, join the Eyre Highway (**Highway 1**) and drive to Stirling North, then turn on to the Quorn road (**Route 47**).*

Quorn

9 Established as a railway town in the late 1870s, the settlement of Quorn sits in a valley in the Flinders Ranges. The railway line was closed in 1957 but a restored section operates as the **Pichi Richi Railway**. A steam locomotive, with carriages from the original Adelaide–Alice Springs Ghan Railway, runs on the 33km track between March and November. Quorn contains many old buildings, such as the 1878 **Mill**, 1891 **Town Hall** and the attractive 1916 **Railway Station**. The **Outdoor Agricultural Implements Museum**, just out of town, features a large display of historic equipment.

ⓘ Council Office, Seventh Street

*Continue on **Route 47**.*

Hawker

10 Hawker was another railway town, but is now better known as the gateway to the Flinders Ranges. Several 1880s buildings remain, including the old **Railway Station**, while the **Fred Teague Museum** has a good collection of minerals, gemstones and Aboriginal artefacts. South of Hawker, the **Yourambulla Caves** contain some interesting Aboriginal rock paintings, and nearby ruined **Kanyaka Station**, once a stately 1850s homestead, is open to the public. From Hawker, scenic flights over Wilpena Pound

and the Flinders Ranges are available, as are escorted 4WD tours.

*Continue on **Route 47**.*

Flinders Ranges National Park

11 This spectacular national park contains much of the central Flinders Ranges – a rugged region of mountains, gorges, grassy plains and towering gum trees – that forms one of the most ancient landscapes on the planet, believed to be more than 500 million years old. The wildlife in this park includes kangaroos and the rare yellow-footed rock wallaby and over 100 species of birds – wedge-tailed eagles, falcons, kestrels and galahs are often seen here.

Remarkable **Wilpena Pound** – a vast, elevated oval amphitheatre, surrounded by sheer red cliffs – is one of the park's highlights. **St Mary's Peak** (1,200m/3,937 feet), on the rim of the pound, is the highest point of the ranges. Vegetation flourishes here and includes the unusual grass tree, while there are many walking tracks for visitors to explore the natural wonders. Wilpena, at the foot of the Pound, has a motel, petrol supplies and other facilities and is the best base for exploring the area. From here, scenic drives can be made to lookouts and Aboriginal carvings.

*Return to Quorn, then drive south to Wilmington and take **Route 56** via Orroroo to Peterborough.*

Peterborough

12 This small town was yet another railway centre. There are a number of historic railway related attrac-

tions here, including a **museum** and the vast old **engine house**. Constructed in 1812, 20-room **Saint Cecilia** was the home of the local bishop, but is now a museum of antique pianos and organs.

ⓘ Main Street

Drive east to join the Barrier Highway (Route 32) and travel south on this major road.

Burra

13 There was little except rolling hills and grassland at Burra prior to 1845, but the discovery of a rich copper lode brought thousands of Cornish, Welsh, Scottish and German miners to the region. The mines functioned for only 30 years, but there are many fascinating remnants of Burra's boom days. The **Bon Accord Mine Complex**; **Burra Mine** and **Enginehouse Museum**; 1856 **Redruth Gaol**; the recreated 1870s buildings of **Market Square Museum**; and 1850s **Paxton Square Cottages**, built to house Cornish miners, are all interesting. This is perhaps South Australia's best preserved old town – you can see it all on the local **Heritage Tour**.

ⓘ Market Square

Drive south on Route 32 for 14km, then take the Clare turn-off.

Clare

14 Named after County Clare by the original 1840s Irish settlers, this picturesque valley town in the northern Mount Lofty Ranges is famous for its agriculture and wine industries. The wineries are a mixture of long-established vineyards (**Eaglehawk Estate**, 1851; **Leasingham Wines**,

Above: rising gradually from the desert, the rugged terrain of the Flinders Ranges is marked by spectacular gorges, canyons and other natural phenomena
Above right: the red kangaroo can reach 2m (6 feet) in height

1893) and more recent boutique-style operations such as the excellent **Tim Knappstein Wines**. Perhaps the most interesting winery is the Jesuit owned and operated **Sevenhill Cellars**, dating back to 1851. Other Clare attractions include the 1850 **Old Police Station** and **Court House**, now housing the **Clare Historical Museum**, and nearby **Bungaree Station**. This large property, established in 1841, has opened its shearing sheds and homestead gardens to the public.

ⓘ Clare Valley Tourist Information Centre, Main North Road

Return to the Route 32 and drive south via Gawler (see page 85) to Adelaide.

Adelaide – Port Wakefield 93 (58)
Port Wakefield – Kadina (Yorke Peninsula) 52 (32)
Kadina (Yorke Peninsula) – Port Pirie 154 (96)
Port Pirie – Port Augusta 92 (57)
Port Augusta – Whyalla 76 (47)
Whyalla – Cowell 108 (67)
Cowell – Tumby Bay 120 (75)
Tumby Bay – Port Lincoln 50 (31)
Port Lincoln – Quorn (via Cowell and Kimba) 460 (286)
Quorn – Hawker 66 (41)
Hawker – Flinders Ranges 75 (47)
Flinders Ranges – Peterborough 270 (168)
Peterborough – Burra 102 (63)
Burra – Clare 43 (27)
Clare – Adelaide 176 (109)

RECOMMENDED WALKS

10 A short walk to the **Jarvis Hill Lookout**, 5km (3 miles) from Hawker, reveals a spectacular view over the Flinders Ranges. There are other short hikes from Hawker, which take in the **Police Hill Lookout**, **Yourambulla Caves** and other interesting local features.

FOR HISTORY BUFFS

14 The historic hamlet of **Mintaro**, 15km (9 miles) southeast of Clare, is well worth a short detour from the main route. Slate has been mined in this heritage classified town for 130 years and the material is much in evidence in the restored buildings here. Nearby **Martindale Hall**, built in 1879 by a local pastoralist, is a fine example of a Georgian-style mansion.

SOUTHWESTERN AUSTRALIA

The vast state of Western Australia, with an area three and a half times larger than Texas, takes up almost a third of the continent yet contains only 1.5 million people – around 8 per cent of the population. These statistics mean that much of the state is undeveloped, and indeed large tracts are either semi-desert or mountainous.

Other than the capital city of Perth, and neighbouring Fremantle, the only towns of any size are on the coast and in the inland mining region of Kalgoorlie–Boulder. The entire coastline is magnificent and there are hundreds of virtually deserted beaches, headlands and capes to explore. In the south and west, the focus of these tours, there are charming coastal resorts such as Geraldton, Margaret River and Albany; historic inland towns like York and New Norcia; the heavily forested south with its towering trees; and an abundance of lovely national parks. Western Australian wines, particularly those produced around Margaret River, are some of the nation's best.

The wildlife is wonderful. You can see everything from dolphins at Monkey Mia, to kangaroos, possums and the furry little quokkas of Rottnest Island, and the state is famous for its unique wildflowers. Western Australia also has a wonderful climate, with warm to hot summers and temperate winters and an abundance of sunshine.

This coastline was explored long before most of the eastern side of the continent – mariners such as William Dampier were sailing here in the 1680s and 1690s – but Perth was not settled until 1829 as the Swan River Colony. The early colonists were all free settlers, but convict labour was used to construct many of the early buildings and roads. The state's growth was slow, however, and real development did not come until gold was discovered in the 1880s. Despite being one of the world's most isolated cities, Perth has made remarkable progress since the 1970s and is now one of the nation's most attractive and go-ahead capitals.

The rest of Western Australia developed gradually – much of the northern part of the state was not even explored until the 1880s. It is recommended that you fly into Perth from any of the eastern capitals to take these tours.

A gentle approach gets a watery welcome from a Monkey Mia resident

City Tour 8
Western Australia's capital, Perth, is a clean and mostly modern city, marked by the distinctive high-rise towers that grew up during the financial boom of the 1980s, but there is still a great deal of history here, particularly in the nearby port town of Fremantle. Perth is well laid out with gardens and parkland and a magnificent, broad Swan River frontage. You can also visit Rottnest Island, a 45-minute boat trip away and the city's favourite weekend retreat.

Tour 18
This very diverse tour of southern WA includes coastal resorts and sandy beaches; the wild, wave-pounded southern coast; the wine-growing region around Margaret River; rolling farmland; forests; and the fringes of the fea-tureless Nullarbor Plain. The 1890s semi-outback mining towns of Kalgoorlie and Boulder still thrive on the gold industry and present a very different picture to the coastal regions. Closer to Perth, settlements such as York and Northam in the fertile Avon Valley contain many old buildings and are an important part of Western Australia's history trail.

Tour 19
Travelling north from Perth, there are more spectacular beaches along a coastline that stretches for thousands of kilometres to the Northern Territory border. This tour has to stop somewhere, how-ever, and we have chosen Shark Bay – approximately halfway up the coast and the home of the famous Monkey Mia dolphins, which you can meet at very close quarters. Other highlights include the strange rock formations of The Pinnacles, the Benedictine monastery town of New Norcia, and spectacular Kalbarri National Park with its incredible plant, bird and animal life.

PERTH & FREMANTLE

Hay Street Mall • Art Gallery of Western
Australia • Western Australian Museum and
Northbridge • St George's Terrace • Kings Park
and the Botanic Gardens • Barrack Street
Fremantle • Perth

First settled in 1829, Perth was colonised by free settlers with
the aid of convict labour. Unlike most Australian cities, Perth
developed slowly along well-planned lines, while real growth
came during the 1890s Western Australian gold rush. Although
several structures from this era remain, a further financial
boom during the 1980s saw many high, shiny towers erected
to change the face of the city forever.

Australia's most isolated city is located on the broad Swan
River, just a few kilometres from lovely Pacific Ocean beaches.
Perth is clean, friendly and has an ideal climate. Twenty kilometres away is Fremantle, Perth's historic port, which has been
transformed into a lovely little city with enormous tourist
appeal. You could easily spend an entire day here.

Although the metropolitan area of Perth is vast, the city centre is quite small and it is suggested that you view the sights
on foot – the same applies to the much smaller settlement of
Fremantle. There is also an optional drive to Perth's beaches,
and a boat trip to Rottnest Island.

*Half-timbered London Court links
with St George's Terrace*

ⓘ Western Australian Tourist
Centre, Forrest Place (corner of
Wellington Street)

*Start the tour at Hay Street Mall,
the heart of the city centre.*

Hay Street Mall

1 The pedestrian mall here, between
William and Barrack Streets, forms
one of the city's major shopping
areas. There are many interesting
arcades to explore, including 1937
mock-Tudor **London Court**. On Hay
Street, but a little to the west of the
mall, the Edwardian **His Majesty's
Theatre** with its wonderfully
restored interior is worth a visit. The
distinctive **Perth Town Hall**, built of
brick in a church-like style, is at the
Barrack Street end of the mall.

*At the end of the mall turn left
into Barrack Street and continue
walking until you reach Beaufort
Street and the Perth Cultural
Centre.*

Art Gallery of Western Australia

2 This art gallery on James Street is
part of the Perth Cultural Centre
and houses a collection of Australian
and European art, and a particularly
fine Aboriginal section. The gallery
also contains a decorative arts section – including jewellery, ceramics,
textiles and glass. Guided tours are
available and the gallery has a bookshop and café.

*Cross the Perth Cultural Centre
Mall to reach the WA Museum.*

Western Australian Museum and Northbridge

3 The WA Museum is particularly
worth visiting for its marine history
– the **Marine Gallery** here contains,
among other displays, the skeleton
of a 25m (82-foot) long blue whale.
Other attractions include interesting
Aboriginal artefacts, a large meteorite and a collection of veteran and
vintage cars. The 1856 stone-built

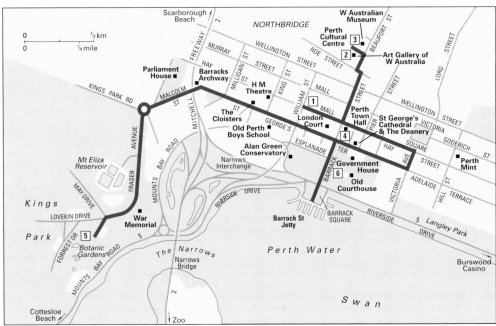

Old Gaol, another part of the museum complex, houses displays on the history of white settlement.

The traditionally European migrant suburb of Northbridge, surrounding the art gallery and museum, is the city's favourite nightlife and dining-out area. There are many restaurants, pavement cafés, bars and nightclubs here and the area has a very cosmopolitan feel.

Return to the city centre by the same route (via Beaufort Street and Barrack Street), turning left into Hay Street, right into Victoria Avenue and right into St George's Terrace.

St George's Terrace

4 Perth's grandest street contains many of the city's most important and historic buildings. **The Deanery**, at the corner of Pier Street, dates from the 1850s and was the residence of the first Dean of Perth. Nearby 1880s **St Georges Cathedral** was designed by the famous church architect Edmund Blacket, the man responsible for many Sydney buildings of the same era. Across the road, National Trust classified 1859 **Government House** is the residence of the Governor of Western Australia and is normally closed to the public.

Beyond William Street the **Old Perth Boys School** (St George's Terrace), built of limestone with convict labour, dates back to 1854 and is now the headquarters of the WA National Trust. Further along on the right, **The Cloisters** was used as a school and dates from 1858. Fronted by the 1860s **Barracks Archway**, all that remains of the original barracks that once housed soldier settlers, **Parliament House** lies at the end of St George's Terrace. This is the seat of the Western Australian Parliament, open to the public at certain times.

Continue towards Kings Park along Malcolm Street and Fraser Avenue.

The reliably fine weather of Perth invites a leisurely souvenir hunt along the numerous arcades off Hay Street Mall, the heart of the city's shopping district. Buys range from didgeridoos to T-shirts

Kings Park and the Botanic Gardens

5 This large area of parkland, on high ground just west of the city, offers both green tranquillity and wonderful views over the city and Swan River. Although there are lawns and formal gardens, a restaurant and playgrounds here, much of the 400-hectare (990-acre) park is untouched bushland that is great for walks or flower and birdspotting. The park is at its best in spring, when the famous WA wildflowers create a riot of colour. Kings Park also contains the War Memorial and an avenue of trees dedicated to some of those who have died in various battles.

Return to the city via Malcolm Street and St George's Terrace, then turn right into Barrack Street.

Barrack Street

6 This pleasant avenue, leading to the city's main wharf, is surrounded by parks and gardens. The **Stirling Gardens** and **Supreme Court Gardens** are to the left – this is also the site of the 1837 **Old Courthouse**, the city's oldest surviving public building. To the right, the **Esplanade Gardens** contain the pyramid-shaped **Alan Green Conservatory**, with its wonderful collection of exotic plants. A wide variety of cruises and ferry trips leave from the Barrack Street Jetty – including runs to Fremantle, Rottnest Island, the zoo and upriver to the Swan Valley vineyards.

Take the boat trip to Fremantle and disembark at East Fremantle. From here you can take the replica Fremantle Tram to the city centre.

BACK TO NATURE

Perth's favourite holiday playground is lovely **Rottnest Island**, a 45-minute ferry ride from Barrack Street Jetty, or 30 minutes from Fremantle. First visited and named 'rats' nest' by 17th-century Dutch explorers, the island is home to the small wallaby-like quokkas which the mariners mistook for rats. Rottnest today is an unspoilt wonderland of white sandy beaches and blue waters. Nature lovers can walk, swim, snorkel and dive, or watch the quokkas, dolphins, whales and abundant bird life.

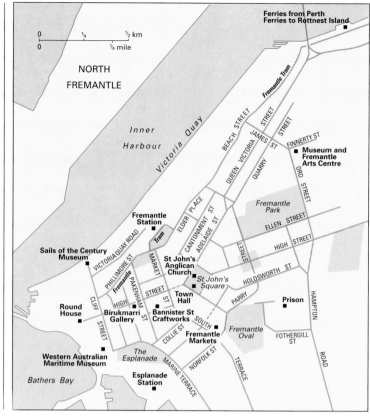

FOR HISTORY BUFFS

A short detour to the eastern part of Perth city brings you to the interesting **Perth Mint**. This handsome limestone building at the corner of Hill and Hay streets dates from the 1890s and long functioned as a branch of London's Royal Mint – gold was also refined here but this process is now carried out elsewhere. Today the building contains a million-dollar collection of coins, gold nuggets, gold bars and jewellery.

Tour the port on the Fremantle Tram

Fremantle

7 There is a great deal to see and enjoy this lovely little port city which, since the preparations for the America's Cup yachting challenge in the mid-1980s, has been transformed from a sleepy harbour into a cosmopolitan delight. Fremantle, known to the local population as 'Freo', contains many historic sites and beautifully restored old buildings. The convict-built **Round House** gaol on the waterfront dates from 1831 and is Western Australia's oldest public building. The nearby **Western Australian Maritime Museum**, housed in a lovely Georgian building, provides a glimpse into the state's long seafaring history and includes relics from many of the state's shipwrecks.

Some other museums and historic sites are the old **Prison**, dating from the 1850s and now containing a museum of penal history, and the **Museum**, which also houses the excellent **Fremantle Arts Centre** with its contemporary works. The former tells the story of the city from the time that Captain Charles Fremantle arrived here in May 1829, ahead of the settlers who later staked their claim on Perth, and declared the entire west coast of Australia British territory. In St John's Square you will find the 1880s **Town Hall** and limestone **St John's Anglican Church**.

More recent additions to Fremantle include the many pavement cafes and restaurants, especially along South Terrace; the excellent indoor **Fremantle Markets**, dating from the 1890s but turned into a modern, 'trendy' market complex (also on South Terrace and open from Friday to Sunday), and a host of arts and crafts outlets. Particularly recommended are the **Birukmarri Gallery**, with its high-quality Aboriginal arts and crafts (47 High Street), and the **Bannister Street Craftworks**, in a converted warehouse at 8–12 Bannister Street. You can also dine out on the waterfront, browse around the city's four harbours, visit the fascinating **Fremantle Crocodile Park** in the harbour area, or see some more maritime history – in the form of a variety of vessels – in the **Sails of the Century Museum** on Victoria Quay.

ℹ️ Town Hall, St John's Square

From here you can return to Perth by boat, or take a train from either the Esplanade station or the main Fremantle station.

Poignant reminder of Coolgardie's rough-and-ready pass. The gold-rush boom town, near Kalgoorlie, was known as Fly Flat in 1892 when a pair of prospectors found 554oz of gold there, beginning an era of raw greed

From Perth City Centre, take the Kwinana Freeway (Route 2) south and follow the Highway 1 signs south to Mandurah.

Mandurah

1 Less than an hour's drive from Perth, Mandurah is popular as both a desirable residential area and a weekend destination for city dwellers. Three rivers meet here, to form the aquatic paradise of Peel Inlet and the Harvey Estuary, and perfect conditions for yachting, fishing, waterskiing and swimming.

About 19km (12 miles) inland, **Pinjarra** is the start of an interesting railway journey to **Dwellingup**. The **Hotham Valley Tourist Railway** runs steam trains on this preserved 1913 line, through farmland and lovely jarrah forest.

Continue south on Highway 1 to Bunbury.

Bunbury and Busselton

2 These popular seaside resorts offer excellent beaches and are favourite holiday destinations for Perth families. The port of Bunbury, with its population of around 25,000, is one of the state's largest towns and provides good swimming and fishing. There are some interesting drives and lookout points here, and the city has a **museum**, pleasant gardens and good facilities. The harbour is worth exploring, and dolphins can sometimes be seen at Koombana Beach.

On the shores of sheltered Geographe Bay, Busselton is surrounded by farming land and ringed by lovely beaches. There is an **Oceanarium** here, with sharks, rays and turtles; the famous 2km (1.2 mile) long timber jetty; and several buildings from the last century. The highlight of these is National Trust listed **Wonnerup House**, which dates back to 1835.

SOUTH COAST WA & THE GOLDFIELDS

Perth • Mandurah • Bunbury and Busselton
Margaret River • Augusta • Pemberton
Walpole-Nornalup National Park and Denmark
Albany • Esperance • Norseman • Kalgoorlie–
Boulder • Wave Rock • York and Northam
The Darling Range • Guildford • Perth

From the wild Southern Ocean coastline to the barren Goldfields region; from towering karri and jarrah forests to the gentle wheatbelt scenery east of Perth – this tour shows you the very best of Western Australia's diverse southern region. The coast to the south of Perth includes pleasant holiday towns like Mandurah, Bunbury and Busselton, while the resort of Margaret River has the added attraction of wineries and limestone caves. From Augusta to Esperance, the coast is exquisite – white sandy beaches, clear blue waters and few people to spoil all this natural glory, while inland there are magnificent forests of tall, hardy eucalypt trees.

Heading north and inland, the scenery becomes more barren and you reach the outback mining towns of Norseman, Kalgoorlie and Boulder, then the strange formation of Wave Rock, in the state's wheat belt area. Closer to Perth there are the picturesque settlements of York and Northam, the wooded hills of the Darling Range and the attractive Swan Valley.

The harbour of prosperous Bunbury, gateway town of the coastal resorts south of Perth

SPECIAL TO ...

In springtime, especially September and October, over 10,000 different species of wildflowers, many of which are unique to Western Australia, bloom throughout this southern region. Flowers such as red and green kangaroo paws, orchids, boronias, blue leschenaultias and many other brilliantly coloured varieties transform areas like the John Forrest National Park, near Perth, and the Walpole-Nornalup National Park. Also special to this region are the towering, strangely named jarrah, marri, tuart, karri, tingle and wandoo trees – these are all giant eucalypts which are unique to southern Western Australia.

BACK TO NATURE

2 The Tuart Forest National Park, off the highway between Bunbury and Busselton, contains stands of tuart trees – slow growing hardwoods that are found only in this region. The tall trees in this 1,786-hectare (4,410-acre) forest are estimated to be between 300 and 400 years old.

i Old Railway Station, Carmody Street, Bunbury

Drive south on the Bussell Highway to Margaret River (Route 10).

Margaret River

3 The attractions of the Margaret River area are many – some of Australia's best wines are produced here in over 50 vineyards; the region is famous for its excellent beaches and surf; and the limestone caves of the Leeuwin-Naturaliste National Park are worth an inspection. This park extends along the coastline from Cape Naturaliste to Cape Leeuwin and contains 28 separate reserves. The caverns, particularly Mammoth Cave and Lake Cave, are quite spectacular, while the Boranup Karri Forest, with its tall trees, is another highlight.

The township itself contains arts and crafts shops and many of the wineries are open for tastings and tours. Some of the best wineries to tour are Leeuwin Estate, Vasse Felix, Sandalford Wines and Cape Mentelle. You can visit Ellensbrook Homestead, the home of the district's first pioneers; and the Clydesdale Museum and Village.

i Corner of Tunbridge Road and Bussell Highway

Continue on Route 10 to Augusta.

Augusta

4 Augusta, with its lovely beaches, is one of Western Australia's oldest settlements, dating from 1830. Jewel Cave, just north of the town, is famous for its sparkling crystal formations, while nearby Cape Leeuwin, capped by a late 19th-century lighthouse, overlooks the junc-

tion of the Indian and Southern oceans and is Australia's most southwesterly point.

Return north on the Bussell Highway, then take the Brockman Highway to Nannup and the Vasse Highway to Pemberton (all Route 10).

Pemberton

5 In the area known as 'Tall Timber Country', the timber town of Pemberton is surrounded by forests of Western Australia's special trees, karri, jarrah and marri. You can take a scenic ride on the early 1900s Pemberton Tramway through these forests, or walk among the trees in the Warren National Park. Other things to do include trout fishing, visiting waterfalls, browsing around the woodcraft shops, or even touring the Pemberton Sawmill. There are also some wineries in the area.

i Brockman Street

Drive northeast from Pemberton and join the South Western Highway (Highway 1).

Walpole-Nornalup National Park and Denmark

6 En route to Denmark you can visit the 18,000-hectare (4,448-acre) Walpole-Nornalup National Park with its tall karri and tingle trees. There are black swans and pelicans on the inlets here, and some lovely walks through the forest – there is a particularly scenic track through the Valley of the Giants.

The small fishing resort of Denmark is best known for its rugged coastal scenery and the gentle lower reaches of the Denmark River. There are also some wineries in the area, including the excellent

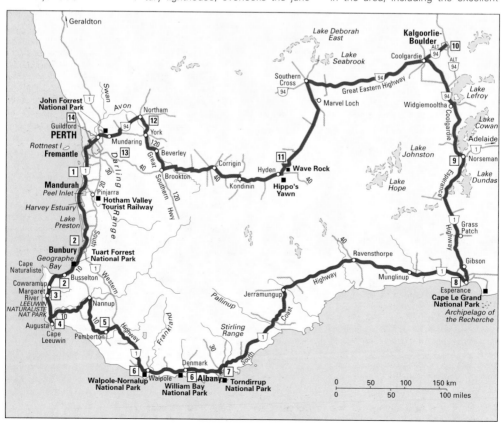

Goundrey Wines, which is housed in the 1928 **Old Butter Factory**. Nearby **William Bay National Park** has superb coastal scenery, and there are several arts and crafts centres in the town.

ⓘ Strickland Street, Denmark

Continue east on Highway 1.

Albany

7 Founded on King George Sound in 1826, Albany was the state's first European settlement and was once an important whaling station. Today, this picturesque area is a popular holiday destination and offers a wonderfully unspoilt coastline. Historic Albany buildings include the 1851 **Old Gaol**, the 1840s **St John's Church** (Western Australia's oldest), and the **Albany Residency**, dating from the early 1850s and now a museum. You can visit **Albany Whaleworld**, a fascinating museum housed in the old whaling station and featuring a whaling ship; and drive to **Torndirrup National Park**. This coastal park is famous for its springtime wildflowers, rugged heathland and the spectacular rock formations of the **Blowholes**,

fauna. Some of these islands, also known as the **Bay of Isles**, can be visited by boat from Esperance.

ⓘ Museum Village, Dempster Street

Drive north on Highway 1.

Norseman

9 Although the most important gold-fields are located further north, the small settlement of Norseman also profited from the discovery of gold in the 1890s. You can visit the **Historical and Geological Museum**, and fossick for gemstones in the area. **Norseman** is the last major town in Western Australia, at the western end of the Eyre Highway and the starting point for the long drive across the Nullarbor Plain to South Australia.

Continue north on the Coolgardie–Esperance Highway (Route 94).

Kalgoorlie–Boulder

10 The combined city of Kalgoorlie–Boulder, with a population of over 23,000, is one of Western Australia's largest settlements. Gold

Natural Bridge, the **Gap** and **Peak Head**.

ⓘ Peels Place

Continue on the South Coast Highway (Highway 1).

Esperance

8 The port of Esperance grew up in the 1860s but its heyday came with the development of the gold-fields to the north in the 1890s. Today, tourism is the boom industry and the area is famous for its incredible white, sandy beaches and clear blue waters. The **Municipal Museum** contains pieces of Skylab, the US space station which fell to earth in the area in 1979. Fifty kilometres to the east, rocky **Cape Le Grand National Park** provides unspoilt scenery and beaches, while, offshore, the 100 or so islands of the **Archipelago of the Recherche** form a haven for native

Kalgoorlie, where people on a fossicking tour get a metal detector

was found here in 1893 and the ensuing rush rapidly transformed this barren area into a thriving township. Unlike many gold boom towns, Kalgoorlie and Boulder have thrived and are still involved in mining nickel and gold.

You can tour the **Hannans North Mine**, visit the **Museum of the Goldfields** and the **School of Mines Museum**, and take a rail journey along the famous **Golden Mile**, the source of most of the area's gold. There are many old buildings here, including the 1899 **Post Office**, the **Boulder Town Hall** and the 1898 **Cornwall Hotel**, while Hannan Street has retained much of its 1890s charm. Other points of interest are the **Royal Flying Doctor Service** base, camel rides and an emu farm at nearby

FOR HISTORY BUFFS

10 Coolgardie, 39km (24 miles) from Kalgoorlie, was once the centre of Australia's greatest gold rush and boasted a population of 15,000 in 1900. The 1890s town is now a shadow of its former glory but many interesting old buildings remain, including the opulent **Marble Bar Hotel**, a reminder of the days when there were 23 hotels here. Other attractions include the **Goldfields Exhibition**, the 1896 **Railway Station** (now a museum) and the Old Coolgardie Gaol.

RECOMMENDED WALKS

10 The Eastern Goldfields Heritage Trail at Kalgoorlie is the best way to see the city's many interesting historical sites. In addition to this easy 4km (2½-mile) trail, you can undertake a shorter heritage walk around the neighbouring town of Boulder.

FOR CHILDREN

12 Balladong Farm at York dates back to 1831, when it was the state's first inland farming venture. Today, this is a delightful and educational place to bring children – restored farm buildings, old machinery, blacksmithing, Clydesdale horses and the chance to feed farm animals are all on offer here.

The cresting granite wall of Wave Rock, streaked by chemicals in the stone reacting with rainwater

Coolgardie, and the **Two Up School**, a gambling establishment which features a game unique to Australia.

ⓘ 250 Hannan Street, Kalgoorlie

*Take the Great Eastern Highway (**Route 94**) to Southern Cross then turn off to Wave Rock and Hyden.*

Wave Rock

11 This extraordinary natural wonder is a few kilometres from the small wheat belt town of **Hyden**. The formation is a seemingly petrified giant wave, 15m (50 foot) high and over 100m (328 feet) long. Wave Rock is, in fact, an overhanging granite wall created by around 3,000 million years of erosion. Other natural formations in the area include the **Hippo's Yawn** and **The Breakers**, while there are Aboriginal hand paintings at nearby **Mulkas Cave**.

*Continue to Hyden and drive on **Route 40** via Brookton, then head north on **Route 120**.*

York and Northam

12 The picturesque Avon Valley towns of York and Northam offer many attractions. Founded in 1830, York is Western Australia's oldest inland town and contains over 20 listed historic buildings. Highlights include the old **Railway Station** (1886), with its rail museum; the 1843 **Residency** (a colonial museum); and the 1854 **Church of the Holy Trinity**. The famous **York Motor Museum** contains over 200 vintage and classic vehicles, and you can also see the 1906 suspension bridge across the Avon River.

Northam became an important road and rail centre during the 1890s and is now the major Avon Valley town. Attractions include parklands along the Avon River, stately **Buckland Homestead** (1874) and

the **Old Railway Station Museum**. You can also take a camel ride, go canoeing, or enjoy a hot air balloon trip here.

ⓘ 105 Avon Terrace, York

*From Northam, take the Great Eastern Highway (**Route 94**) to Mundaring.*

The Darling Range

13 The small settlement of **Mundaring**, high in the wooded Darling Range, is best known for its weir. **Mundaring Weir**, completed in 1902, was constructed to supply water by pipeline to Kalgoorlie and the goldfields, over 550km (340 miles) away. Water is still piped from the weir to 3 million hectares of land and over 100 towns in southern WA. The weir is in a pleasant bush setting, and there is a museum on the site. **John Forrest National Park** is a bushland reserve famous for its jarrah forest and springtime flowers.

Continue on the Highway.

Guildford

14 The historic river town of Guildford is at the heart of the Swan Valley, an area of high-quality vineyards and wineries – **Houghtons Winery** is particularly recommended. **Guildford** also contains the National Trust mansion, **Woodbridge**.

*Return to Perth via the Great Eastern Highway (**Route 94**).*

Perth – Mandurah 75 (47)
Mandurah – Bunbury 101 (63)
Bunbury – Margaret River 100 (62)
Margaret River – Augusta 43 (27)
Augusta – Pemberton 168 (104)
Pemberton – Denmark 187 (116)
Denmark – Albany 54 (34)
Albany – Esperance 480 (298)
Esperance – Norseman 204 (127)
Norseman – Kalgoorlie–Boulder 205 (128)
Kalgoorlie–Boulder – Wave Rock 390 (242)
Wave Rock – York 290 (180)
York – Mundaring (Darling Range) 99 (61)
Mundaring – Guildford 20 (12)
Guildford – Perth 15 (9)

Dolphins can be hand-fed at Monkey Mia Beach

*From Perth City Centre, take the Mitchell Freeway (**Highway 2**) north. Leave the highway on **Route 82** to Sorrento.*

Northern Beaches

1 Perth's clean, sandy Indian Ocean beaches, such as **Scarborough** and **Sorrento**, are a wonderful playground for the city's inhabitants. At Sorrento, the marine village of Hillary's Boat Harbour, with its shops, cafés and entertainment is a major attraction, while Scarborough offers white sands and surf.

*Drive north on **Route 71** to Burns Beach, then join **Route 60** and continue north.*

Yanchep

2 The resort town of Yanchep, with its good beaches, fishing and nearby lake system, is a popular destination for Perth day visitors. **Yanchep National Park** preserves 2,800 hectares (6,920 acres) of bushland and wetlands, and an extensive network of limestone caves. Guided tours of fantastic **Crystal Cave** are available. There are koalas here and the park is famed for its springtime wildflowers. There are more good beaches at the nearby resort and marina of **Two Rocks**.

i Yanchep National Park

*Continue north to join the Brand Highway (**Highway 1**), then drive north and take the Cervantes turn-off.*

Nambung National Park

3 This coastal national park is famous for the strange formations known as 'The Pinnacles'. Thousands of limestone pillars and needles have been eroded over hundreds of years to form fantastic craggy shapes, up to 5m high. The remainder of the national park contains other pillars in the 'Painted Desert', dunes, multi-coloured sandplains and numerous empty sandy beaches. Nambung is also home to a wide range of wildlife, including

CENTRAL & NORTHERN WA COAST

Perth • Northern Beaches • Yanchep Nambung National Park • Dongara and Port Denison • Geraldton • Kalbarri National Park Shark Bay and Monkey Mia • The Midlands Scenic Way • New Norcia • Perth

This long tour takes in the beautiful coastline immediately north of Perth; Nambung National Park with its famous stone pillars, The Pinnacles; the unspoilt coast around Dongara and Geraldton; wild Kalbarri National Park and the wonderful dolphins of Monkey Mia, on Shark Bay. Inland, on the return journey to Perth, you will pass through some of Western Australia's wheatlands and wildflower regions and visit the fascinating Benedictine township of New Norcia, with its unusual architecture and priceless art collection.

Although settlement did not spread north from Perth into most of this region until the 1840s and 1850s, the coast was explored by English and Dutch seafarers as far back as the early 1600s. The first known landing on the continent by Europeans took place at Shark Bay in 1616.

kangaroos, emus and many birds. The small fishing and seaside resort town of **Cervantes** is the base for visiting the national park, and you can take guided tours from here.

*Return to **Highway 1** and continue north.*

The Pinnacles, reminiscent of the standing stones of Brittany

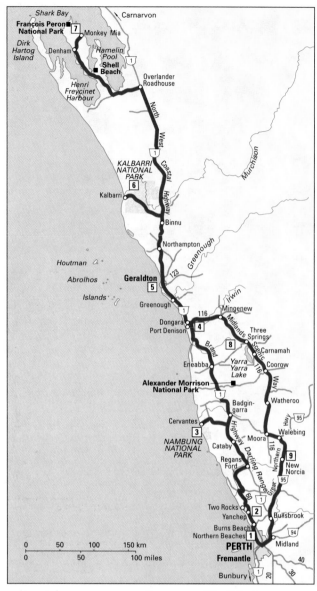

es, excellent fishing, scuba diving and surfing.

The interesting **museum** contains shipwreck *memorabilia* and relics, including items from the Dutch ship *Batavia* which was wrecked in 1629, natural history displays and Aboriginal items, while the grand Byzantine-style **St Francis Xavier Cathedral** comes as a surprise in this rather remote settlement. The best way to see the local sights is to drive the 30km (18-mile) **Geraldton Heritage Trail**.

i Bill Sewell Complex, Chapman Road

Continue on Highway 1, through Northampton, then take the Kalbarri turn-off.

Kalbarri National Park

6 The 186,000 hectares of Kalbarri National Park form a spectacular wilderness of gorges, rugged plains and surf-pounded coastline. Over millions of years the Murchison River has carved 80km (50 miles) of white and red banded gorges through the ancient sandstone plateau to create a dramatic landscape. The coastline is equally majestic, with precipitous red cliffs plunging into the Indian Ocean. The park contains over 500 plant species, including many colourful wildflowers, and is home to wildlife such as kangaroos and rock wallabies, and over 170 species of birds, including emus.

The resort of **Kalbarri**, on the estuary of the Murchison River, is the perfect base for visits to the national park. Activities on offer here include swimming, boating, fishing, diving, waterskiing, canoe safaris, and joyflights over the park's remarkable gorges. You can also visit **Kalflora**, a centre which focuses on the local wildflowers.

i Grey Street

Return to Highway 1, continue north, then take the Denham turn-off.

Shark Bay and Monkey Mia

7 This vast bay to the north of Kalbarri contains 1,500km (930 miles) of coastline, and innumerable inlets, bays, gulfs and islands. The old pearling centre of **Denham**, Australia's most westerly town, is the major settlement here. The area's main attraction is the **Shark Bay World Heritage and Marine Park**, centred on the beach of Monkey Mia. Since the 1960s, this has been the site of fascinating encounters between man and wild dolphins – these creatures regularly swim up to the beach to be hand fed and petted by humans. A **Dolphin Information Centre** has been established here, and the feeding is controlled to prevent the dolphins from becoming dependent on this source of food.

The tip of the peninsula contains **François Peron National Park** (parts of which are accessible only by 4WD vehicle). This park is composed of sandy plains and gypsum claypans, and is home to birds, dolphins, turtles and dugongs. **Shell Beach**, 40km (25 miles) from Denham, is made up of billions of

SPECIAL TO ...

6 Long before James Cook explored Australia's eastern seaboard, seafarers were familiar with the continent's west coast. **Wittecarra Creek**, south of Kalbarri, was the landing site of Australia's first, albeit unwilling, permanent European inhabitants. In 1629 the Dutch ship *Batavia* was wrecked offshore and some of the crew mutinied. Two of the culprits were abandoned here by the captain to fare as best they could. Their fate is unknown, but a cairn marks the spot of this involuntary landing. **Dirk Hartog Island** in Shark Bay was the site of Australia's first known European landing in 1616.

Dongara and Port Denison

4 The quiet town of Dongara, on the banks of the Irwin River, was first settled in the early 1850s as a farming and coalmining settlement. Many 19th-century buildings remain – the four-storey **Royal Steam Flour Mill** (1894), limestone **Russ Cottage** (1870), the 1870 **Old Police Station and Courthouse**, and **Priory Lodge** are all worth visiting. Dongara's main street is famous for its enormous 85-year-old Moreton Bay fig trees, which are listed by the National Trust. Nearby Port Denison is a holiday resort, popular for fishing, windsurfing and reef diving.

i 5 Waldeck Street, Dongara

Continue northwards on Highway 1.

Geraldton

5 Known as 'Sun City' because of its warm, sunny climate, the prosperous port of Geraldton is the administrative centre of the state's mid-west. Famous for its lobsters, this city on the shores of Champion Bay was first settled as a mining centre in the 1840s. Today, Geraldton is better known as a holiday resort with white sandy beach-

tiny non-fossilised white shells that reach a depth of up to 10m (32 feet).

☐ Knight Terrace, Denham

Return to the North West Coastal Highway and drive south via Geraldton and Dongara. Take Route 116 to Mingenew.

The Midlands Scenic Way

8 Part of the return journey to Perth is known as the Midlands Scenic Way. **Three Springs** has a heritage path through the region's wildflowers and the area from here to **Coorow** offers a number of wildflower drives (details available locally). **Carnamah's** main attraction is the **Yarra Yarra Lake**, a salt lake system with unusual water colours, while the **Alexander Morrison National Park** is worth a visit.

☐ Midlands Road, Mingenew

From Coorow, continue on Route 116, then turn on to Route 95 out of Moora.

New Norcia

9 Set incongruously in the farming plains, the settlement of New Norcia is an extraordinary surprise. Benedictine monks came to the state in the 1840s to establish a mission for Aborigines, and eventually a small town of grand classical, Byzantine and gothic buildings grew up here. The complex includes a

monastery, a boarding school, and historic **New Norcia Hotel**, which provides accommodation for visitors. The **Museum and Art Gallery** contains displays on the settlement, rare antiques, and a world-class collection of European religious paintings.

☐ Great Northern Highway

Continue on Route 95 (Great Northern Highway) and return to Perth via Bullsbrook.

Perth – Sorrento 20 (12)
Sorrento – Yanchep 40 (25)
Yanchep – Nambung NP 200 (124)
Nambung NP – Dongara 208 (129)
Dongara – Geraldton 70 (43)
Geraldton – Kalbarri 167 (104)
Kalbarri – Monkey Mia 400 (248)
Monkey Mia – Mingenew 555 (345)
Mingenew – New Norcia 248 (154)
New Norcia – Perth 135 (84)

Right: paradise regained – happy co-existence between man and beast at Monkey Mia. Below: Kalbarri Park's stunning gorges

FOR CHILDREN

2 Children will never forget the experience of meeting the dolphins at Monkey Mia, but another attraction for the young is at Yanchep. At the **Wild Kingdom Wildlife Park** here, children can hand feed the kangaroos and handle the cute and cuddly hairy-nosed wombats.

BACK TO NATURE

5 Sixty-four kilometres (40 miles) offshore from Geraldton, the **Houtman Abrolhos Islands** form a network of reefs and islands that has been a graveyard for many ships. The islands are used for lobster fishing, but the area is also an important breeding ground for terns, shearwaters and other seabirds. Boat trips to the islands can be made from Geraldton and Kalbarri.

FOR HISTORY BUFFS

4 The historic hamlet of **Greenough**, north of Port Denison, was founded in the 1850s and eleven of the old sandstone buildings here have been restored by the National Trust. You can take a guided tour and also visit the **Greenough Pioneer Museum**.

RECOMMENDED WALKS

9 The many attractions of New Norcia are best seen on the 2km (1.2-mile) **Heritage Trail**. The walk is easy and takes in the most important buildings and historic sites. If you feel energetic, there is also a scenic 1.7km (1-mile) river walk here.

NORTHERN & CENTRAL AUSTRALIA

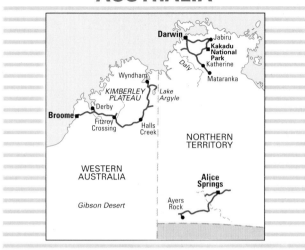

Tour 20

This tour covers the most exciting sights of the Northern Territory's 'Top End'. Darwin is a surprisingly cosmopolitan city and offers history, Aboriginal arts, crafts and culture, and sophisticated nightlife at its modern casino. A trip to view the scenic, Aboriginal and wildlife wonders of Kakadu National Park is a must, as is the drive south to Katherine and its famous gorge. Other attractions include the gold town of Pine Creek, Mataranka and its thermal pool, and the oasis of Litchfield National Park.

Tour 21

After flying into Alice Springs and exploring this interesting town of 25,000 or so people together with its hinterland of dramatic cliffs, gorges, rivers, and even a lush oasis of palm trees, that make up the MacDonnell Ranges – the tour heads south. There is much to see here, including the mysterious Henbury Meteorite Craters and magnificent Ayers Rock and The Olgas. You can also ride camels, go hot air ballooning, spot strange Australian flora and fauna, and visit a Royal Flying Doctor Service base on your unique Red Centre experience.

The Broome coast, glimpsed between curtains of red rock, is the finest in northwest Australia. Its shallow waters have long been the source of oysters yielding mother-of-pearl

The still relatively untamed north and 'Red Centre' of Australia is a very special place. The vast tracts of uninhabited coastline, rugged hills and tropical wetlands of the far north are complemented by the deserts and red mountains of Central Australia. The population is small, the scenery spectacular and the wildlife intriguing: here you can see crocodiles, kangaroos, goannas, dingoes, thorny devils and a fantastic variety of birdlife. Aboriginal culture and traditions are alive and well here, and Kakadu National Park contains ancient rock art that forms one of the world's most important primitive art sites.

The isolated Northern Territory capital of Darwin is the country's least 'Australian' city. With its white buildings, Aboriginal, Islander and Asian population and tropical vegetation, this could be Indonesia or Malaysia. Nearby World Heritage protected Kakadu National Park is the undoubted gem of the north, but the lesser known rivers, gorges and sandstone hills of Western Australia's Kimberley region, especially the extraordinary Bungle Bungles, are a close second. Broome, the tropical gateway to this spectacular landscape, has a long history of pearling and cattle farming.

At the heart of the continent – the Red Centre – lies the colourful outback town of Alice Springs. The Alice is still a rather rough and ready place, but a modern town that thrives on tourism, mining and cattle rearing. Further south are two unmistakable symbols of Australia – Ayers Rock (Uluru) and the nearby Olgas (Kata Tjuta).

Explorers first passed through inhospitable Central Australia in the 1840s. The far north of Western Australia, or at least sections of its coastline, was first visited by European seafarers during the 1830s but it was not until the Kimberley region was explored in the late 1870s that the true nature of the land was revealed. Darwin dates from 1869 and Alice Springs a couple of years later, while the Broome area was not officially settled until the early 1880s.

These three tours are all of the fly/drive variety. You can fly to Darwin and Alice Springs from most major cities, while the easiest access to Broome is from Perth. This northern area of the continent experiences a wet season from November to March and is best visited in the cooler winter months.

Tour 22

From the historic port of Broome, with its palm-fringed streets, stunning 20km (12-mile) long white beach, and colourful multinational population, this tour takes you inland into the wild and beautiful country of northern Western Australia. The old port of Derby, spectacular Geikie Gorge National Park, the mining town of Halls Creek and manmade Lake Argyle are all on the itinerary. The highlight, however, is the Bungle Bungle (Purnululu) National Park, a remarkable area of strangely shaped sandstone hills that has come to wide attention only during the last decade. Much of this region can be driven through only during the dry and cooler season, from April to October, and many of the roads are less than perfect, but it's all worthwhile to see such splendid and unique natural sights.

Rust-red Ayers Rock changes hue dramatically under various lighting and weather conditions

THE FIRST AUSTRALIANS

No one is absolutely certain, but it is believed that Aboriginal people first came from southeast Asia to what is now Australia around 40,000 years ago. To put this into perspective, official European settlement began only 200 or so years ago in 1788. Apart from the occasional coastal foray by 17th- and 18th-century European explorers, and the visits of seafarers and fishermen from Malaya and Indonesia from the 1650s onwards, Aborigines led an undisturbed tribal life of nomadic hunting and gathering based on the seasonal availability of game, seeds and fruits until the First Fleet landed in 1788.

'From the beginning': Aboriginal people venerated their land, but had no concept of owning it

killing, on behalf of the new arrivals increased and the Aborigines turned to guerilla warfare.

The Aborigines were little match, however, for knives, muskets and, ultimately, far superior numbers. Smallpox and influenza ravaged the Sydney Aborigines, while other introduced killers such as venereal disease and alcohol also took a heavy toll. As the settlers spread to Tasmania and further into the continent, this dismal situation was exacerbated and the Aboriginal population was abused, hunted, poisoned, massacred and eventually decimated. One Sydney tribe, which had numbered around 400 in 1788, was reduced to just four people by 1845.

The Tasmanian Aborigines

The most distressing tale is that of the Tasmanian Aborigines. European settlers moved into Tasmania in 1804 and the first massacre of the native people occurred within three months of their arrival. Eventually the situation degenerated to one of genocide. In 1831 a group of Aborigines were moved to Flinders Island in Bass Strait, and by the end of the following year there were 100 remaining here and perhaps another 100 on the main island. By 1863 there were just seven known Aborigines alive. It was long believed that William Lanney, who died in March 1869, and Truganini (died May 1876) were the last remaining male and female

Conflict

Initially the Aborigines kept their distance from the white man, but conflict arose as the natives realised that the intruders were here to stay and intended to find new uses for the land. Land to Aboriginal people is not something to be owned, but an integral part of life which is to be deeply respected and cared for, and which provides shelter, water, food, skins for clothing and fire. Europeans understood nothing of this and wanted the land for farming, to build houses on, to create wealth from, and to own. This lack of understanding of the Aborigines' viewpoint inevitably led to their displacement from traditional hunting, living, and even sacred, sites. General antagonism, and then

Set out compass-like in the desert, this Aboriginal painting in the Northern Territory is at once stunning and evocative

Tasmanian Aborigines. Some must have escaped the net, however, as there are several thousand Tasmanians today who claim Aboriginal roots.

The traditional life

Back in 1788 there were perhaps 300,000 Aboriginal people, spread among some 500 tribes, living on the continent. Each clan or tribe had its own language and territory, based on traditions which went back to the creation ancestors who first inhabited the land. The lifestyle was nomadic, and dependent on the seasonal availability of fish, game and other 'bush tucker'. Possessions were few and were essentially those required for survival and hunting, such as spears, boomerangs, baskets and nets. The importance of the land has already been mentioned, but the essence of this belief was, and is, that the ancestral spirits not only created the land during the Dreamtime – they inhabit it in the form of trees, rocks, waterholes, rivers and other landforms. It is not, therefore, surprising that the 18th-

undoubtedly a great deal of racism to be overcome, many Aboriginal people still live in great poverty, and alcoholism is a persistent problem. But, while all is definitely not perfect, issues such as rights to the profits from mining and quarrying on Aboriginal land, education and general welfare are very much to the fore in the 1990s. Aboriginal people are working in the tourism industry as national park rangers, and some have started their own safari operations. Aboriginal art and perfor-

The deep, haunting tones of a didgeridoo take great skill to produce, and the instrument itself is a work of art

century Aborigines lived in harmony with the land and its animals, birds and seasons.

Despite this poor life by western standards, Aboriginal people had an extraordinarily rich culture, based on their ancestral mythology and links with the land, and expressed through storytelling, song, dance, ritual and arts. Today, thankfully, many reminders of these fascinating artistic traditions still exist in the form of ancient rock art, and in the resurgence of Aboriginal arts such as carving, painting, weaving and dance.

Aborigines today

Despite 200 years of deprivation the modern Aboriginal, or Koori, people are experiencing a resurgence of hope and pride. Incredibly, Aborigines were granted the right to vote only in 1967, but there has been great progress on the subject of land rights – Ayers Rock, for example, has 'belonged' to Aboriginal people since 1985. The recent Mabo land claim High Court case is causing great controversy, but there seems no doubt that the result will be that Aboriginal people will receive more legal recognition and the right to their traditional lands.

On the down side, there is

Art in a non-literate society had story-telling and ceremonial roles

mance is much admired internationally and many people now make a good living through such arts.

Not so long ago there were few famous Aborigines other than tennis player Evonne Goolagong, artist Albert Namatjira and a few other sporting heroes, but the picture has changed a great deal in recent years. Kooris who now lead their fields include Cathy Freeman, the international-class sprinter, world-famous rock band Yothu Yindi (lead singer Mandawuy Yunupingu was Australian of the Year in 1983), writer and painter Sally Morgan; and many Aboriginal artists, performers and sporting stars.

8 days – 1,131km (701 miles)

DARWIN TO KAKADU & KATHERINE

Darwin • Kakadu National Park • Pine Creek
Katherine and Nitmiluk National Park
Mataranka • Litchfield National Park • Darwin

After flying in to Darwin and hiring a vehicle, you can explore this tropical northern city before heading off to the highlights of the Northern Territory's 'Top End'. World Heritage listed Kakadu National Park is a unique environment of spectacular scenery, incredible wildlife and some of Australia's most impressive Aboriginal rock art. From here you travel south to the old goldmining town of Pine Creek and on to lovely Katherine Gorge and Mataranka Pool, delightful oases in this otherwise arid country. The return to Darwin along the Stuart Highway is via the small town of Adelaide River, the pools and rainforest of Litchfield National Park, and the fauna sanctuary of Berry Springs, the Territory Wildlife Park.

Al fresco shopping in a market in Darwin

Darwin

1 Port Darwin harbour was first discovered in 1839 and named in honour of Charles Darwin. Settlement began 30 years later and the region boomed once gold was discovered in the 1880s. Darwin was bombed by the Japanese during World War II and further devastated by Cyclone Tracy, which hit on Christmas Day 1974. The city has re-created itself, however, as a modern and very relaxed environment that is home to just 76,000 people of 45 different ethnic groups.

Few of Darwin's old buildings have survived, but the 1883 colonial-style **Government House** and the 1920s **Old Admiralty House** are interesting. Out of the city centre, **Fannie Bay Gaol** now houses a museum; also at Fannie Bay is the **Northern Territory Museum of Arts and Sciences**, with its excellent Aboriginal arts and culture section and marine display. You can visit the **Indo Pacific Marine**, an exhibition of living coral reefs; while **Aquascene** gives you the opportunity to hand feed ocean fish. The tropical **Botanic Gardens** are also worth a visit, as are the colourful **Thursday Mindil Beach markets**. Other attractions include strolling through **Smith Street Mall**, at the city's heart, and the new waterfront **Wharf Precinct**; harbour cruises; the **Diamond Beach Casino**, and several Aboriginal art and craft galleries. South of town, the **Aviation**

SPECIAL TO...

At the **Darwin Crocodile Farm** (on the highway 40km (25 miles) from Darwin) saltwater and freshwater crocodiles are bred for their skins and meat – you can sample barbecued croc and other unusual delicacies here!

SCENIC ROUTES

2 Although the most important Kakadu sights are off the main roads, the entire area is very scenic and driving through this national park is a delight – keep your eyes open for wildlife too!

FOR HISTORY BUFFS

Adelaide River, on the highway south of Batchelor, became an important military centre during World War II. The town was bombed and the war cemetery here contains the graves of the 480 or so people killed during these air raids. The 1888 railway station features historical displays and memorabilia from the war.

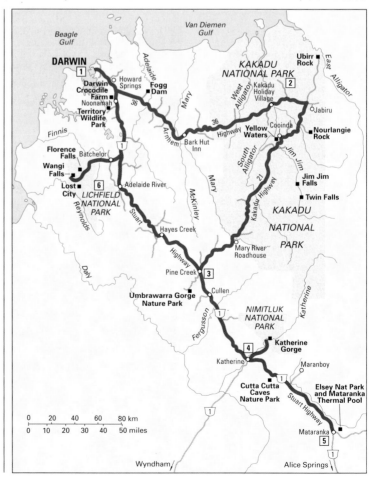

Museum features a massive B52 bomber.

ⓘ 33 Smith Street Mall

*Leave Darwin via the Stuart Highway (**Highway 1**) then take the Arnhem Highway to Kakadu National Park.*

Kakadu National Park

2 The highway into Kakadu is sealed and suitable for most vehicles. Once inside the park, head for the visitor centre on the highway before setting off to see more of this very special environment. (See **Kakadu**, page 112, for full details.)

*Continue through the national park on the Arnhem Highway, turning south on to the Kakadu Highway, which in turn joins the Stuart Highway (**Highway 1**) at Pine Creek.*

Pine Creek

3 Gold was discovered here in 1872 and ten years later Pine Creek became the terminus of the now defunct North Australian Railway. An open-cut goldmine was established here in 1985 and the small settlement is experiencing a new boom. For visitors the main attractions are **Miners Park**, with its old mining machinery and *memorabilia*, the **Railway Station Museum**, the National Trust **Museum**, and the opportunity to take guided mine tours. To the southwest lies **Umbrawarra Gorge Nature Park**, with its crystal clear pools.

*Drive south on the Stuart Highway (**Highway 1**).*

Katherine and Nitmiluk National Park

4 The highlight here is undoubtedly **Katherine Gorge**, located in the Nitmiluk (Katherine Gorge) National Park. This is where the Katherine River has cut a series of 13 dramatic gorges through the sandstone plateau. The river flows between sheer 60m-high walls and forms a delightful oasis. You can take a boat tour through some of the gorges and admire the brightly coloured walls, adorned with ancient Aboriginal paintings. Fauna abounds in the park – there are some 58 reptile and amphibian species here, including the freshwater crocodile and tortoises. Nitmiluk is now owned by the local Aboriginal people, who lease it to the government.

Katherine was an important Stuart Highway centre as far back as the early 1870s, and the railway later brought growth to the town. Today, the 5,700 people here are involved mainly in the cattle and tourism industries. Attractions include the **Museum**, the **Railway Museum**, tours of the **School of the Air**, and the **Low Level Nature Reserve**. You can also visit 1879 **Springvale**, the Northern Territory's oldest homestead, and National Trust listed **O'Keeffe House**.

ⓘ Corner of Stuart Highway and Lindsay Avenue

Continue south on the Stuart Highway.

See the Katherine River's gorges from a tour boat or your own canoe

Mataranka

5 Mataranka is at the heart of 'Never Never' country, so called because those who fall in love with this region can never leave it! The highlight here is the **Mataranka Thermal Pool**, a natural swimming pool surrounded by lush rainforest, with waters at a constant 34°C. You can also visit **Elsey National Park** and the **Museum of the Never Never**.

Return north on the Highway. Take the Batchelor turn-off.

Litchfield National Park

6 Although less well known than Kakadu, Litchfield National Park is becoming increasingly popular. The park is famous for its cool, clear swimming holes, the lovely Florence, Wangi and Sandy Creek waterfalls, lush rainforest and sandstone plateau scenery. The **Lost City**, with its amazing rock formations, is another highlight, as are the huge termite mounds. Most of the park's roads are rather rough and a 4WD vehicle is necessary to reach many of the sights. Access into the park is via the small settlement of **Batchelor**, a uranium mining centre during the 1950s and 1960s. There is accommodation here, and the town has fine tropical gardens.

Return to Darwin on the Stuart Highway.

Darwin – Jabiru (Kakadu NP) 250 (155)
Jabiru – Cooinda (Kakadu NP) 55 (34)
Cooinda – Pine Creek 165 (102)
Pine Creek – Katherine 90 (56)
Katherine – Mataranka 112 (70)
Mataranka – Batchelor (Litchfield NP) 355 (220)
Batchelor – Darwin 104 (64)

BACK TO NATURE

3 Cutta Cutta Caves Nature Park, to the south of Katherine, contains a series of limestone caves that are home to the rare orange horseshoe bat. Also within the park are strange weathered limestone formations believed to be 500 million years old.

FOR CHILDREN

At the **Territory Wildlife Park** (at Berry Springs, south of Darwin) you can meet the local fauna at close quarters. There are kangaroos, wallabies, dingoes, buffalo and banteng (Bali cattle) here, as well as a lagoon with native birds, an aquarium, a rainforest aviary and a nocturnal house.

RECOMMENDED WALK

The wetlands around **Fogg Dam**, on the way to Kakadu, form an important bird sanctuary where brolgas, herons, ibis and many other water birds congregate. There is also an enjoyable 3.5km (2-mile) walk through the rainforest here.

KAKADU, AYERS ROCK & THE OLGAS

Native Australian: a cheeky budgerigar displays green plumage, but related strains have been bred in many colours

Three of the best reasons to visit the Northern Territory are the presence of the spectacular natural wonders of Kakadu National Park, to the east of Darwin, and Ayers Rock and The Olgas, in Uluru National Park to the south of Alice Springs.

'X-ray' rock art: uranium deposits in Kakadu are attracting mining interests worryingly near some of Australia's finest Aboriginal art

KAKADU NATIONAL PARK

Kakadu National Park is a very special place indeed. Australia's largest national park covers some 20,000sq km and was added to the UNESCO World Heritage list in 1987. Kakadu contains an incredible range of animal, bird and plant life and remnants of at least 25,000 years of Aboriginal occupation. It is appropriate that the park is now owned by the local Gagudju Association, who lease the land to the National Parks and Wildlife Service. Most of Kakadu is the floodplain of the East, South and West Alligator Rivers – in the wet season this area is transformed into a vast freshwater lake, teeming with birdlife. Rainforest, woodlands and mangrove forests are also found on the lowlands. Behind all this, the 250m-high (820-foot) high Arnhem Land escarpment rises abruptly in a series of mighty sandstone walls, broken by gorges and waterfalls, that runs for 600km (370 miles).

Kakadu highlights are the spectacular 215m (705-foot) high Jim Jim Falls, the smaller Twin Falls, and Yellow Waters, a remarkable wetlands area with prolific birdlife. The world-famous Aboriginal art here is some of Australia's most impressive and dates back 20,000 or so years. Ubirr Rock contains extraordinary 'X-ray' paintings which detail the interiors of fish and animals, while Nourlangie Rock's human and mythical figures are depicted in beautiful natural ochres, reds, blacks and whites.

Bordering the national park to the east is the vast expanse of Arnhem Land. This Aboriginal owned land is generally closed to visitors, but guided tours are available from the settlements of Jabiru and Cooinda. Jabiru is the only town of any size within the park and, controversially, uranium is mined nearby at the Ranger site. Tours of the mine, scenic Kakadu flights and many other guided excursions are available from Jabiru.

Fauna

There is a great variety of wildlife here. On the plateau, rock wallabies, euros (small kangaroos), bats and quolls (native cats) thrive; while the lowlands are home to dingoes, feral pigs, water buffalo, marsupial mice and possums. There are many reptiles, including goannas, tree snakes and frilled lizards, while both varieties of crocodile are common in the waterways. Fish species, including the large barramundi, are abundant.

The bird life of Kakadu is extremely prolific. Waterbirds, including brolgas, geese, pelicans, jabirus and herons, are plentiful while the woodland areas are home to cockatoos, brightly coloured lorikeets, hawks and owls. Unique to the Kakadu area are the white-lined honeyeater, banded pigeon and the chestnut-quilled rock pigeon.

Flora

Kakadu's vegetation is as varied as everything else in this outstanding natural reserve. There are knotted mangrove forests on the tidal flats; pandanus palms on the beach areas; wetland paperbark forests; eucalyptus woodland and rainforest; and even scrub, rough spinifex and grasses on the high plateau.

ULURU AND KATA TJUTA

Uluru (Ayers Rock)

The statistics behind one of the world's most famous sights are astonishing. Uluru is the world's largest monolith – 348m high, with a 9km circumference. The rock is merely the tip of a vast sandstone underground 'mountain', which is around 600 million years old. Some visitors make the strenuous, 1.6km (1-mile) climb to the rock's summit, while others prefer to accept the Aboriginal view that Uluru is sacred and not to be walked on. An interesting option is to walk around the rock – there are ancient carvings and paintings here and a variety of guided walks are provided by the Aboriginal rangers.

Ayers Rock was first sighted by a European in 1872. Surveyor Ernest Giles named it in honour of Sir Henry Ayers, the Premier of South Australia. To Aboriginal people, however, Uluru is far more significant. This is a sacred place which features prominently in Tjukurpa (the

While visiting The Olgas, carry sufficient food and water. Even experienced climbers must take care because of loose rocks

Pretty he's definitely not, but how impressive: the swift-running, flightless emu

creation period), and an important ritual and spiritual site. As the sun moves across the sky, Uluru changes colour from deep red to mauve, pink, brown, and even blue. Special sunset viewing areas provide the best vantage points for this spectacular and much photographed event.

Kata Tjuta (The Olgas)

About 40km (25 miles) away from Ayers Rock, Kata Tjuta (Aboriginal words for 'many heads') are part of the same great underground rock formation as Uluru, and are equally important in Aboriginal legend. The less imposing Olgas, however, are composed of 30 or so rounded formations, culminating in the high point of 546m (1,790-foot) Mount Olga. Ernest Giles, who first came across these remarkable domes in 1872, named Mount Olga after the wife of the King of Spain. It is possible to walk through some of the gorges between the domes – this is an excellent way to view the rock surface and surrounding vegetation, but many of the walks are difficult. Always check with the rangers before attempting such a hike.

Fauna and flora

Although not as rich in birdlife as Kakadu, this Central Australian region is home to the magnificent wedge-tailed eagle, kestrels, and plains birds such as honeyeaters and crested pigeons. Also common here are red kangaroos, camels, dingoes, echidnas, the very large perentie lizard, tiny geckos and the peculiar looking thorny devil. You can often see emus and flocks of budgerigars on the plains.

There is little vegetation in this arid Red Centre area other than low-growing mulga and spinifex, and the occasional white-trunked ghost gum, fig tree or desert oak. After rain, however, the desert comes alive with wildflowers such as the hibiscus-like Sturt's desert rose, or white daisies.

PRACTICAL CONSIDERATIONS

The Northern Territory experiences two distinct seasons: November to March is hot, humid and wet (particularly in the north), while the remainder of the year is cooler and drier. There are plenty of ways of seeing the sights – everything from air to walking tours are available. It is essential to make accommodation bookings in advance, especially in the popular winter months. Visiting Kakadu and Central Australia is generally a safe experience, but do remember that you are in a very rugged region and always carry sufficient fuel and water. Keep an eye out for snakes, and beware of crocodiles in the north – do not swim or *even stand* in creeks, rivers or pools.

Kakadu National Park

There are numerous places to stay in Kakadu, with everything from good quality hotels to campsites. The town of Jabiru is the park's main centre, with fuel supplies and plenty of accommodation.

Ayers Rock Resort

This attractive modern resort has been created to provide accommodation and facilities for the increasing number of visitors here. The resort contains hotels, motels, backpackers' accommodation, serviced apartments, caravan and camping sites, as well as shops and fuel outlets.

7 days – 1,128km (702 miles)

ALICE SPRINGS & THE RED CENTRE

Alice Springs • Simpsons Gap National Park and Standley Chasm • Hermannsburg and Finke Gorge National Park • Alice Springs • Henbury Meteorite Craters • Uluru (Ayers Rock) and Kata Tjuta (The Olgas) • Alice Springs

Alice Springs is your starting point for this tour around Australia's 'Red Centre'. The undoubted highlights are Ayers Rock (Uluru) and The Olgas, but there is much else to see in this rugged region at the very heart of the continent. Alice Springs, affectionately known as 'The Alice', has many attractions and is the centre of a fascinating geological region, dominated by the magnificent MacDonnell Ranges. These reddish quartzite hills are probably 850 million years old and run in a broken band to the south of town. The tour includes highlights of the Western MacDonnells, while the attractions of the eastern part of the range are options. Further south, the fascinating Henbury Meteorite Craters are on the itinerary before you arrive at Uluru. It is suggested that you fly to Alice Springs and hire a vehicle there. At the end of the tour you can either return to Alice, or continue to South Australia on the Stuart Highway – Adelaide is over 1,500km (930 miles) from the Ayers Rock Resort. The best time to visit is during the cooler months from May to September.

SPECIAL TO . . .

1 The **Frontier Camel Farm**, 7km (4 miles) from Alice Springs, provides great entertainment. You can ride on these strange, lurching animals and the farm also contains a museum dedicated to the Afghan camel drivers and their beasts of burden.

FOR HISTORY BUFFS

In the Western MacDonnell Range, 100km (62 miles) from The Alice, **Arltunga Historical Reserve** contains remnants of the area's goldmining era. Gold was discovered here in 1887 and at one time there were 400 people living at the site. Today, all that remains are ruined buildings, old mining equipment and a restored gaol and police station.

Alice Springs

1 Back in 1871 Alice Springs was merely a telegraph station on the line stretching across the continent from Adelaide to Darwin. Originally a rough and ready outback settlement known as Stuart, 'The Alice' is a modern well-maintained town and home to around 25,000 people. There are many hotels here, Lasseters Casino, an 18-hole golf course and good tourist facilities.

Most of the stone buildings at the **Old Telegraph Station** have been restored and form an outdoor museum. Other old structures include the 1907 **Stuart Town Gaol** and **Adelaide House**, the original 1926 hospital. The **Royal Flying Doctor Service** operates from a base at Alice Springs and visitors are welcome to visit their museum. The **Strehlow Research Centre** offers displays on the local Aranda people, while **Minerals House** provides a glimpse into the area's complex geo-

Camels were invaluable in opening up the Red Centre. See them close up at the Frontier Camel Farm

logical make-up. The Adelaide railway line arrived here in 1929 and the **Ghan Preservation Society** runs a railways museum and operates a steam train a few kilometres from town. Other Alice Springs attractions include camel rides, the **Chateau Hornsby winery**, an **Aviation and Auto Museum**, and the opportunity to buy Aboriginal paintings and artefacts.

i Centrepoint Building, corner of Hartley Street and Gregory Terrace

From Alice Springs travel west on Larapinta Drive, then turn right at the Simpsons Gap turn-off.

Simpsons Gap National Park and Standley Chasm

2 Just 17km (11 miles) west of Alice, Simpsons Gap National Park contains a section of the western MacDonnell Ranges. Steep gorges, magnificent gum trees, and the famous 'gap' – a wide break in the ridge – can all be visited. Nearby Standley Chasm, a cleft in the range, is a remarkable 100m (328-foot) high gorge that is only 5m (3 miles) wide on average. The best time to visit the chasm is around midday, when the overhead sun dramatically transforms the cliffs into a flaming red.

Return to Larapinta Drive and continue driving west.

Hermannsburg and Finke Gorge National Park

3 In 1877 Lutheran missionaries arrived here to establish a mission for local Aborigines. They built a school at Hermannsburg, which operated until 1982, when the settlement passed into Aboriginal hands. Australia's most famous Aboriginal artist, Albert Namatjira, was born at the **Mission** in 1902, and there is a **Namatjira Memorial** here.

To the south lies Finke Gorge National Park, a 46,000-hectare (113,600-acre) region of dramatic red gorges, rivers and valleys. The highlight here is the lush Palm Valley oasis, where around 3,000 ancient red cabbage palms thrive. These trees are several hundred years old and are unique to the area. The Finke River is one of the world's oldest watercourses, although it is normally dry. Note that this area is not accessible during or after heavy rain.

Return to Alice Springs via Hermannsburg and Larapinta Drive.

Alice Springs

4 The inaccessibility of some of the region's most important sights, and their long distances from Alice Springs, make air tours an excellent sightseeing option. Joyflights over the MacDonnell Ranges, Kings Canyon, Ayers Rock and The O'gas are all available from Alice Springs, as are shorter hot-air balloon trips.

Head south from Alice on the Stuart Highway (Route 87) and take the Henbury turn-off.

Henbury Meteorite Craters

5 Just off the Stuart Highway, a reserve protects these craters, believed to have been formed by a meteorite plunging to earth some 5,000 years ago. It seems that the various craters (the largest is 180m /590 feet wide and 12m/40 feet deep) were created by the meteorite breaking up before landing.

Continue south on the Stuart Highway to Erldunda, then take the Lasseter Highway to Uluru National Park.

Uluru (Ayers Rock) and Kata Tjuta (The Olgas)

6 These remarkable natural features will be the highlight of your Central Australia tour – see the Ayers Rock and Olgas feature for details. The nearby **Ayers Rock Resort** village provides accommodation and full tourist facilities. In addition to the natural wonders here, attractions include the **Uluru Experience**, a slide presentation on the area; the **Mulgara Gallery**, where resident Aboriginal artists work at their crafts; and Aboriginal music.

ⓘ Visitors and Information Centre, Ayers Rock Resort

Either return to Alice Springs, or continue to South Australia on the Stuart Highway.

Alice Springs – Simpsons Gap NP
17 (11)
Simpsons Gap NP – Hermannsburg
110 (68)
Hermannsburg – Alice Springs 127 (79)
Alice Springs – Henbury Meteorite
Craters 130 (81)
Henbury Meteorite Craters – Ayers
Rock Resort 307 (191)
Ayers Rock Resort – Alice Springs
437 (272)

Spectacular Standley Chasm

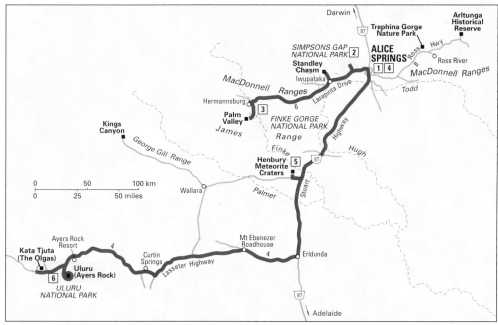

8 days – 1,387km (862 miles)

BROOME & THE KIMBERLEY

Broome • Derby • Geikie Gorge National Park
Purnululu (Bungle Bungle) National Park
Wyndham • Kununurra and Lake Argyle
Northern Territory

The vast, remote Kimberley region contains some of Australia's most fascinating natural wonders. From the historic West Kimberley pearling town of Broome, just 18° south of the Equator, you travel to the 1880s port of Derby and then on a long inland loop that takes in cattle country and spectacular Geikie Gorge National Park. The East Kimberley contains the wonderful rock formations of Purnululu National Park, the isolated towns of Wyndham and Kununurra, and manmade Lake Argyle. Most of this rugged region was untouched by Europeans until the 1880s and the area is still very isolated and sparsely populated.

This itinerary involves flying into Broome, with two options at the end of the tour – either fly out of Kununurra, or continue driving into the Northern Territory. From Kununurra it is over 500km (310 miles) on sealed roads to Katherine, where you can link up with Tour 20. Although the highway is now sealed all the way from Broome to Kununurra, many of the off-road sights require a 4WD vehicle – these can be hired in Broome. Note that all roads in the region can become impassable during the wet (November to March) season.

The Kimberley Plateau, a 'last frontier' with bizarre land forms

Broome

1 Tropical, multicultural Broome, on Roebuck Bay, has a fascinating history. Pearl fishers were the first occupants of the site in the early 1870s and by 1910 the town had become the pearling capital of the world. In addition to the wonderful coastline here, **Chinatown**, the **Heritage Trail**, **Crocodile Park**, the **Bird Observatory**, pearl displays and shops, **Mangrove Walk** and the **Broome Historical Society Museum** are all of interest. **Cable Beach**, a 20km (12-mile) stretch of white sand, lapped by clear turquoise waters, is one of the most appealing attractions. There is an upmarket resort here and Broome offers a wide variety of other accommodation.

i Corner of Bagot Road and Great Northern Highway

Follow the Great Northern Highway (Highway 1), then take the Derby turn-off.

Derby

2 The modern town of Derby is the administrative centre for the West Kimberley region. Historic buildings include the **Old Derby Gaol** (1880s), and 1920s **Wharfingers House**, which now contains a museum. The Royal Flying Doctor Service base is open to the public, and the **Boab Prison Tree**, just out of town, is also worth a visit. This huge hollow tree, a variety that is found only in this region, is believed to have been used as a lock-up for prisoners. Adjacent to the tree, **Myall Bore** is an artesian well which feeds a 120m (390-foot) long cattle trough.

i 1 Clarendon Street

Return to the highway and continue to Fitzroy Crossing.

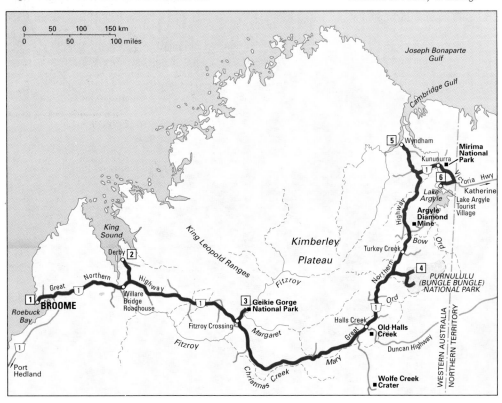

Geikie Gorge National Park

3 This magnificent 3,000-hectare (7,410-acre) national park is just 16km from the small highway town of Fitzroy Crossing. The highlight here is 14km-long Geikie Gorge, which was formed by the erosive action of the mighty Fitzroy River. The gorge's limestone cliffs contain fossil deposits and the river is home to freshwater crocodiles and stingrays. Cruises are available, but a scenic flight is probably the best way to view the gorge – especially as the park is open only from April to October.

Continue driving on Highway 1 via Halls Creek until you reach the turn-off to the Purnululu National Park. (Note that the nearest accommodation to the park is in Halls Creek.)

Purnululu National Park

4 One of Australia's most spectacular natural wonders, the Purnululu National Park became well known only in the early 1980s. Also known as the Bungle Bungles, these extremely fragile striped sandstone hills resemble beehives and reach a height of 300m (984 feet). It is difficult to drive around the park, even with a 4WD, and access is limited to prevent further erosion. For this reason (and the fact that the park is closed from January to March) it might be best to take a scenic flight over the formations. These are available from **Halls Creek** and **Kununurra**.

Return to Highway 1 and continue north until you reach the Wyndham turn-off.

Wyndham

5 The 1880s port town of Wyndham, on Cambridge Gulf, has retained several old buildings including the **Port Post Office**, **Durack's Store** and the **Old Court House**. You can visit the huge **Boab Tree**, some 2.5m (8-foot) wide, and the **Afghan Cemetery**, the last resting place for many Afghan camel drivers who worked here in the early days. You can view crocs at the **Wyndham Crocodile Farm**, which breeds both the freshwater and estuarine varieties. There are also Aboriginal rock paintings, a scenic drive to **Five Rivers Lookout** and bird-rich lagoons in the area.

ⓘ Old Post Office, O'Donnell Street

Return to the highway and drive on to Kununurra.

Kununurra and Lake Argyle

6 The town of Kununurra, lying on the shore of Lake Kununurra, dates from the 1960s, when it became the base for irrigation scheme workers. Although very isolated, the town has excellent facilities and visitors can enjoy fishing, lake cruises and visiting an Aboriginal crafts centre. The **Argyle Diamond Mine**, 80km (50 miles) to the south, produces high quality stones and the diamonds, including the unique local pink variety, are sold in Kununurra.

Vast Lake Argyle, created in 1972, is part of the Ord River Irrigation Scheme which waters large tracts of this dry country. The lake, Australia's largest manmade reservoir, contains nine times the amount of water of Sydney Harbour and is home to around 60 bird species. **Lake Argyle Tourist Village** provides accommodation and facilities for visitors, and offers cruises on the lake.

ⓘ Ord Tourist Bureau, Lot 75, Coolibah Drive, Kununurra

To drive to the Northern Territory, continue east on the Victoria Highway (Highway 1).

Broome – Derby 222 (138)
Derby – Geikie Gorge NP 276 (171)
Geikie Gorge NP – Purnululu NP 476 (296)
Purnululu NP – Wyndham 312 (194)
Wyndham – Kununurra 101 (63)

The setting sun plays over Lake Argyle

SPECIAL TO . . .

From Halls Creek on the highway it is 150km (93 miles) to the 850m (2,788-foot) wide and 50m (164-foot)-deep **Wolfe Creek Crater**. 'Discovered' in 1947, this vast circular depression was created by an enormous meteorite falling to earth. The unsealed road is generally accessible between May and November.

FOR HISTORY BUFFS

At the 1880s mining settlement of Old Halls Creek you can visit mudbrick ruins, the cemetery and old mine shafts. This was Western Australia's first goldrush town and the short-lived boom brought 10,000 people to this very remote part of the continent.

BACK TO NATURE

6 On the outskirts of Kununurra, **Mirima National Park** is a rugged region of ancient sandstone hills and valleys. The park contains Aboriginal rock painting sites and the ubiquitous baobab, or boab, trees. Marked walking tracks provide excellent views of the surrounding area.

FOR CHILDREN

1 There are a number of attractions here. The **Broome Crocodile Park** features crocodiles and alligators; the **Wonderful World of Birds** has a collection of colourful Australian parrots; and you can see dinosaur footprints at **Gantheaume Point**!

INDEX

References to captions are in *italic*.

ACKNOWLEDGEMENTS

The Automobile Association would like to thank the following photographers and libraries for their assistance in the preparation of this book.

J BORTHWICK 10a,21, 24a, 32b, 34a, 40, 110, 112a, 112b, 113b
CHRIS FAIRCLOUGH COLOUR LIBRARY 84
FFOTOGRAFF 94/5, 103a, 105a
FOOTPRINTS 44/5 (N Hanna), 46a (C Lima), 47 (A Dalton)
INTERNATIONAL PHOTOBANK 24/5, 33, 56a, 58/9, 67a, 91, 92/3
LONE PINES SANCTUARY 89a
D McGONIGAL 16, 26a, 36, 37, 44a, 67b, 73a, 73b, 106/7, 109b, 115, 116, 117
QUEENSLAND TOURIST & TRAVEL CORPORATION 30, 31
SPECTRUM COLOUR LIBRARY 1, 3, 8/9, 26b, 27, 29, 38a, 38b, 39, 41, 43, 46/7, 49, 52a, 52b, 55, 70, 77, 80, 83, 85a, 85b, 98, 108b, 109a, 111
TOURISM SOUTH AUSTRALIA 81, 82, 87a, 87b
WESTERN AUSTRALIA TOURIST COMMISSION 5, 102
ZEFA PICTURE LIBRARY (UK) LTD Cover, 15

The remaining photographs are held in the Automobile Association's own library (AA PHOTO LIBRARY) with contributions from A BAKER 13b, 18a, 18b, 20, 23a, 23b, 28, 32a, 34/5, 42, 50, 51, 54, 56b, 57, 60, 61b, 63a, 64, 65a, 69, 71a, 71b, 72, 74, 76, 78, 79, 88a, 88/9, 90, 96, 97, 99a, 99b, 101, 103b, 105b, 107, 113a, 114; P KENWARD 2, 10/11, 11a, 13a, 14, 17, 89b, 93; C OSBORNE 61a, 63b, 65b, 68

Copy editor: Dilys Jones